PUBLIC VALUES LEADERSHIP

PUBLIC VALUES
LEADERSHIP

Striving to Achieve Democratic Ideals

▲

BARRY BOZEMAN
and **MICHAEL M. CROW**

Johns Hopkins University Press | BALTIMORE

Johns Hopkins University Press
2715 North Charles Street
Baltimore, Maryland 21218-4363
www.press.jhu.edu

Library of Congress Cataloging-in-Publication Data

Names: Bozeman, Barry, author. | Crow, Michael M., author.
Title: Public values leadership : striving to achieve Democratic ideals / Barry Bozeman,
    Michael M. Crow.
Description: Baltimore : Johns Hopkins University Press, 2021. | Includes bibliographical
    references and index.
Identifiers: LCCN 2020054184 | ISBN 9781421442013 (hardcover) | ISBN 9781421442020
    (ebook) | 9781421442211 (ebook open access)
Subjects: LCSH: Leadership—United States. | Public interest—United States. |
    Common good. | Social responsibility of business—United States.
Classification: LCC HD57.7 .C77 2021 | DDC 658.4/092—dc23
LC record available at https://lccn.loc.gov/2020054184

A catalog record for this book is available from the British Library.

*Special discounts are available for bulk purchases of this book. For more information,
please contact Special Sales at specialsales@jh.edu.*

Contents

Preface
A Personal Story behind Public Values

This book is more relational than most, its style is more personal than most, so it makes sense to start with an account of the authors' four decades of continuous friendship and intellectual partnership. Let us take you back to 1981, an eventful year in which Ronald Reagan was sworn in as US president, the space shuttle *Columbia* launched, Major League Baseball went on strike, Beyoncé was born in Houston, Texas, and Sandra Day O'Connor walked into a building at 1 First St., Washington, DC, and was seated on the US Supreme Court, becoming its first female justice.

Somewhat less earthshaking than any of the above events, 1981 is fondly remembered by Barry Bozeman and Michael Crow as the year they did *not* meet; in fact, they did not even come within 402 miles of meeting. Shopping for doctoral programs in public affairs and having no travel budget, Crow saw that Bozeman was presenting a research paper in Detroit, at the March 1981 Annual Conference of the American Society for the Advancement of Public Administration. Hoping to meet Bozeman, one of the "finalists" in Crow's search for a mentor focused on science and technology policy and public administration, Crow hopped into his 1977 Toyota and drove nine hours from his home in Carbondale, Illinois, where he was directing a coal research laboratory, to Detroit's Cobo Hall, where Bozeman was scheduled to give a paper at 2:00 p.m. on March 23. Crow found the room, but also a sign saying "session canceled." He later found out that Bozeman, having his session canceled, did not come to Detroit but, rather, was at that exact time sitting in his office at Syracuse University's Maxwell School of Citizenship and Public Affairs, contemplating the melting snow and wondering about the accumulation of black ice on the road.

Undeterred (a lifelong and accurate descriptor for Crow), Crow made his way in April 1982 to that same Maxwell School office in which

Bozeman had been ensconced during their 1981 nonmeeting, but this time Crow was forearmed with an appointment. Following his usual travel plan, Crow piled into his car, along with two friends who came along just for the road trip, and headed to Syracuse. They pulled into the parking lot in the late afternoon, and the two friends stayed in the car. Crow, dressed for success in a three-piece suit, a bit wrinkled after a 10-hour drive, met Bozeman just as he was leaving his office. Bozeman, often described before and after—always accurately—as a "space cadet" who is untethered to his calendar, had forgotten about the appointment and was heading to the Little League baseball team he was coaching. Accordingly, he was dressed in his beat-up Gulf Oil baseball cap, a down vest (April in Syracuse), and sweatpants. Feeling only a little guilty for forgetting the appointment, and wishing to test Crow's mettle, Bozeman asked, "Why don't you go with me and pitch batting practice? We can talk there." Crow, his athletic years still not far behind him, did not flinch from the challenge. After returning to the car and explaining to the road trip friends that the presumed homeless person in the greasy Gulf Oil cap was, in fact, Bozeman, the entire retinue drove to a field near Fowler High School and participated in practice, along with the other kids.

After loosening his tie and taking off his coat and vest, Crow proved a decent batting practice pitcher and also a pretty good doctoral program recruit. That afternoon's teamwork was the prelude to more than 35 years of Crow and Bozeman partnership. Their quick affinity related to similar interests and values but also common experience. The two had lived much the same life. Neither of Bozeman's parents had graduated from high school, with his dad being for much of Bozeman's childhood an itinerant construction worker and his mother a homemaker. Since the construction industry was not unionized in the South (for the most part it still is not), when Glenn Bozeman's construction project ended, it was time to move to a different job, often with a different company, helping put natural gas systems in places like Red Bay, Crestview, Alexander City, Cheraw, DeFuniak Springs, Guntersville, Humbolt, and many other small southern towns that remain unfamiliar to most people. By the time Bozeman had entered the seventh grade and his family had settled down for a while, thriving and finally stable because Glenn had become a foreman, he had attended 21 different schools.

Crow, likewise, had attended school all over the United States and also other parts of the world. His father, also not a high school graduate, was an enlisted man in the US Navy, ultimately rising to the rank of chief petty officer. Crow's mother died when Crow was 12 years old, and his father raised Michael and three other children. Like Bozeman, Crow's interest in school was in part rooted in his desire to participate in athletics, Crow going to Iowa State University for track and field, Bozeman landing at Palm Beach Junior College, motivated chiefly by the opportunity to play on a good baseball team. Despite important differences between their personalities and life experiences, the two were united by a remarkable convergence of intellectual interests as well as the crucible of working-class lives lived in innumerable small towns. Each knew early on about the value of adapting to change.

Authors' Respective Career Paths

Having put the origins vignette on the table and having provided some basis for our decades of kinship, we can now turn safely from a third-person perspective to first-person plural. Let us say a bit about our book and why we wrote it. This book represents our coming full circle in our professional relationship, back to where we began (no, not batting practice, but joint research and writing). For the first 10 years or so of our relationship we worked closely on a number of research projects, ones yielding several research grants, three books, and quite a few published research articles. When Crow landed in academic leadership jobs, first at Iowa State and then at Columbia University, the collaboration continued but was more focused on institution building, including, for example, working together, along with our good friend and colleague Dan Sarewitz, to create the Center for Science Policy and Outcomes. Despite collaboration in institution building and some respective attention to academic administration (Crow was executive vice provost at Columbia; Bozeman went on to be founding director of the Georgia Tech School of Public Policy), for a time our respective careers diverged, with Bozeman spending most of his professional life on academic research and Crow, while continuing to do research, focusing his time and energies in academic leadership positions.

With this book we come back to joint research and writing, intent on taking advantage of not only career convergence but also divergence. The convergence: despite dissimilar roles, Bozeman and Crow have been intensely focused on public values and "publicness." The divergence: Crow's work has centered on achieving public values in institutions, Bozeman's on studying public values and developing theory, research, and even some occasional practical applications of public values concepts and thinking. We hope to bring together the knowledge from these intersecting but quite different professional lives, one a life of scholarly work devoted primarily to writing about practical problems, the other the life of a practitioner applying ideas to public problems.

Shared Values

While each of us has gone down a different path—indeed, many different paths—there are a few core ideas and values that both of us have embraced for nearly 40 years. These ideas, in one form or another, emerge in every chapter of this book. Some of these ideas will seem controversial, some less so.

Let's start with an uncontroversial idea that permeates our book—an embrace of *pragmatism as a guiding philosophy*. US intellectuals and many ordinary citizens pride themselves on pragmatism having been "invented" by Americans, and pragmatism is often described as the only truly original American philosophy. While the invention claim is subject to debate, it is also largely beside the point. The influence of American thinkers on pragmatism is undeniable. Giants such as Walter Lippmann, William James, John Dewey, and especially C. S. Peirce—all Americans—are the best-known nineteenth- and twentieth-century thinkers who were instrumental in shaping the philosophy of pragmatism. Pragmatism is to philosophy what jazz is to music—American to its roots.

There are many definitions of pragmatism, including some that only a philosophy professor would espouse, but the basic idea is not difficult to convey—that our thinking should focus on outcomes rather than a system of beliefs that stand independent from outcomes. Pragmatism is as much about rejection as it is about axioms—it rejects absolutism, it rejects metaphysical thinking, and it rejects obsession with formality at the cost of observation and opportunity. Pragmatism is a codified philosophy, but it is also a mindset that is widely influential, especially in the United States. Our reading of history suggests that many of the founders of the American republic, though some were well steeped in philosophy, were pragmatic to the core. George Washington, for example, was much more concerned about politics as the art of the possible than as an object of speculation. Pragmatism remains highly influential today, though nowadays we tend to use the term "entrepreneurism" or "social entrepreneurism" to signify a "can-do" approach focused on outcomes and impacts rather than dogma.

Now for a more controversial tenet of our book: the firm rejection of "market failure" reasoning. The part of market failure that presents the rub, indeed a perpetual annoyance, is the relegation of government to a residual category of institutions, a last resort. Even those not intimately familiar with market failure reasoning may be familiar with the idea that government should provide goods and services only when markets have clearly failed, that there is no positive role for government—it just steps in when, for one reason or another, markets are not efficient.

Market failure reasoning affects public policy and administration to a degree that may not be immediately obvious but that we feel is both enormous and insidious. We will have more to say about the failures of market failure throughout this book, but for the present let us consider a question that has long puzzled us, one that perhaps the reader has an answer to. We do not. The question is this: How can a nation that takes pride in its pragmatism insist on an economics-based ideological solution to nearly every policy problem? Why would anyone continually try to fit a big, fat, round problem into their favorite, tiny, square ideological hole? How did we get to the point that our demonstrably pragmatic nation has embraced an unbending and damaging set of ideological assumptions to which almost everyone, liberal or conservative, pays tribute? We have rejected "one best way" ideas in so many realms, including public administration practice, so why do many people still believe that the role of government (or presumably the nonprofit sector) is to slink into the foreground only after we have demonstrated that markets do not work? As we note in the very first chapter, as well as in many other places in the book, we love markets, as well as government agencies, nonprofits, public-private partnerships, and any organizational form that can solve pressing social problems. We loath organizations that exist for no reason other than to perpetuate themselves and extract a toll, a rent, from the rest of us. We are pragmatists. We want institutions and organizations that achieve public values. The exception: organizations explicitly formed for private benefit and private profits. All we ask of them is that they not *thwart* public values.

What do we mean by "public values"? For present purposes let us describe public values as *consensus* values concerning the rights and privileges due to all US citizens (yes, public values tend to be culturally and politically framed). While values count as public values only if there is vast agreement about ends, that does not necessarily imply any agreement about means. Nor can we expect that public values necessarily are consistent with one another. Sometimes they clash, such as liberty and public safety, for example. Our book is about public values leadership, developing and managing organizations, institutions, and people who can and wish to achieve public values impacts. We have ideas about how to do so, and we invite the reader to sift through these ideas, consider them, argue with them, and improve them.

The Book's Intended Audience

Like most authors, we would like to think that the audience for our book is everyone. Like most authors, we know that a book written for everyone generally appeals to no one.

Our book is written primarily for students of public policy administration and for practitioners in public and nonprofit organizations.

However, our intended audiences converge. A large percentage of public affairs policy and administration graduate students, and a significant percentage of undergraduate students, either are working in public or nonprofit organizations while they are enrolled or have done so before enrolling in such a program. That convergence makes this book a little more daunting to write, but also more fun because almost everyone in our projected audience will have not only some strong ideas of their own but also some ideas grounded in directly relevant experience. We welcome these strong ideas, even strong disputes, because this book is not a didactic textbook, but rather a conversation between the authors and the readers. Sometimes it is even a conversation just between the authors as we strive to highlight points of disagreement (all too few) or compare experiences from two very different but related careers. Indeed, this book is so conversational that we even end with an unusual concluding chapter—a conversation. But the authors' conversations are not designed to pre-empt others'. Quite the contrary. This book succeeds or fails according to its effectiveness not only in informing but also in provoking and stimulating deliberation, self-reflection, and argument, both with oneself and with others.

Even if our book is primarily intended for students and practitioners, we would be pleased if it proved to have some utility for academic professionals engaged in teaching or research on public affairs–related topics, but please understand that the book was not written *primarily* for you. We present no great leaps forward in theory, but rather spend most of our energies trying to sort out the relevance of theory and context for practice. In some cases, actually quite a few, we even reflect on our own experiences, ones that may be utterly divorced from theory and research, in an effort to determine whether these experiences, personal though they may be, have any significant implications for practice. This, too, explains the tone of the book, though the major explanation is simply that it is a lot of fun writing a personalistic, shoot-from-the-hip book. If you are in need of a more conventional (i.e., sleep-inducing) book, then we have several to recommend, starting with most of the ones we have written. We particularly recommend M. Crow, B. Bozeman, W. Meyer, and

R. F. Shangraw, *Synthetic Fuel Technology Development in the United States*. We can endorse it personally since we sometimes keep a copy on our nightstand to deploy if we need to fight insomnia.

Yes, we do meander. But before we finally get to the task at hand, we have one final and important obligation—to briefly thank the many people who have helped make this possible. First, we thank the public values leaders we interviewed at length for giving us their time and valuable insights. Their wisdom appears at various points in the book, including an entire chapter devoted to cases of public values leadership. Several of them also commented helpfully on an earlier draft of this book. Second, we are much indebted to several people who read all or part of our book draft and provided extremely valuable comments and criticisms. We thank Steve Elliott, Stuart Bretschneider, Alex Murdock, Derrick Anderson, and especially Gregg Zachary (who has written books that people actually read). We are especially indebted to Kathryn Scheckel, who coauthored and, indeed, was lead author on one of the chapters, one focused on the Starbucks-ASU Alliance. When the chapter was being written, Ms. Scheckel was ASU's director for the Starbucks Alliance.

We are very grateful to the two anonymous reviewers from Johns Hopkins University Press, each of whom provided good advice, advice we implemented, and which we feel made this a better book than it would otherwise be. One of the comments of an anonymous reviewer is worth paraphrasing here because the reviewer provides a useful warning to the reader: "The personal tone was confusing at first, but . . . over the course of several readings, I found the friendliness and intimacy of the tone to be more of a bonus than a negative. I love it, but didn't at first, and so everyone should know that this is a risk." Yes, a risk. You may, indeed, get more Bozeman and Crow and less scholarly literature than you bargained for. However, at least you have been warned, and, to put a more positive face on it, we hope you, too, will adjust to the "intimacy of the tone" and ultimately decide that it is "more of a bonus than a negative."

Finally, and most importantly, we are grateful to our families and especially our spouses, Dr. Monica Gaughan (professor, Arizona State

University), Bozeman muse and confidant, and Dr. Sybil Francis (president and CEO, Center for the Future of Arizona), Crow muse and confidant. We are inspired by our sons, John Bozeman and Ryan Crow, who have careers actively contributing to public affairs, and by our daughters, Brandyn Bozeman, Rosa Gaughan Bozeman, Brittany Crow-Miller, and Alana Francis-Crow, each of whom has the determination and courage that our society (and most others) still requires for women to succeed.

PUBLIC VALUES LEADERSHIP

INTRODUCTION

We seek to advance ideas about how people and organizations can achieve public values. What are public values? Concern with public values provides the motivation for this book, and we devote the entire next chapter to public values concepts, complexities, and disputes. But for now, it suffices to note that public values are the "big ones," the ones that transcend particular people, groups, and organizations and relate to all citizens. Public values are the fundamental rights and benefits to which all citizens are entitled.[1] They include such consensus-based values as liberty, health and life, security and public safety, opportunity, sustainability, and freedom of speech, among others (Bozeman 2019). One finds public values in places such as the Constitution, landmark court cases, and history books. They are not ephemeral.

Given their importance to society as a whole, agreeing on public values is often relatively easy, but achieving them is almost always difficult. In part this is because vast resources are required to achieve some public values (e.g., public health, security), but also because they sometimes conflict with one another, they may be at odds with private values and preferences, and people disagree about how to achieve them.

It requires some audacity to write a book about achieving public values, the very values that are by definition the most important ones in a society. But audacity is not the same as hubris. We appreciate the complexities of the topic, and we are in touch with the fact that we are jumping into a discourse and a set of arguments that are even older than the United States, the nation that is our primary (though not exclusive) focus.

We pay our respects to the complexities of public values by proffering no magic bullets or easy solutions. Instead, the book is intended as a dialogue with the reader. Our chief goal is to motivate the reader to ponder and actively criticize the ideas we present and, ultimately, to develop their own ideas about the best ways to achieve public values. True, in most cases we argue forcefully for our point of view, but not in an effort to preempt others' views, but rather to give them clear targets to shoot at.

In many chapters we provide questions directed to the reader, questions designed to provoke the reader to think critically about public values. The book includes many prescriptions, some explicit, others a bit more subtle. However, these are not magisterial lessons burned into stone tablets. The prescriptions we provide exemplify both our unabashed commitment to saying what we think and, at the same time, our effort to provoke readers' contemplation and discussion of their own values, thoughts, and perhaps alternative conclusions about lessons. We would be disappointed were the reader to examine all of our provisional lessons and conclude, "Okay! Now I understand and now I know just what to do." Throughout the book, at various points and in various ways, we try to poke and prod the reader. We hope you will poke back.

Our book relies on three different types of knowledge, each having known strengths and weaknesses. First, we do, indeed, rely a good deal on our own direct experiences. As we note in the preface, one of the authors (Bozeman) has spent much of his career writing and conducting research about public values, and the other (Crow) in trying to achieve them, especially within the context of higher education institutions. However, we well understand that our experiences do not fit to every circumstance and that others working to achieve public values may have different experiences, ones that are equally valid and, in some cases, more instructive. Thus, in addition to our own experiences and ideas, we present the ideas of people who are "public values leaders." This august group (identified and discussed later in this chapter) includes a diverse set of people who have in common their success in achieving public values and their willingness to share insights and experiences with us.

As implied thus far, our book is more personal than most books about management and leadership, and we begin below with a personal experience case study that examines some of the difficulties of achieving public values, even when everyone agrees about the public values objectives to be achieved. The case deals with water resources, health, and public safety, issues that would likely find their way to almost anyone's public values list.

The case below evokes all three of the working assumptions on which we base the book, ones we refer to as the premises of public values management. At this point let us simply list and identify them:

1. Core public value premise: It is possible and desirable for individuals and organizations to pursue and achieve public values.
2. Sector agnosticism premise: No sector "owns" public values; they may be achieved in the public, private, and nonprofit sectors and, often, by partnerships among organizations, often from different sectors.
3. Pragmatism premise: Public values achievement almost always requires pragmatic approaches, not ideologically centered approaches.

We elaborate on these points in chapter 3 and touch on them throughout the book, including the personal experience case below. The case below provides insights into each of these three premises, showing the interrelationships among them and how easily core public values—in this case provision of clean, healthy water to all citizens—can be thwarted even when most people agree on goals. The case is the antithesis of sector agnosticism, showing how deeply rooted market-based ideology gives rise to a reflexive private-sector favoritism that can run roughshod over attempts to solve large-scale public values problems. In this case, and in so many others, the pragmatism that so many profess and that is America's only original political philosophy (West 1989) is easily set aside when citizens are in the throes of unbending ideology.

The case illustrates why simple pragmatism so often proves difficult. The case also provides a good "origins story" about interest in public values research and theory, so it is longer and more elaborate than most of our personal experience cases. After presenting the case, we return briefly to its role in launching a public values research agenda.

A Quick Note on Cases and Illustrations

Throughout the book, we use several modalities to convey contextual material, so a few words on organization and nomenclature may help. We begin below with a "personal case," a report of one or both of the authors' personal experiences. A "mini-case" is brief, usually less than a page, and typically functions as an example or, sometimes, even counterexamples. "Deep cases" are more extensive, providing considerable detail, and sometimes conclude by asking readers to reflect on and possibly discuss (if they are reading the book with others, such as in a class) reactions to discussion questions. Finally, we present "comments," mostly by public values managers and leaders, throughout the book. These modalities are labeled and presented in a somewhat different format than the other material in the book.

Here is an example of one of the modalities we employ, the personal case. This particular personal case is a touchstone for the book because it describes reasons behind the first glimmer of contemporary public value theory.

Personal Case (Bozeman). City of Atlanta Water Policy and Market Frameworks
My focus in this case is on issues related to choosing who should provide public values, a decision that more often than not also determines exactly what public values are served and for whom. This personal experience

case emphasizes the difficulty of making public values decisions when there has been so little progress in developing ways of talking about public values or tools for understanding and assessing public values. This case and all of the book's personal experience reports are presented in first person.

Enter the Three Men in Rubber Boots

Our story begins more than 20 years ago, when I was director of the Georgia Tech School of Public Policy. On a brisk October day in Atlanta, I had just settled into my office at the D. M. Smith Building when the landmark Georgia Tech factory whistle blew the first of its 11 hourly piercing alerts. That whistle marked the time as 7:55 a.m., the beginning of the workday. I was just recovering from the whistle's sonic blast when I noticed a call on the intercom. Rita Davis, the school's administrative assistant, who was in the anteroom to the director's office, let me know that there were three men outside my office, politely requesting a meeting.

School directors have plenty of meetings, but this one seemed strange. First, the men had no appointment and stated no business. Second, they obviously did not know me at all, or they would have never expected me to be at work so early. A 7:55 appearance was a rare event. Rita did not identify the men by name, again unusual, violating the usual protocols. I was curious, not least because of the surprise registered in the usually unflappable Rita's voice; I said, "Please, send them in."

The three men who entered resembled one another in some respects. All looked to be between 40 and 50 years old, all were African American, and all were dressed in sturdy work clothes and rubber boots, not the attire of the usual student, faculty, or administrator clientele. After declining coffee or water, the three got right down to business.

"Dr. Bozeman, we're from the municipal workers' union, we work at the water department. We don't have a lot of time, we're already going to be late for work, but we read what you wrote in the paper yesterday and we would like to get your help."

The day before meeting them, I had published an op-ed in the *Atlanta Journal-Constitution*, weighing in on Mayor Bill Campbell's plan to privatize water and sewer operations in the city of Atlanta. Campbell hoped to find some way to solve an infrastructure crisis that everyone agreed was reaching emergency levels. The chief source of the city's water, the Chattahoochee River, was so polluted that swimming was banned at several points. The city had already been subjected to millions of dollars of fines from the US Environmental Protection Agency owing to runoff of raw sewerage into the water system. Atlanta's water system was antiquated, and the sewer system still had some wooden ducts and no adequate capture of runoff water. Some of the pipes installed in 1875 remained in service, and many others had been fixed with a patchwork of materials, some haphazardly.

Many observers agreed that the city would need to invest millions of dollars to renovate the sewer and water systems, but tax dollars were already strained and bonding capacity stretched. Mayor Campbell was now campaigning forcefully for a sweeping solution. According to Campbell, as well as many greater Atlanta business leaders and some city officials and politicians, the only viable solution was to sell or privatize the system and take advantage of the efficiencies of private markets.

The op-ed I had written was not exactly radical, except perhaps in the context of metropolitan Atlanta's dominant market ideologies. The gist of my op-ed was this: evidence shows that in some cases privatization of municipal services works very well, and in other cases privatization causes more problems than it solves. I argued (and had a good deal of research to support the idea) that privatization's likelihood of success is not random but instead depends on a variety of situational factors, including political will, knowledge of contracting and contract management, and a close partnership with the contractor. That mixed review was the most skeptical opinion about water and sewer privatization that had yet appeared in print or on radio and television. Thus, the men from the municipal employees' union were not exactly thinking of me as their knight in shining armor, but they did view me, quite correctly, as the rare Atlanta dweller who had not made up his or her mind on the topic.

"I can understand why you guys oppose this possible privatization; some of you would probably lose your jobs," I said. "I understand that. I sympathize. But is there any other reason you oppose it?" The youngest worker, who unexpectedly seemed to be the spokesperson for the group, replied, "There is nothing about this whole mess that's our fault. Lots of people think that if they can just get rid of these lazy government workers everything will be okay. They don't know us. We do our job and we serve the public. We like having a job. But we also think what we are doing is important and we want to keep doing it."

The workers really had only one request. They asked me to contact one of the few members of the Atlanta City Council who seemed to be listening to them, Councilwoman Clair Muller. At the time Muller was an eight-year veteran of the City Council, and she would later be described in the local newspaper as "the city's reigning technocrat, with an unparalleled knowledge of virtually every aspect of city operations."

After a brief telephone conversation, Councilwoman Muller asked me to meet for lunch the next day at Mary Mac's Tea Room, a fifty-year-old Midtown landmark, as well known for its relaxed atmosphere conducive to business as for its fried green tomatoes and chicken and dumplings. We got right down to business. While no enemy of privatization per se, Muller voiced a number of reservations about the Campbell privatization plan, particularly questioning the Campbell administration's ability to manage what would surely be an enormous contract, in all likelihood far bigger than anything in the history of Atlanta.

Still trying to get up to speed with local politics, I asked many questions about the history of water and sewer infrastructures and also the political alignments related to this history. I told Muller about my interest and background in studying privatization of government services, the primary reason for my cautious outlook on the impending service delivery choices. I also told her that I had not made up my mind about this major policy problem and that I would need a lot more information before doing so. "Don't put me in any advocacy camp," I said, "at least not right now." I thanked her and assumed that my involvement with the issue had essentially ended.

The Atlanta Sewer and Water Privatization Advisory Committee

A couple of weeks after our initial meeting, Muller called me and asked if I would cochair a "blue ribbon" committee she was putting together to do fact-finding and make recommendations to the City Council on the Atlanta sewer-water privatization issue (later sewer issues were to some extent set aside and the focus was on water). After hearing about the planned objectives and activities of the committee and its projected membership, including respected local businesspeople, other academics, and political leaders, I accepted the offer. Shortly thereafter, the committee began its business, most of which involved public testimony, chiefly by technical or professional experts but by many ordinary citizens as well.

During the more than six weeks of meeting and testimony, the committee heard from an amazingly diverse set of citizens, including construction company presidents, consultants, politicians, academic researchers, neighborhood organizers, and mothers and fathers worried about the health of their families. The majority of citizens, especially business representatives, the largest group of those appearing before the committee, were strongly in favor of privatization. Many of these witnesses provided opinions wrapped in the language of neoliberal, market failure economics. Some of the more sophisticated provided information about benefit-cost streams and discount rates on marginal utility; others referred to market failure arguments, opining that government should be involved only in cases of obvious market failure, and since in this case the failure seemed to be related more to governance than to the market, it was obviously time to take advantage of market competition and achieve an efficient and effective outcome. Many of these arguments were quite persuasive.

Interestingly, those who were not so keen on this particular privatization choice were not much different in their approach and arguments than were the people who were in favor of privatization. Thus, some argued that maybe there was some market failure here since previous vendors had not been forthcoming. Others argued that this was a case where the government needed some role, even if not an exclusive one, because there were obvious externalities in the provision of water and sewer services, a typical economic rationale for government to be involved. Most of those in favor of maintaining a government role said the same exact thing: "I feel it is in the public interest for government to provide such a basic public service." Most did not offer much elaboration on that point.

One of the most eloquent speakers was one of the men who had appeared in my office the previous October. The city worker described in detail the nature of his work, the work of his crew, their level of commitment to the job, and many instances where they had gone above and beyond their work requirements, mainly because they viewed themselves as "public servants working in the public interest."

The committee concluded its business recommending that privatization might not be the answer given that there was no evidence that problems were due to government performance. While the committee identified major problems related to capital cost and revenue shortfalls, it was not clear that these problems were going to be resolved by contracting with the private sector, especially given the need to build into the contract a profit margin for the contractor.

Mayor Campbell dismissed the report as a political setup and gave his opinion that privatization would save more than $20 million over the life of the contract (Jørgensen and Bozeman 2002). The mayor, with the backing of a small majority of the City Council, proceeded to develop bidding rules for contractors. In November 1998, the city of Atlanta signed a contract with United Water Services for what was at the time the longest and most costly contract for water services in the history of the world. United Water was one of the largest such companies, operating 32 privatized water systems in cities on four different continents. The week the contract was signed, the local newspaper reported that the signing "caps a tumultuous year-long process characterized by political infighting among local officials, apprehension in the community among city employees and a bidding blitz from five corporate behemoths" (Hairston 1998, D1). There was a sigh of relief in most quarters, though not the City Water Department.

Hopes Dashed

The Atlanta water privatization case is now viewed by many as a public policy and political disaster of epic proportions. United Water, a well-established and reputable company, took over operations shortly after the contract was signed. Only a few months afterward, the new mayor, Shirley Franklin, issued a notice that the contractor was not in full compliance with the 20-year contract, noting problems related to staffing, billing, meter installation, and system repairs. This grievance came at just about the same time as United Water was asking for an additional $80 million to perform services that the city insisted on but that the company claimed were not correctly specified in the contract. The city gave United Water 90 days to solve the problems. United Water, in turn, provided letters signed by Mayor Bill Campbell (who would soon be in prison for unrelated bribery charges) stating that the company would be paid an additional $80 million, off contract. This was contested by the city and by Mayor Franklin, who claimed that the letters of agreement were neither valid nor legal. United Water dropped its claim for an additional payment of $80 million.

Not long after the contract dispute, a fire swept through an Atlanta public housing project, destroying many homes, this despite the rapid response of the Atlanta Fire Department, which arrived on the scene only to find that the fire hydrants had not been inspected recently and had insufficient water pressure to drive water through a fire hose.

Alleging poor service, poor water quality, and fraudulent billing, Mayor Franklin demanded that United Water quit or be fired and that the contract be terminated. United Water resigned from the contract, after fulfilling four years of the 20-year agreement. The company paid $6 million to settle all legal claims with the city. The city hired 364 employees and reconstituted its water department. In short, the chief outcome of the privatization effort was the expenditure of a great deal of taxpayer money, only to return to essentially the same government-run system in place before the privatization.

Lesson: Public Values Leadership Requires Pragmatism

Some may conclude that the Atlanta water case is a government-is-good, business-is-bad morality tale. We feel that is the wrong conclusion. The case shows that there is plenty of "bad" to go around (corruption, poor contracting and oversight, performance and performance management problems, toxic politics)—no single sector or organization gets all the discredit. The case also shows that while blaming people is easy enough, carefully parsing culpability is more challenging.

Even today it is difficult to identify and carefully sort all of the ingredients in the seeming disaster of the Atlanta case.[2] Some argue that the public-private partnership failed because the city did such a poor job of providing information about the woeful state of its infrastructure (that was the United Water argument, one that seems to have some validity). Others argue that political corruption is front and center in understanding what went wrong. Many of those who followed the case feel that, plain and simple, the company did not live up to what it promised, that it was just interested in making money, not in providing service. Others are less critical of United Water's service, arguing that giving the system back to the city did not improve service and may have made it worse. Some dispassionate analytical types claim that neither government nor business was at fault, that most problems were a result of Atlanta's gigantic growth spurt and the difficulty of responding as rapidly as needed to population-driven challenges. Most importantly for present purposes, the case does not tell us that privatization is good or that it is bad—which, I guess, is where the case started.

Discussion Questions
- Question 1: In the authors' view, much about the Atlanta case related to the specific and long-standing political culture of Atlanta. Here is the thought experiment for the reader: Consider your own hometown. If it were to be embroiled in a vital but controversial public works (water, or whatever may be relevant to your region) policy choice about privatization versus government or possibly a public-private partnership provision of services, how might the distinctive political culture affect outcomes? Do you think that the hometown's history and political culture would impede or perhaps facilitate decision-making, and in what ways?
- Question 2: As the case points out, those citizens who were interested in making a strong case for privatization often

effectively framed their arguments in economic terms, such as cost-efficiency or cost-benefit analysis, but those who thought that the city might be better off by continuing to have government as a provider of services tended to speak vaguely about "the public interest" or even cloaked their own arguments in business terms. If you had decided that public provision of water might lead to better outcomes, how might you frame your argument? Can you think of ways to make such a case with more compelling and precise arguments than "I think it is in the public interest"?

Out of the Shadow of Market Theory

The Atlanta water privatization case remains important today because the city's water problems still remain, despite some progress. But it is also personally important for Bozeman and Crow because it stoked an interest in public values theory that has not receded and has, since the late 1990s, developed along multiple paths forged by multiple people.

The origin story's motivations might be presumed to have been grounded in reaction to the hypercapitalist assumptions pervading a public values problem, but that was not a new experience, so not a new motivation. What was jarring to Bozeman were the ways in which those who were in favor of government provision of services, as well as those who were open-minded and pragmatic, nonetheless frequently articulated their ideas using (and sometimes misusing) economic reasoning and terminology. Disputants on every side of the issue spoke of market failure (though arriving at different judgments about it) and framed the issues in terms of economics-driven cost-benefit analysis concepts. The "public interest" was much alluded to, but never in any concrete or instrumental fashion.

During this experience, Bozeman concluded that existing public interest theory (more about that later) was not sufficiently precise to compete with the analytical precision of neoliberal microeconomics theory and measurement. In Bozeman's view, economic values often supplant public interest values for no other reason than this analytical mismatch. Worse, the mismatch often results in the supplanting of vital but conceptually murky public interest values with the more easily communicated and measured values central to economics.

The Atlanta case suggests the dangers of relying on dominant ideologies as opposed to reasoned pragmatism, and it shows how public values come to be held prisoner to ideology. The case shows that blind allegiance to ideology often gets in the way of public values objectives. Stereotypes about sectors and rigid ideas about sector roles get in the way of achieving public values. Somehow, we never learn from countless historical instances showing us that business, government, and nonprofit sectors all provide not only good solutions to social problems but also terrible ones, and all gradations of quality in between those extremes. In our view, achieving public values requires a focus on outcomes and approaches that work—pragmatism. Ideology makes sense in some realms, especially political persuasion, but in many instances public values can best be achieved with diverse policies, organizational designs, and institutional arrangements.

Public values theory, at least our version of it (Bozeman 2002, 2007), was created in an effort to rehabilitate venerable but often ambiguous public interest theory, to offer more precise premises, concepts, and perhaps even measures, so as to diminish the need to use theories developed for a very different purpose, namely, market efficiency, owing simply to the lack of any satisfactory alternative. Indeed, a central thrust of public values theory involves developing alternatives to the decision-making criteria included in market failure theory (e.g., spillovers and externalities, market monopolies), ones pertaining to values affecting the broad public rather than issues related to the technical efficiencies of prices for goods and services.

We shall see in the next chapter that by the usual criteria we bring to assessing the precision and robustness of theories and the measures that flow from them, public values theory is still a work in progress. But at least it seems fair to say that it results in expanded discussion and gives some hope of moving analysis of public issues out of the long shadow cast by market failure reasoning. We are on a mission—to do all we can to support the discussion, the analysis, and, especially, the application of public values—and we invite the reader to join us, with the attitude that the perfect (that is, perfect public values theory and measures) cannot be the enemy of the good (expanded public values deliberation and action). For the rest of the introduction, however, we set aside analytical cudgels.

The Atlanta case tells us much about ideological rigidity and dominance, political incompetence, corruption, and the squandering of vast sums to little good purpose. It is a depressing story of public values thwarted, made all the more depressing when we consider that most actors shared public values objectives. We counterbalance with an instance of public values achievement, albeit one with some bittersweet elements.

Mini-case. The Public Value of Private Safety: The Safe Arrival of Kayla T.

Public values–focused organizations and institutions come in many shapes, sizes, and sectors. Often groups of organizations, working together informally in networks or in formal alliances, serve public values. In doing so, they sometimes achieve great public values successes.

On a late October Saturday evening, just after sunset, Kayla T. (not her real name), a 17-year-old junior at McClintock High School in Tempe, Arizona, finishes her six-hour shift as a weekend worker at the Target store in the Tempe Marketplace Mall. She is tired after a day at the cash register, her fatigue exacerbated by sleep deprivation the night before. Kayla went to sleep much later than usual after attending a Friday night football game with her McClintock Chargers traveling to nearby Tempe High School for the season's most important rivalry game. The Chargers suffered a dispiriting beatdown by the archrival Buffaloes, and Kayla stayed out late with friends, drowning their athletic sorrows at a nearby Zoyo ice cream and frozen yogurt shop. Now Kayla is bicycling home, hoping to get a quick nap before meeting up with a bunch of friends and heading back to the mall to see an old James Bond movie playing in the theater's vintage film series.

Kayla lives with her parents near downtown Tempe, about two miles from the Target store. Tempe has extensive bicycle lanes, and Kayla looks forward to a little exercise, especially now that the weather in Tempe has finally cooled off a bit. She unlocks her bike, one of those retro fat tire bikes that she and her friends prefer, hers in pink and purple with white tires; she puts on her helmet, turns on her bicycle light, and proceeds down Rio Salado Parkway, a busy winding road with too much traffic, but also with a well-demarcated bike lane. This is rush hour, but—important because of Kayla's desperation for a nap—it is also the quickest route to her home. Kayla is a little nervous with so many cars whizzing by and with some more athletic superbikers on her tail, ones in fancy bike shirts on expensive ultralight carbon bikes, passing her on the left-hand side outside of the bike lane.

In a little more than 20 minutes Kayla is safely home; she puts up her bike, greets her mom and her little sister Samantha, heads to her room, and sets the alarm to ensure that she will meet her friends, and ten minutes later she is fast asleep.

The point of this story is that nothing melodramatic happens; it is a "day in the life" story. Kayla lives; she suffers no traffic accident; she doesn't even have a flat tire. The story is a happy one, in part because of the work of public values–based individuals and organizations. To what can we attribute this happy if unexciting outcome of Kayla arriving safely at home? Sure, Kayla is a responsible commuter. But let us also consider that the Tempe City Council adopted a "traffic smoothing" strategy and worked with local bicycle shops and a Tempe nonprofit group advocating for bicycle safety to build and publicize new and expanded bike lanes so that people like Kayla, part of Tempe's increasing bicycle commuter population, could be healthy, help curb pollution, and, most of all, do so safely.

Lesson: Good Things Happen Because Bad Things Don't

Sometimes when we think of achieving public values, we imagine highly visible sets of actions consuming prodigious resources and resulting in splashy outcomes. But in many cases, public values come in small packages, and public values successes entail quietly avoiding public values failures. (In chapter 1 we discuss public values failure in detail, providing specific criteria for assessing public values.)

Deep Case. Public Values Controversy: Mothers Against Drunk Driving
Of necessity, we start this case with a real-life nightmare outcome. On May 3,
1980, 13-year-old Cari Lightner, a California girl, was walking with a friend, not
riding, in a bike lane. Cari was hit from behind by an automobile and killed
instantly. Rather than stopping, the driver accelerated and sped away. Soon
the police arrested him. A few days later, the police told Cari's mother, Candy
Lightner, that the man who killed Cari by vehicular homicide had only two
days before been released from jail on another drunk driving, hit-and-run
case. On May 8, Candy Lightner assembled friends, and the group pledged to
start an organization that would do something to combat drunk driving. One
of the friends suggested the name Mothers Against Drunk Driving (MADD).
The organization came to national prominence and has been credited by
many for its role in putting drunk driving on the public policy agenda,
affecting public opinion, and organizing public actions against drunk driving.

The sharp decline in drunk driving in the United States between 1980
and the present relates not only to changing norms and policies but also
to demographic factors. However, there seems little doubt that just a few
determined people with a vision for a shared public value, public safety,
managed to design an institution that ultimately had significant impacts
in the realization of the value it pursued. Did Kayla make it safely home
in October because of MADD? We cannot know. Social outcomes are
remarkably complex and "overdetermined." But there seems little doubt
that MADD has contributed to public values and to the safety of citizens
throughout the United States.

The history of MADD provides important lessons about achieving
public values, about both the role of the individual and the role of
concerted efforts by multiple institutions and organizations. It is not the
archetypal case of public values–based institutional design, but that is
only because there is no archetype, but rather many routes to public
values–based institutions. In some cases, as with MADD, institutions
begin with a charismatic leader with a strong emotional appeal, but
other cases begin with no single leader and not even much charisma. In
some cases, as with MADD, the institution has its beginnings in informal
groups and grassroots movements; in others, a public values–based
institution is developed from existing organizations coming together in

common purpose. In still other cases, public values–based institutions have political roots, either encouraged by or established in law and public policy. There is not one template, but, as we shall see here, one can identify patterns that cut across almost all efforts to design public values–based institutions.

As mentioned above, it is easy to identify the precipitating causes and the time of origin for MADD. However, MADD was not the first organization formed to fight drunk driving. This is important to note because there is no requirement that a public values–based institution be the first organization of its type or that it be innovative. The key is the ability to attain public values, whether or not the institution is the "first mover." MADD was preceded by another citizen activist group, Remove Intoxicated Drivers (RID), established in New York State by Doris Aiken. The circumstances were similar. Aiken learned about the traffic deaths of Karen and Timothy Morris, who were killed by a drunk driver on December 4, 1977, siblings who were the only children in the Morris family. Several days later, Bonnie Morris, the victim's mother, called Aiken to enlist her help in getting the district attorney to even return her phone calls. After a series of public meetings, some media coverage, and the attention of public officials, RID was launched. It continues today, with chapters or representatives in 42 states, and with Doris Aiken at its head until her death in 2017. However, RID, which started earlier and shares many characteristics with MADD, has for many years had a much smaller footprint than MADD. In comparing MADD and RID, one lesson is that there is no requirement to be first, and another is that public values–based institutions, even ones with quite similar origins, can evolve in very different ways.

It is not always easy to see just why some grassroots organizations take off and others do not. The success of MADD has attracted researchers' interests (Weed 1987, 1993; Fell and Voas 2006; Hurley 2014), and the history of MADD often is viewed as a prime example of institution-building success. All seem to agree that the charismatic leadership of Candy Lightner proved important, but not more so than early linkages to mass media and to elected officials. One of Lightner's early allies, Cindi Lamb, whose child was paralyzed by a drunk driver, was introduced to Lightner and her nascent organization by Sandy Golden, a Washington, DC, television correspondent who was developing a story on drunk driving. The combination of a coast-to-coast alliance, likable spokespersons, and mass media coverage attracted the interest of members of Congress, initially Michael Barnes (D-MD). The more attention garnered, the more Lightner began to rise as a national spokesperson for the anti–drunk driving cause. The National Highway Traffic Safety Administration (NHTSA) began actively assisting, including helping Lightner and Lamb at press events, most importantly a national press conference in which the two activists joined Congressman Barnes, Senator Claiborne Pell (D-RI), and Joan Claybrook, then head of the NHTSA.

Spurred by the publicity, in 1980 MADD was incorporated as a California corporation and had formed chapters in Maryland and California. In 1981, the organization was featured in stories in the *Los Angeles Times* and *Family Circle* and in guest appearances on *The Today Show* and *The Phil Donahue Show*. By this time MADD had ascended to national leadership in the anti–drunk driving cause (Fell and Voas 2006). Naturally, the publicity and the public awareness of MADD did not immediately or directly translate into social or political influence. It seems clear that one significant milestone was the establishment by President Reagan in 1982 of the Presidential Commission on Drunk Driving. MADD advocates were instrumental in urging the creation of the commission and were invited by the Reagan White House to attend ceremonies for its establishment. They were featured prominently at the meetings of the commission, complete with Candy Lightner photo ops with President Reagan. One result was the increased legitimacy of the organization as a public policy advocate.

In the early 1980s MADD formed a new set of alliances, this time with the scientific community working on issues of substance-based impairment and accidents. Because of work by this diverse coalition of advocates and researchers, federal legislation was developed establishing a national minimum drinking age of 21 (the National Minimum Drinking Age Act of 1984). MADD continued to partner with White House policy makers and the Office of the Surgeon General (including their sponsorship of the Workshop on Drunk Driving), bringing together a diverse coalition of advocates, policy makers, and scientists.

By its tenth anniversary in 1990, MADD, by this time one of the few "household name" advocacy organizations, had accomplished much in its legislative programs at both the federal and state levels and felt confident in establishing an ambitious goal: "20 by 2000," aiming to reduce alcohol-related traffic deaths by 20% by the new millennium. The goal was met three years early. Not only were programs adopted throughout the nation, including most conspicuously a lowering of blood alcohol rates permissible for driving, but also the membership of MADD and the resources available to it continued to climb. Spin-off groups were developed, such as Students Against Drunk Driving. MADD played a significant role in the 1998 federal Transportation Equity Act for the 21st Century, which set a minimum one-year suspension of driver's licenses for DUI second offense, as well as provisions for impoundment of vehicles.

The Bittersweet Part

Notwithstanding its considerable influence and success, MADD, like nearly any public values–based institution, has had to withstand threats to its success and very survival. First, there was the nasty empirical reality that drunk driving fatalities, which had trended downward for so long, stopped doing so, despite the best efforts of advocates. From 1982 to 1993 alcohol-related traffic fatalities decreased steadily from more than 26,000 to a low of 17,732. But declines were not sustained and for the next decade ranged from the high 16,000s to the mid-17,000s.

More specific to MADD, Candy Lightner resigned as CEO, partly because of a conflict with the board of directors. By the early 1980s, MADD had transitioned into a more traditional business-like approach, focusing on resources and strategic planning and less on advocacy. According to some observers, it was this major transition, this proliferation of the organization's formal bureaucracy, that ultimately sustained it, but these changes were accompanied by considerable internal conflict (McCarthy and Wolfson 1996).

What has been the specific role of MADD in improving traffic safety? It not possible to give an exact accounting of the full impact of an organization operating for a relatively long time on a public value issue that has involved a great many other organizations, including ones often working in partnership.

It is possible to point to tens of thousands of lives saved from reductions in alcohol-related traffic deaths from the beginning of MADD until today, and there is a long list of public programs, at state, federal, and sometimes municipal levels of government, that have been created coincident with aggressive MADD advocacy. In short, there seems little doubt that MADD has contributed to achieving the public values it set out to achieve, but the magnitude of its effectiveness is not so easily gauged.

Since MADD has received some scholarly attention, there are various views about its success. As mentioned above, some feel that the ability of the organization to develop from a loose coalition into a formal bureaucratic structure has been a source of strength. However, critics point to the fact that almost half of its $45 million annual income goes toward salaries, a high number for a nonprofit organization. Some attribute MADD's seeming success to the fact that the organization emerged at a time in which the policy agenda was ripe, especially in touch with the moralistic tone set by the Reagan administration. While almost everyone credits MADD founder Lightner with much of the early success of MADD, it seems clear that the ability to quickly and effectively partner with other organizations has been instrumental at all points of MADD's history. Sometimes the partners are not "obvious" ones. Another point of criticism: at one point the hospitality industry played an important part in MADD support and funding, chiefly because they wished to distinguish between the social drinker and the "problem drinker" (McCarthy and Wolfson 1996). But MADD has many partnerships, including with researchers, government agencies, and mass media.

As we write this, MADD has evolved and adapted a good deal. One of their most important programmatic changes has been a strong emphasis on victim services, programs that have helped with recruitment and with expanding advocacy.

Lesson: The Power of the Few

As is so often the case with a protracted effort to achieve public values, the MADD case is a complex one where different people draw different lessons. Here are ours. Lesson One: the MADD case shows that it is possible to begin with humble resources and go on to contribute greatly to public values, especially when working closely with many different people in different organizations, people who bring their own resources and energy.

Lesson: Fraught Public Values Heroism
Lesson Two: if one is looking for credit, it is best to believe in heavenly rewards in the afterlife. This is, we think, not an overly cynical conclusion. Even when society does anoint public values heroes, the acclaim often is fleeting or symbolic. Symbols of accomplishment have their place, but achieving public values usually requires more than one or two heroes.

What's in the Rest of the Book

While it is conventional at this point to go over the content of a book, chapter by chapter, we have trust in the readers' ability to look at the table of contents and, just on that basis, determine which chapters appeal. So, instead, we review below some of the more unusual features of the book, including one we are especially pleased with—the inclusion of views, based on interviews, of several people we consider public values leaders.

Lessons from Public Values Leaders

While much of this book is the gospel according to Crow and Bozeman, we include perspectives of many others who cooperated with us in putting together this book. We refer to them as "public values leaders" because, in our view, that is exactly what they are. Of course, that is not all they are. Some are politicians, some are lifelong public servants, some work in industry, and others are leaders in nonprofit organizations or institutions of higher education. Despite diverse backgrounds, these leaders do have some things in common that we feel unite them as public values leaders. We do not expect that a public value leader focuses only on public values, we do not expect that public values leaders are saints and never make mistakes, and we certainly do not expect that public values leaders will necessarily play the role of the charismatic hero leader. Often leadership is about stamina, patience, and the ability to work with others. What these people have in common is this: much of their work has been guided by a desire to achieve the most fundamental rights and benefits to which all citizens should be able to lay claim, but which are sometimes denied. The people we interviewed for this book have worked for human rights, education and social development, health and well-being—in short, the public values about which most of us agree. Each has accomplished great things, sometimes through highly visible public values attainment, and other times in a cloak of near anonymity.

There is no political or ideological litmus test for public leaders (remember—pragmatism and agnosticism about sector). People of many different political persuasions can and do contribute to public values achievement. We shall see that all public values leaders are not from the same mold. One of the refreshing elements of these interviews is a clear indication that there are many different valid and effective approaches to leadership and many different routes to achieving public values. The list includes not only people who are well known to most of the general public but also people who have a regional or local reputation for achievement. One also finds people from all sectors—business, politics and public administration, and nonprofit organizations.

In addition to sharing our only criterion, having contributed to significant public values achievements, about the only other thing the leaders all have in common is that one or both of the authors (but usually Crow) have long been acquainted with them. That explains the fact that they are not geographically representative. Many are from Arizona or from Washington; the two authors spend the majority of their time in those two locales and meet more people from these two places than, say, Alaska or Nebraska. But it will not surprise you to know that we feel there are good, strong public values leaders in every state in the United States and, indeed, throughout the world.

Despite the geographic bias, the list is in other ways diverse, including people from different sectors, different political leanings, and different genders, races, and ethnicities. Their respective contributions to this book are enormous, and we are enormously grateful for their generosity in granting time for in-depth interviews. You will find the public values leaders' contributions used in a variety of ways. Most conspicuously, our chapter 6, "Case Studies in Public Values Leadership," features five extended cases, what we call here "deep cases" so as to distinguish them from the many other illustrations, comments, and briefer cases employed. We feature these public values leaders not because their accomplishments exceed others but because our interviews with them focused more on one particular case, rather than several smaller episodes, ones that are more amenable to extended treatment. We also chose these leaders because they represent different sectors, including nonprofit, higher education, city management, business, and gubernatorial politics.

In addition to the deep cases, we also feature public values leaders in mini-cases and sometimes just in brief comments or observations, ones we feel edify the particular points we are making (or, in some cases, contrasting points or perspectives). The names and affiliations of the public values leaders are given in table 1, but, of course, we provide more information about them and their activities in other places in the book. We invite you to do a little research on your own and find out more about these extraordinary people.

Lessons from History, Assorted Personal Experiences, Arizona State University, Participant Observation, and Even Scholarly Sources

In writing this book, we grabbed about anything that we felt would help us make useful points about public values management and leadership, including even some theory and research from academic publications, including research on exactly what we mean by "public values." Extended historical accounts include such diverse elements as the origins

TABLE 1
Public Values Leaders and Their Affiliations

Public Values Leaders	Affiliation
Jeb Bush	Former Governor of Florida Jeb Bush and Associates, LLC. Biographical information: https://www.britannica.com/biography/Jeb-Bush
Antonia Hernández	President and CEO, California Community Foundation Biographical Information: https://www.calfund.org/about-ccf/ccfstaff/presidents-office/
Freeman Hrabowski	President, University of Maryland at Baltimore County Biographical information: https://president.umbc.edu
Linda Hunt	CEO, Dignity Health Biographical information: https://www.dignityhealth.org/arizona/about-us/executive-leadership/linda-hunt
Tony Penn	President and CEO, United Way of Tucson and Southern Arizona Biographical information:https://www.unitedwaytucson.org/our_board
Anne-Marie Slaughter	President and CEO of New America Biographical information: https://www.newamerica.org/our-people/anne-marie-slaughter/
Brian and Kelly Swette	President and CEO, Sweet Earth Incorporated Biographical information: https://www.sweetearthfoods.com/who-we-are#mission
Deborah Wince-Smith	President, Council on Competitiveness Biographical information: https://www.compete.org/about/senior-staff/3182
Steven Zabilski	Executive Director, St. Vincent de Paul Biographical information: https://www.catholicsun.org/2017/01/22/steve-zabilski-20-years-of-serving-the-common-man-at-st-vincent-de-paul/
Ed Zuercher	Phoenix City Manager Biographical information: https://www.phoenix.gov/citymanager/executive-team/ed-zuercher

of food safety policies, the eradication of smallpox, the fight against drunk driving, and many others. Some of the history is personal history, including everything from Bozeman's work on a citizen's advisory commission on water and sewer privatization to Crow's work developing the Starbucks-ASU Alliance for education. There are extended sections based on Crow's experiences managing the largest university in the United States. While we are not bashful about drawing from our own experiences and warned at the beginning that this is a more personal book than most, we can say in our defense that we certainly do not view our experiences as definitive or unique, and we invite the reader to not only reflect on them but also argue with the lessons we draw from them.

Perhaps most unconventional, but certainly in keeping with the personalistic tone of the book, our concluding chapter presents a conversation between the authors, a conversation reflecting on and extending the public values, management, and leadership topics explored in the book. In the unconventional final chapter please accept our invitation to engage in a "conversation" with the authors, though necessarily at some remove.

For readers more at home with the conventional, the next chapter comes closest. In chapter 1 we dig into the nature of public interest theory, its relation to public values, and its contrasts with market failure theory.

Public Values Theory

A Short, Practical History

Introduction: Caveat Lector

Whereas most chapters in this book have a strong orientation toward practicality, this chapter is a bit more philosophical and theoretical than the others.[1] We expect that many readers will likely be content with the uncomplicated public values concept we presented right at the beginning of the introduction—public values as the "fundamental rights and benefits to which all citizens are entitled." That definition conveys enough meaning that one armed only with it and with no extra frills will easily be able to move through this book. Satisfied with the simple but functional public values concept we already introduced? Then you may wish to move along to chapter 2 or beyond. We shall catch up with you later.

We are professional nerds of long standing (a nerd in this case defined as one who actually enjoys reading philosophy), and we expect that some percentage of our readers will likewise have a bit of nerd affinity. Such kindred spirits will be unsatisfied with the introduction's simple, functional public values concept, a serviceable concept, but one that leaves out analytical details and nuance. These readers will want to dig more deeply into the public values concept and related concepts from which it evolved. This chapter is for you. Indeed, let us start right away by providing the public values concept central to this chapter: public values are "those values providing normative consensus about (a) the rights, benefits, and prerogatives to which all citizens should (and should not) be entitled; (b) the obligations of citizens to society, the state, and one another; and (c) the principles on which governments and policies should be based" (Bozeman 2007, 131).

Later in this chapter we dissect this definition in some detail. Other topics explored here are as follows: (1) the relation of public values theory to public interest theory; (2) the steps in the development of public values and public failure criteria, especially the possibilities of public values theory as a complement to more familiar and in some respects quite limited market failure theory; (3) the literature on public values theory and research, including the work of major contributors throughout the world; (4) a brief report of some research on citizens' and policy makers' views about which values are perceived as public values and why; and (5) the limitations of public values theory and why those wishing to apply it need be aware of its shortcomings. Since public values theory is in some respects a response to the dominance of economic reasoning in public policy making (as suggested in the introduction), we spend quite a bit of space detailing why we think economic approaches are insufficient to address many public issues and decisions.

In the introduction, we provided a personal case and other explanations as to why we became interested in developing public values theory. However, public values theory did not emerge out of the ether. Here we discuss some of the theoretical or philosophical precursors of public values theory.

Public Values Theory Antecedents

The term "public values," in the specific meaning discussed here, has been around for only a short period of time (see Bozeman 2002), but it has many antecedents. From Aristotle's Lyceum to the 1787 Constitutional

Convention in Philadelphia and beyond, there has been continual discussion of concepts linked closely to public values, including such familiar terms as "public interest" and "the common good." Sometimes ideas related closely to public values have been expressed in language predating the invention of public values theory, often in poetic language, such as "certain inalienable rights," or as inspiration words, such as "government of the people, by the people, for the people, shall not perish from the earth." None of these ideas or concepts move far away from the other accepted lexical meaning of "public" as "concerning the people as a whole."

Public Interest Theory: Taproot of Public Values

As implied, political theorists have a long history of developing ideas about the nature, rights, and duties of citizens, often under the term "the public interest." Not only do such ruminations predate contemporary political science and public administration, not to mention public values theory, but ideas about the public interest have been with us for centuries. In his *Politics*, Aristotle was preoccupied with what he referred to as the "common interest" (to koinei sympheron) (Swanson 1992). Many centuries later, Scottish philosopher David Hume, in his *A Treatise of Human Nature: Being an Attempt to Introduce the Experimental Method of Reasoning into Moral Subjects* (1739), proposed that rules of justice require an appeal to the "public interest" and that rules be justified by their correspondence to the public interest (MacIntyre 1969). Hume's work in moral philosophy (if not his work on empiricism) was influenced by one of the most eminent philosophers of the seventeenth century, John Locke. In his *Second Treatise of Government*, Locke contends that "the peace, safety, and public good of the people" are included among the "transcendent political purposes." Both Hume and Locke were key figures influencing the thinking of the framers of the US Constitution. Their influence on the "Founding Father of the Constitution," James Madison, is particularly noteworthy (Lutz 1984).

During the early years of formal political science scholarship, many noteworthy scholars gave considerable attention to ideas about the public interest. For example, much of the work of Pendleton Herring (1936) centered on public interest theory and was widely disseminated in the discipline owing to Pendleton's academic acclaim and his presidency of the American Political Science Association. In political science, public interest theory began to wane in the late 1960s as the "behavioral revolution" emerged. The political science discipline began to take the "science" part of its name more seriously. As a field that had been dominated by history, law, and case studies began to gravitate to quantitative data and statistics, and, more importantly, as the discipline embraced philosophy of science and empiricism, public interest theory was found wanting. Indeed, it was and is. One interested in precision, explanation, and measurement finds little to love in public interest theory.

Glendon Shubert (1957) mounted one of the most effective attacks on the structure and content of public interest theory by dismissing public interest as a set of myths. That same year, Frank Sorauf, another highly respected scholar, denigrated public interest theory and charged it scathingly with perpetuating "fables about the political process" (Sorauf 1957, 638). Interestingly, neither of these well-regarded political scientists was much involved in public administration or, until their critical writings, public interest theory. Shubert was a judicial politics researcher, and Sorauf was best known as a student of political parties. After working briefly and with considerable success to drive a stake through the heart of public interest theory, neither spent any significant time afterward on public interest theory.

In retrospect, it seems a bit surprising that so few circa-1960s public administration scholars, who had previously embraced public interest theory with fervor, came to its defense. Perhaps this reluctance is explained by the fact that public administration as a field was widely under attack in what was then its traditional disciplinary home, political science. Public administration had come to be viewed as insufficiently scientific to meet the new standards for behavioral political science. In the wake of internal disciplinary turmoil and schisms, public interest theory was essentially collateral damage and left bleeding on the sidewalk. Both political science and public administration scholars turned attention to more timely and fashionable topics. Public interest theory never really recovered from the intellectual attacks and the changes of scholarly fashion witnessed in the late 1950s and early 1960s. One scanning the second half of the twentieth century for academic studies aimed at developing public interest theory searches in vain.

Despite the decline and, indeed, near death of public interest theory in academia, practitioners carried the flame, not only talking about the public interest but also weighing their concepts of the public interest in public policy decisions. References and appeals to the public interest permeate public law, and especially regulatory law, in the United States and other democratic nations (Varuhas 2014). The term finds life in the contemporary political deliberations of pundits and the discourse of ordinary citizens. Public interest may have largely disappeared from academic journals, but it retains a strong hold on citizens and public administration practitioners.

The Demise of Public Interest Theory, the Rise of Private Interest Theory

Some of us grieved at the death of public interest theory, even if we did understand its fatal pathology. The critics weren't wrong. Public interest theory was and is too general and ambiguous and fails to generate measures or even precise concepts. Developing analytical rigor proves difficult when we consider the most familiar scholarly definition of public interest: "what men would choose if they saw clearly, thought rationally, [and] acted disinterestedly and benevolently" (Lippmann 1955, 40).[2] Any concept requiring for its application knowledge of the rationality, benevolence, and disinterestedness of behavior, and with no accompanying evidence, has limited utility in the actual design of institutions and public policy. Nor do we find other versions of public interest theory that lend much hope of yielding research or explanatory theory. Public interest theory proves more a symbol than a theory, either empirical or normative (Cochran 1974). Other than its symbolic value, public interest theory has only one thing going for it, but it is not a small thing: it pushes us to contemplate the nature of a just, beneficent, and inclusive society.

As scholars began to forsake public interest theory owing to its limitations as a theory and policy makers continued to be frustrated by public interest theory's lack of practicality and its ineffability, few alternatives emerged to the United States' other theory of governance, not public value or public interest but rather aggregated individual interest (i.e., utilitarianism). In many ways this has provided most unfortunate. Even if public interest theory did a poor job of showing how one might develop instruments, measures, or even specific propositions related to the particular contexts of public decisions, its general contours and symbolic values at least suggested the possibility of making decisions based in part on concerns not easily embraced in standard economic approaches.

As we shall discuss in more detail below, public values theory can be thought of as an effort to retain the ideals of public interest theory but with less ambiguity and imprecision. We understand that economic analysis and economic models have much to contribute to understanding and analyzing policy. After this brief discussion, we move to public values criteria we feel should complement market failure theory. We shall see that both approaches to making decisions about provision of public goods and services have their limitations.

Market Failure as a Theory of Public Policy

Economists have generated a great many approaches to valorizing market reasoning and economic efficiency as means of making public decisions and highlighting limits to government. These include, among others, principal-agent models (Morduch and Armendariz 2005), transactions cost theory (Buchanan 1973), proprietary property rights theory (Alchian and Demsetz 1973), benefit-cost analysis (Maass 1966; a technique that has many embedded theory assumptions; see Dasgupta and Pearce 1972), and, most venerable, various forms of utilitarian theory (Posner 1979).[3] The various economics-based approaches have at least one thing in common: compared to public interest theory, each is more precise and yields propositions that are potentially testable or directly applicable. Thus, the theories have given rise to a wide variety of policy instruments, including, for example, many forms of privatization and contracting out (see Brooks 2004 for an overview), tax credits (Bloom, Griffith, and Van Reenen 2002; Wu 2005), pollution (and other negative externality), credit trading and offsets (e.g., Krupnick, Oates, and Van De Verg 1983; Needham et al. 2019), and tournaments (Dechenaux, Kovenock, and Sheremeta 2015; Glaeser et al. 2016), among others.

Our chief interest here is not in the various approaches above, except as they touch on our primary target, market failure theory. As a way of thinking about public allocation of goods and services, market failure theory has, we feel, been more influential than any other theory of public finance, chiefly because it has found its place in the thoughts of ordinary citizens who have little experience with formal economics and, as a result, is the framework most often applied to policy (Zerbe and McCurdy 2000). While many of the basic ideas in market failure are quite old, it emerged as a coherent, or at least a systematic, theory in the 1950s. Those most often credited with formulating market failure theory are the economists Paul Samuelson (1954) and Francis Bator (1958). In our view, Bator's version is more accessible and multifaceted, but Samuelson had a huge effect on popularizing the theory because he was the author of the best-selling textbook *Economics* (Samuelson 1948), now in its 19th edition (Samuelson and Nordhaus 2009), its impact only somewhat tempered by Samuelson's death in 2009. A significant percentage of all college students since 1945 have been assigned this landmark textbook.

The policy relevance of market failure theory is its attendant failure criteria, but Donahue (1991, 18) provides a useful and succinct account of the underlying idea of market failure, noting that it occurs when "prices lie—that is, when the prices of goods and services give false signals about their real value, confounding the communication between consumers and producers." The chief cause of market failure is when goods are "nonrival," with one person's consumption having no substantial effect on its availability to others. Other reasons why markets fail include the following:[4]

1. Imperfect information. Information needed for buyers and sellers to make rational decisions is for some reason inadequate. Usually either the buyer or the seller has more information (asymmetric information, which results in an imbalance of power between the two and, thus, market failure).
2. Monopoly. The market is controlled by a single provider of a good or service, making competition impossible and, thus, resulting in market failure.
3. Transaction costs. When there are high costs of conducting market exchange, markets fail because this type of cost introduces an inefficiency that has nothing to do with the value of the good or service. A common example is the commission one pays to a stockbroker or to those who broker tickets to events.
4. Externalities (spillover effects). In a perfect market, only the buyer and seller experience any cost or benefit. When costs or benefits affect parties not directly involved in the market exchange, then these are deemed externalities and defined as market failure. An example of a market failure is a transaction between a smoker and a seller of tobacco products. The seller receives a market price for the tobacco, and the buyer "benefits" from the enjoyment of the habit (and pays its cost in terms of personal health). But when other parties experience unpleasantness or poor health due to secondhand smoke, then there are negative externalities. Education is an example of a positive externality. Benefits accrue not only to the individual but also to society because the individual has greater human capital, is likely more productive, and contributes to the society's overall economic wealth and perhaps to an increased tax base.
5. Missing or incomplete markets. Sometimes needed goods and services are not available in the market because there is insufficient incentive to produce them or because no one had identified a method to produce them. The former case includes problems with intellectual property rights—if authors or inventors cannot be sure they can capture profits from the time and energy

invested in goods and services, they will likely not produce or will underproduce the good or service.

6. Volatile markets. In some cases, goods and services will be produced at a less-than-optimal level (not meeting demands) because economic and social forces make markets highly unstable. A good example is agricultural products. As weather extremes become more common and crop failure more likely and less predictable, growers have less incentive to produce agricultural goods sufficient to meet demand.

The Public Bottom Line

This is not a course in economics. Thus, while there are many intellectually and practically interesting implications of market failure theory, our concern is the fact that market failure theory is so often employed in decisions about allocation of duties between the public and private sectors. The market failure prescription is straightforward:

- Step One: Determine whether, in fact, there has been a market failure, and if there is none, leave the market alone and let it oversee all transactions of interest, providing all goods and services.
- Step Two: If there is a market failure, then it is time to seek to somehow regulate the market—through government, social agreement, or social manipulation of practice, or by having the good or service provided by others. One of these "others" is government, but others also include voluntary organizations, charities, nonprofit organizations, and private foundations, among others.
- Step Three: Allow government to "intervene" in the marketplace, but only if its intervention addresses market failures and does so better and more efficiently than is possible with other private providers.

This account, thus, means that government is a "last resort" provider of goods and services and should stay out of any domain where there is not clear evidence of market failure. The presumption is that markets inevitably prove more effective at producing any good or service when markets are efficient. Government is the residual category. Now let us consider why this characterization is both wrong and injurious.

The Failures of Market Failure

It is easy enough to understand the popularity of market failure as a guide to public policy, especially in the United States. The market failure model fits well with the economic individualism at the core of American political culture (Feldman 1982; Shen and Edwards 2005). The preference for market approaches to problems not only predates the market failure model but also was in many respects built into the nation's founding (McNamara 1998, 101), in both sensible ways (e.g., early laws about patents and property rights) and pernicious, evil ways, including the legal validation of owning and selling human beings. But it should surprise no one who has studied the economics of frontier culture (Bazzi, Fiszbein, and Gebresilasse 2020) and the libertarian forces underpinning the founding of the United States (Egnal 1975; Perkins 1988; Innes 1995) that so many citizens and policy makers agree with Thoreau's idea that the government that governs best governs least. Indeed, this is such a popular notion that we often erroneously attribute it to Founding Father Jefferson, perhaps because a national cultural touchstone fares better when associated with the polymath president and primary author of the Declaration of Independence than an eccentric misanthrope best known today for glorifying his preference for living alone in the rural Massachusetts woods.

Doubtless, there are some things to like about market failure as a guide to making decisions about public policy choices and the role of government. Unlike public interest theory and most political science theories, market failure theory provides some relatively simple guidelines, ones that are based on explicit assumptions. However, the explicit assumptions are deficient and shortsighted.

In our view, the most grievous problem with the market failure model is its core assumption that the choice among institutional actors to provide goods and services should be based on pricing efficiency and that pricing efficiency should be privileged among the many possible values obtaining in society. Pricing efficiency may or may not be a way to govern private economic transactions, but it is no way to govern a society and collective choices.

Many vital collective choice (and public value) considerations seem to us at least as important as maximizing transactional economic efficiency, and these other values cannot be easily accommodated in the market failure model except through the most tortuous logic. First, it seems to us that collective choice, even when based on market considerations, should perhaps give some attention to whether people in society have resources to participate in markets. The market failure makes no distinction between economic outcomes for people who are working hard to provide socially significant goods and services, such as emergency medical personnel or front-line health care workers, many of whom are working at minimum-wage jobs, and those who possess vast amounts of multigenerational wealth, live on trust funds, and provide no direct benefit to society except, perhaps, by generating economic spillovers with their consumer purchases. Market failure is ahistorical, not giving any attention to how and why certain classes of consumers came to be advantaged over others.

Relatedly, most economists are beginning to conclude, along with social and political analysts, that at a certain point the degree of inequality in a society begins to have deleterious effects for the economy as a whole (Stiglitz 2012; Block and Somers 2014; Bartels 2018). Few, even in the upper echelons of the economy, benefit in the long run from an ever-increasing disparity in wealth and income. Conventional market failure reasoning pays no attention to this set of concerns, in part because market failure not only is ahistorical but also gives no consideration to long-term impacts. Market failure is a theory of the moment, and that moment is the execution of a discrete economic transaction.

Market failure gives no encouragement to anyone who feels that government often has a positive role. True, market failure theory grudgingly offers criteria for "government intervention," but only as a last resort, and, importantly, government is only one possible institutional intervention. The idea that government might actually take a lead in activities where an efficient market exists or may exist soon is anathema. Market failure tends to ignore those many instances when businesses work with government as cooperative partners, with business pursuing market approaches even as government simultaneously pursues any of a great many possible policy instruments alongside business. For example, at various stages in the history of the development of the internet and the World Wide Web, and even the commercialization of the internet, markets worked reasonably well and government activity supplemented market activity (Rogers and Kingsley 2004; Leiner et al. 2009).

Perhaps the most glaring problem with market theory is this: if governments should have a role to play only when markets fail, then there is virtually no limit (by market failure criteria) to government expansion. While not having fully lodged in the mind of many citizens, most economists (e.g., Robinson 1953; Stiglitz 1979; DeJong and Whiteman 1992; Barnett, Block, and Saliba 2005) recognize that the perfectly efficient market is not a practical goal but rather a useful ideal concept that almost never corresponds with any empirical reality, expect perhaps in the case of very simple person-to-person transactions. Even if one wished to be quite methodical in applying the market failure model, reality would require challenging and difficult work aimed at answering the following question: "What kinds of market failure at what acceptable tolerances?"

The fact that market failure presents a series of evaluation criteria for "intervention" gives it a veneer of analytical precision, but, on closer examination, the veneer could hardly be thinner. On close scrutiny market failure criteria present little of use in making broad-based decisions about collective action. In some respects, the idea of externalities proves useful, but even this criterion needs tempering. Externalities almost always exist with any complex collective choice; the only issue is the extent of externalities and determining who bears the benefits and costs of externalities—issues to which economics contributes but which market failure theory does nothing to clarify.

In our view, market failure often just muddies the water, especially for decisions where economic efficiency is not the primary consideration.

It is well past time for market failure to be more widely recognized as a sometimes useful but limited ideal type, one not as different from the public interest ideal as it seems.

Enter the Public Values Alternative

Since the turn of the millennium, a number of scholars have contributed formulations concerning public values, some of them as self-conscious compliments of market failure or other dominant economistic approaches to public policy (a particularly useful overview is provided by Van der Wal, Nabatchi, and De Graaf 2015). While we touch on some of this literature, the predominant focus is on the version of public value theory associated with Bozeman's early work, not only because it occurs early in the theory development chronology but also because one of the prerogatives of an avowedly personal book is to be personal in focus. Below we examine some of the personal motivations for developing public value theory, not as some sort of self-hagiography but because the motivations relate closely to the problems of market failure discussed above. However, we shall also see later in this chapter that public values theory has its own problems that are worth knowing about and, if possible, addressing.

Motivations for Developing Public Value Theory

Remember the "Men in Rubber Boots" story in the introduction? This episode shows one motivation for beginning work on the Bozeman version of public values theory, namely, a concern that no viable public values–focused alternatives to the individual-interest, utilitarian models pervading economic theory could be found. Thus, a first effort (Bozeman 2002) was to create a "public failure model" that would be in some respects analogous to the "market failure" model that dominates so much of economics and, ergo, public policy reasoning. As we see below, public values failure criteria were intended to serve as a counterpoint to market failure and, in many respects at least, turned market failure criteria upside down.

A second public values motivation was "the times" and a frustration with the view that everything that could be privatized should be privatized. Not only were the US federal government (Milward and Provan 2000) and other national governments (Rhodes 1996; Davies 2000) being privatized and "hollowed out" as rapidly and thoroughly as possible, but some municipalities were striving to replace government with full-scale contractor provision of all goods and services (James and Lodge 2003; Anttiroiko, Bailey, and Valkama 2013).

Some readers will recall that in the first decade of the 2000s, the United States became embroiled in what proved to be a controversial ("weapons of mass destruction") war in Iraq. Holding aside for the moment many of the controversies surrounding the war, one motivation for thinking about public values criteria was the fact that this was the first US war to completely set aside one of the most hallowed ideas of "public goods theory," a close counterpart to market failure theory.

In public economy, those who do not pay the price can be excluded from enjoying the benefits of the good, with the advantage that the producer can profit and has an incentive to keep producing the good. By contrast, a good is "nonexcludable" if it is not possible, when the good is produced, to exclude individuals from benefiting from the good, even if they do not pay the price. This leads to inefficient markets, in part because the producer does not receive a price for the good that fully reflects its use and benefit. Another issue is whether a good can be "depleted." If a producer brings tomatoes, smartphones, automobiles, or (in the United States at least) medical insurance to the market, it is easy enough to hold most benefits of production of these goods and services from those who do not pay its price. However, some goods and services are "nondepletable," meaning that once it is produced, one person's enjoyment of the good or service does not reduce its availability to others. At first blush the idea of a nondepletable good or service may seem counterintuitive and perhaps even in violation of the laws of physics. But the idea is clarified with a couple of examples. Knowledge is an example of a nondepletable good. Let us say we are interested in learning how to solve differential equations and, after a good deal of work, we have full command of the knowledge needed to do so. In obtaining this knowledge we have not affected the ability of some other person to use this same knowledge.

A primary assumption of modern economics is that knowing whether a good or service is a public or a private good tells us much about whether it is best to have government or the private sector produce the good or service. In reality this is not always easy because, while "public goods" and "private goods" are quite distinct, a great many goods and services, ones usually referred to as "quasi-public goods," are partly depletable or partly exclusive. However, fine-grained differences (i.e., reality) aside, no one really disagrees that government should focus on producing public goods, chiefly because we cannot expect businesses to do so given their economic character; businesses cannot make a profit from pure public goods.

Now we move—perhaps a little more slowly than the reader would prefer—to the point. The classic example of a public good, one that is both nondepletable and nonexcludable, is national defense. One review (Coyne and Lucas 2016) of 20 of the leading introductory textbooks of economics showed that all 20 included national defense as their primary example of a pure public good. While it costs a great deal to provide national defense, once it is provided, one person's use does not diminish its availability to others, and, of course, how could we possibly develop an efficient price for national defense? Hence, we pay for national defense from tax dollars, and we have the government-funded armed services to thank for keeping us safe. At least this was the way things used to work.

Older readers may recall the ties of the Bush administration to the Blackwater Corporation and the large-scale privatization of the Iraq War. At one point, the number of civilians fighting or supporting the war nearly matched the number of US military. In the Iraq War, scandals were associated with civilians and mercenaries, including the conviction of former Blackwater employees for the 2007 massacre of 14 unarmed civilians (Roberts 2014). The increasing privatization of government services is, of course, a tendency that began greatly accelerating during the Reagan administration (Henig 1989). There is nothing new about scandals in various privatized activities, including not only national defense but also many other privatized services, most notoriously perhaps in privatized health and prisons.

Question: when the "pure public good" of national defense responsibilities moves from provision by government to business contactors, when even wars are "run like a business," in direct contradiction to the most basic lessons in public finance and in microeconomics textbooks, is it not time to rethink the utility of microeconomics theory for guiding choices about goods and services affecting every citizen? National defense is, indeed, as close to nonrival and nondepletable as goods and services get.

The turning over of a pure public good to contractors also raises this question: how exactly, and in contradiction to the basics of economic theory, can businesses be induced to invest in the provision of pure public goods and services such as national defense? We think that the answer is easy enough: government load shedding almost always means that businesses must be paid a handsome fee, one that includes a significant profit margin, to provide the public goods formerly provided by government. While it is certainly the case that businesses in some cases strive to achieve public values, most companies in the businesses of war and prisons may be more motivated by windfall profits. One might suggest that, even at a price premium, businesses do a better job of delivering goods and services.

Question: if not even national defense is a "public good" or, to put it another way, a fundamental responsibility of government, then what is? One answer to that question is that there is no need for government, period. This answer is not as uncommon as one might think. Consider, for example, experiments in local government to entirely do away with government, except in its role of overseeing private contractors (Kuttner 1999; Gilroy et al. 2011; Anttiroiko, Bailey, and Valkama 2013). Our answer is that if not even national defense is a public good, then perhaps it is time to reevaluate the utility of public goods theory and, generally, microeconomics in determining who should achieve public purposes and how.

Even many public administration scholars, usually circumspect about run-government-like-a-business claims, were jumping on the bandwagon under the label "new public management" (NPM). At the risk of being accused of oversimplifying an oversimplification, suffice it to say that NPM is a how-to theory about making government run like a business (those who wish for a more sophisticated account can refer to Lane 2000; Schedler and Proeller 2000; Pollitt, Van Thiel, and Homburg 2007). NPM was never as influential in the United States as in Europe and the United Kingdom and Commonwealth, chiefly because few in the United States would find novelty in the primary premises of NPM, most of which had long held forth in the United States. Indeed, most US public administrators, including many following closely to the guidelines of NPM, have never heard of NPM, but rather are employing such approaches as privatization, contracting out, and performance management based on ideas that preceded NPM. While the NPM still holds sway, especially in the United Kingdom, its novelty has worn off, and many are beginning to do retrospectives to determine its impacts (Pollitt and Dan 2013; Chandler 2017).

In the United States, NPM did not fare as well with scholars as it did in many other countries. Having been educated in a nation where most citizens believe that "government should be run like a business," a management philosophy saying much the same thing had, for most scholars, little appeal and no novelty. US public administration scholars tend to have little sympathy for stereotypical or ideological thinking about the allocation criteria for public versus private sector (Perry and Rainey 1988; Rainey and Bozeman 2000; Walker et al. 2011; Bromley and Meyer 2017), in part because so many organizations cannot be easily categorized as public or private (Emmert and Crow 1988; Vakkuri and Johanson 2020).

Public Values Failure Criteria: Market Failure Turned Upside Down

Bozeman's (2002) earliest work on public values took a sort of backward approach, focusing not on particular public values (except by implication) but rather on public values failure criteria. This approach, as discussed, grew out of a dissatisfaction with market failure theory and its influence in public policy. Thus, even before developing an explicit conceptualization of public values, the first shot across the bow was an attempt to suggest failures in public values, with the public values implicit in the failures. The resultant "public values failure criteria" (Bozeman 2002), along with subsequent additions (Bozeman 2007; Bozeman and Sarewitz 2011; Bozeman and Johnson 2015), have remained central to public values theory. Indeed, the criteria have been applied in a remarkably diverse set of domains, including, among others, higher education (Anderson and Taggart 2016), climate science (Meyer 2011), knowledge inequality (Monroe-White and Woodson 2016), public utilities (Steenhuisen, Dicke, and De Bruijn 2009; Marie 2016), teaching (Shareef 2008), and management of parasport events (McPherson et al. 2017).

Table 2 provides a list of public values failure criteria, including the ones in the original formulation (Bozeman 2002) as well as two later additions (public sphere and progressive opportunity), along with definitions and illustrations. We shall refer to these criteria at other points in this book, reiterating definitions.

In all likelihood, it is apparent to the reader, even without close inspection, that some of these criteria are "inspired" (in a negative sense) by traditional market failure criteria, but several others seek explicitly to address concerns not touched on in market failure criteria or any familiar microeconomics-based approach to making public policy–relevant decisions.

Among the assumptions included in the original formulation of public values failure criteria, a couple are worth noting since they are relevant to much of the subsequent argument provided here. First, there is not an implication that either business or government (or nonprofit or hybrid organizations) "owns" public values. The focus of public values theory is on achieving public values, not on sorting institutional providers. Relatedly, the approach does not assume that market failure and public failure are at opposite ends of a spectrum, but that collective action may be a combination of public values failure and market success, public values success and market failure, public and market success, and public and market failure. The intent is not to segregate

TABLE 2
Public Values Failure Criteria

Criterion	Definition	Illustration of Public Value Failure and Success
Creation, maintenance, and enhancement of the public sphere	*As a public value:* Open public communication and deliberation about public values and about collective action pertaining to public values. *As a public value enabling institution:* The space, physical or virtual, in which the realization of the public sphere value occurs.	Failure: An authoritarian regime seizes control of the internet or other social media in an effort to exert control of protestors and thereby thwarts open public communication. Success: A deliberative democracy group is established to bring together diverse stakeholders in a local environmental dispute and these stakeholders engage in free and open public values–related communication.
Progressive opportunity	An "equal playing field" is less desirable than collective actions and public policies addressing structural inequalities and historical differences in opportunity structures.	Failure: "Merit-based" policies that fail to distinguish the effects of opportunity structures on achievement. Success: Compensatory education programs.
Mechanisms for values articulation and aggregation	Political processes and social cohesion should be sufficient to ensure effective communication and processing of public values.	Failure: Combination of US Congress's seniority system and noncompetitive districts leading, in the 1950s, to legislative bottlenecks imposed by just a few committee chairs who held extreme values on civil rights, national security, and other issues. Success: The US Congress's seniority system reforms taking into account such factors related to relevant subject matter experience and expertise.
Legitimate monopolies	When goods and services are deemed suitable for government monopoly, private provision of goods and service is a violation of legitimate monopoly.	Failure: Private corporations negotiating under-the-table agreements with foreign sovereigns. Success: Uses of patent policy in allocating intellectual property rights.
Imperfect public information	Similar to the market failure criteria, public values may be thwarted when transparency is insufficient to permit citizens to make informed judgments.	Failure: Public officials developing national energy policies in secret with corporate leaders of energy companies. Success: City council's widely advertised and open hearings about proposed changes in zoning.

TABLE 2 (*continued*)

Criterion	Definition	Illustration of Public Value Failure and Success
Distribution of benefits	Public commodities and services should, ceteris paribus, be freely and equitably distributed. When "equity goods" have been captured by individuals or groups, "benefit hoarding" occurs in violation of public value.	Failure: Restricting public access to designated public use land. Success: Historical policies for the governance of national parks.
Provider availability	When there is a legitimate recognition about the necessity of providing scarce goods and services, providers need to be available. When a vital good or service is not provided because of the unavailability of providers or because providers prefer to ignore public value goods, there is a public values failure due to unavailable providers.	Failure: Welfare checks are not provided owing to the lack of public personnel or failures of technology for electronic checking transactions. Success: Multiple avenues for rapid and secure delivery of income tax refunds.
Time horizon	Public values are long-run values and require an appropriate time horizon. When actions are calculated on the basis of an inappropriate short-term time horizon, there may be a failure of public values.	Failure: Policy for waterways that consider important issues related to recreation and economic development but fail to consider long-run implications for changing habitat for wildlife. Success: Measures taken to ensure long-term viability of pensions.
Substitutability vs. conservation of resources	Actions pertaining to a distinctive, highly valued common resource should recognize the distinctive nature of the resource rather than treat the resource as substitutable or submit it to risk based on unsuitable indemnification.	Failure: In privatization of public services, contractors have to post bond-ensuring indemnification but provide inadequate warrants for public safety. Success: Fishing quotas or temporary bans allowing long-term sustainable populations of food fish.
Ensure subsistence and human dignity	In accord with the widely legitimated Belmont Code, human beings, especially the vulnerable, should be treated with dignity and, in particular, their subsistence should not be threatened.	Failure: Man-made famine, slave labor, political imprisonment. Success: Institutional Review Boards' protections of "vulnerable populations," including children, prisoners, and the mentally ill.

Source: Adapted from Bozeman (2007) and Bozeman and Johnson (2015).

providers of public values but rather to ensure that these values are provided (Rutgers 2015). This is quite consistent with the assumptions that run throughout this book, an emphasis on pragmatism instead of ideology and a sector agnosticism, rejecting the stereotypes that market failure theory (and in some cases political theory) have reinforced.

Building on the Criteria

By the time Bozeman got around to writing his book on public value theory (2007), giving more depth to the ideas that he and others had previously addressed in a series of articles (e.g. Bozeman 2002; Jørgensen and Bozeman 2007), interest in public values theory had, if not exactly caught fire, at least lit a few sparks, especially in Europe. A scholarly tradition developed (for an overview see Van der Wal, Nabatchi, and De Graaf 2015), focused mainly but not exclusively on conceptual work, but also including the odd bit of survey research and case studies.

After having developed a set of public values concepts and the aforementioned public values criteria, public values researchers set about developing propositions about public values and, at least in some cases, testing them. As a result, we now know more about how public values emerge, how they change, how they are enacted, and the complexities of trading off public values against other deeply held values, including not only private economic values but also political values, ideological values, and organizational goals and objectives. We have come to understand, at least to some small degree, how persons pursuing public values in their organizations differ from those driven by more conventional values. Unfortunately, we must confess that public value theory, no matter how much we prize it, is rife with shortcomings, simplifications, and unanswered questions. Not unlike market failure theory, the more serious one becomes about application in managerial action, the more glaring the shortcomings.

Let us consider some of the continuing difficulties of public values theory. Since this is the optional theory chapter, the reader possibly expects that at least one chapter will be devoid of cases and illustrations. Not true. We use the case below to illustrate some of the practical difficulties of public values theory.

Mini-case. Governor Winchester's "Safety through Firepower" Policy Initiative: An Apocryphal Tale Illustrating the Difficulties of Identifying Public Values

First-time political candidate Smith W. Winchester rode his pledge to "make our state safe again" all the way to the governor's office of a medium-sized southwestern state. Since Governor Winchester, a successful entrepreneur and owner of the nation's second-largest online plumbing fixtures retailer, had never before run for office and had provided few specifics in his campaign proposals, the voters did not know exactly what to expect. However, there was some agreement that he would likely fulfill his central and most resonant campaign pledge "to make our citizens safe again." No one was sure just how he would make the state's citizens safer, but since he was a renowned supporter of gun rights, there was little expectation that it would be through gun control policies. Perhaps stiffer criminal penalties or beefed-up police forces?

Finally, Governor Winchester's State of the State message provided the details of his citizen safety measures—citizens would be safer because policies would be advanced to make the state the most gun friendly in America. This approach horrified some citizens, who viewed the ease of gun acquisitions as a core aspect of the state's crime problems, but it elated others who agreed with Governor Winchester that the "bad guys" would think twice about wreaking havoc on citizens when most of the them would be well armed.

The governor's new proposals were sweeping, including repealing all limitations on both open and concealed carry of handguns, overturning background checks, and creating two innovative programs not found in any other state. The first program provided income-limited tax credits for families purchasing their first firearms; the second provided rebates to those choosing to enroll in firearms training courses.

One of the more controversial parts of the governor's "Firepower Safety" legislative package (as it soon came to be known) was to remove all limits on bringing guns to college campuses. In an unfortunate incident shortly before the election, a deranged student had illegally brought a handgun to his geology class and fired on fellow students, seriously wounding three of them. The governor addressed these criticisms head-on, saying, "That is exactly why we need this preventive safety legislation. If the other students had holstered pistols on full display, do you think this unbalanced student would have opened fire? If he had, what is the likelihood he would have gunned down three innocents before anyone managed to take him out?"

The new gun ownership policies were met with enthusiasm in the state legislature, dominated by Winchester's party, and the chances of passing all aspects of the legislation seemed very good. Then, the leading newspaper in the state, the capitol city's *Daily Clarion*, began a campaign against the legislation, including several days' worth of news articles and opinion pieces. The *Daily Clarion*'s hard-hitting articles made all the following arguments, excerpted and quoted below:

> The governor was bought by and is owned by the National Rifle Association. They provided more campaign funding to the governor than did any other nonprofit organization and the NRA public affairs director, Ross Remington, actually wrote many of the policy proposals included in the Governor's reprehensible package.

> Is it only coincidental that Governor Winchester happens to have more than a million dollars in stock in our state's major small arms manufacturing company, a company that would likely benefit more than any other from his tax credit proposal?

> Why is the governor oblivious to the fact that thousands of state university professors, staff, and administrators signed petitions against guns-on-campus policies?

> The *Daily Clarion*'s reader poll shows that 54% of our state's citizens are against expanded gun ownership policies and 61% are opposed to guns-on-campus policies.

Governor Winchester, far from being chastened by the *Daily Clarion*'s campaign, professed "outrage" and "disgust" with the "discredited liberal media." He called a press conference, where he read the following opening statement before entertaining questions:

It is a sad day when the tyrants of the far-left media establishment feel they can derail a vital legislative package aimed at making the citizens of our great state safer and more secure. I am outraged that I need to spend even one minute defending myself or this farsighted and innovative legislative package from the inaccuracies, fabrications and phony polls presented by the *Daily Clarion*. Today, I am going to unmask the lies settled right below the surface of these misleading accusations.

Let me take each allegation point by point. First, I am proud to be a member of the NRA, a distinction I share with a great many of our state's citizens. I was delighted to have the NRA donate to my campaign—as I am sure were the other 137 legislators, all Constitution-loving upholders of the Second Amendment, who were fortunate enough to receive campaign contributions from the NRA. Nor is it a secret that I sought out the advice of NRA's Mr. Ross Remington in developing my legislative package. He is one of the state's foremost experts on gun policies and gun safety.

The *Daily Clarion* got one point right: I do own stock in our state's leading firearms manufacturer, a point that could not have been clearer when during the campaign I freely released my financial statement. I am proud to own stock in one of the leading companies in the state and, if you look at my financial statements, you will see that I own stock in six different, diverse, job-creating businesses located in our state. I invite everyone who loves this state, including the out-of-state owners of the *Daily Clarion*, to donate to our state's foremost businesses.

Now let's talk about the alleged opposition to our policies in support of the Second Amendment. It is true enough that a lot of college professors signed petitions against our public safety reforms but, God love 'em, professors are about the only consistently liberal group in our state. They did sign this petition and many of these same professors also signed petitions this year for such politically correct notions as trigger warning requirements and free speech districts—as if every area of this state were not already a free speech district. More important, a poll conducted by the student government at our largest university showed that more than 60% of students are in favor of carry-on-campus. The students could teach the professors something here. The students know that they will be safer if they don't have to come to campus involuntarily disarmed.

I think my personal favorite among these various lies and distortions is the *Daily Clarion*'s readers' poll. Yes, readers' poll. Readers of the liberal media are hardly a representative group. I have authorized an independent poll and the early results from the Acme Survey Research firm's telephone polling of a representative group of 2,023 citizens of this state show that 71.3% favor our gun reforms generally and that 77.2% favor our new guns-on-campus policies. These are not "readers," these are our fellow citizens.

In conclusion, let's forget about the senseless allegations and the muddle-headed attempts to thwart progress. Let's get on with the business of increasing our citizens' liberties and making our state the safest, most secure state in the union.

Questions?

Public Values Conceptual Issues

This fictional case illustrates several problems with a public values basis for policy making and institutional design. Let us assume that decision makers were to embrace our suggestion to take public values into account in their design of institutions and policies. Doing so suggests that they have, first, some notion as to what constitutes a public value and, second, reason to believe that the causal mechanisms and probable outcomes of their designs would, in fact, enhance the public values in question. Elsewhere (Fukumoto and Bozeman 2019) we refer to the first requirement as the Identification Problem and to the second as the Instrument Problem. The case above well illustrates both problems. To these we can add a third concern, the Motivation Problem: how do we know that those seeming to promote public values are doing so honestly as opposed to as a cover for other values, ones perhaps less public-spirited? Does it really matter whether public values designs are genuinely motivated as opposed to a smokescreen for personal interests?

The Identification Problem

The Identification Problem in public values pertains to the difficulty of knowing a public value when you see one. The literature on public values (for an overview see Van der Wal, Nabatchi, and De Graaf 2015) shows no consensus on public values; indeed, there is no preferred method for identifying public values. Scholars have suggested that public values can be found in literature (Williams and Shearer 2011), in the nation's founding and historically significant documents (Jørgensen and Bozeman 2007), from polls of citizens and leaders (Van der Wal, De Graaf, & Lasthuizen 2008), and in public participation and deliberative processes (Davis and West 2009; Nabatchi 2012). Most agree that public values are mutable, at least in the long term, further exacerbating the Identification Problem.

In the Governor Winchester case above, what is the public value(s) pursued, if any? Clearly Governor Winchester's policies suggest at least two major values. They suggest values related to personal safety and to liberty, specifically liberty as it pertains to ownership, display, and use of weapons. One need not dig deeply to see these values manifested in the proposed policies. But are these values upon which the functional case turns actually public values in the meaning provided above? Just as important—and this is frequently a problem with public values—are the two values at odds?

The Instrument Problem

The identification issue is related to the Instrument Problem. Public values can be achieved only if the instruments designed to achieve them are effective. In this case, as in so many others, we do not actually know how instrument relates to outcome. We shall see below that a higher percentage of US citizens feel that gun ownership is itself a public value. Many feel that gun ownership provides a means of enhanced personal safety and agree with our fictional Governor Winchester's notion of mutually assured destruction, that is, to increase the presence of weapons, a strategy that worked for years in nuclear weapons policy and can work as well at a small personal scale. The idea is that those tempted to use weapons will think twice if they know that others around them are armed. At the same time, many other people feel that the increased presence and availability of weapons make citizens less safe. There is some evidence supporting each view, so who is right? At this point, the best answer, despite intense feeling among disputants, is that we do not know for sure. This is a key problem in public values. If we are to achieve a public value, say, public safety, we also need to be operating under the correct causal assumptions—and doing so is rarely easy.

Approaching the Instrument Problem: Taking Solace from Its Generality

To reiterate, the Instrument Problem reminds us that even if we have identified an appropriate public values basis for policy and institutional design, there is no guarantee that doing so will ensure that the policy or action instruments employed to achieve the public values will be effective. While this is, indeed, a formidable problem, we do not feel that it is an obstacle to pursing public values–based policies and designs. We have no solution for the problem, only our claim that the problem is independent of the values basis of actions. Yes, it is true that a poor policy or action instrument may foil an excellent public values basis, but the same is true for small group values bases, or for economic efficiency bases, or even individual personal values bases. We know from everyday life that when we as individuals pursue a course of action that we feel will enhance some treasured personal value, we often choose instruments that turn out to be flawed, sometimes our causal reasoning is flawed, or, in some cases, the relevant environment has changed, perhaps casting asunder our best-laid plans. Thus, this is certainly a criticism of public values–motivated actions, because it is a criticism of all human actions taken under conditions of uncertainty, which is to say all human actions.

The best approach to guarding against ill effects of the Instrument Problem is careful design, care not specific to public values–based action. One can strive to develop the best possible causal reasoning, testing out as many alternative plausible outcome hypotheses and contingencies as possible, and once the instrument has been set in motion, one can evaluate results using the best available social technologies developed for outcome evaluation, all of which are as applicable to public values–based instruments as to any others.

The Motivation Problem

The Motivation Problem, likewise, is well illustrated in the Governor Winchester case. Are Governor Winchester's motives pure? Does he really want to advance public safety and liberty, or is he more concerned with his personal investments and past and future campaign donations? Is he pandering, or is he trying to enhance public values as he sees them? In a very real sense, it is almost always impossible to know people's motivations. However, it seems feasible in some cases to make judgments based on evidence. The problem in our fictional case, and so often in reality, is that the evidence from which we wish to make inference sometimes is less than clear-cut. Reasonable people could look carefully at the press allegations and the governor's rebuttal and come to completely different conclusions as to whether he is a selfless public servant pursuing public values–based policies or a self-interested trickster achieving his own agenda, the public be damned. When we consider the recent trends in ever-lower confidence in mass media[5] (Graber and Dunaway 2017) and the vast ideological gulf among groups of US citizens[6] (Rempel 2018), disagreements about motivations seem almost certain to occur.

Just as important for present purposes, does it really make any difference whether the hearts of leaders and decision makers are pure? Or is it better to focus only on results? Either way, this much is true: we cannot know motivations in any absolute sense; therefore, is the search for indirect evidence worthwhile? Perhaps. If we have some insight into motivation, no matter whether indirect and inferred, it may be easier to make judgments about the plausibility of instrumental claims and about likely future behavior.

The Motivation Problem: How and Why to Ignore It

The Motivation Problem concerns the sincerity of public values expressions. We know that a great many decision makers and leaders cloak their actions, sometimes even destructive actions, in the most public-spirited and benevolent rhetoric. How do we know when public values–based policies and designs are truly motivated by good intent?[7]

We feel there are two answers to this question, one more important than the other. First, by watching patterns of behavior over the long term, it is usually possible to make better inferences about motivation as related action. The better answer: it is not possible to gauge motivation, and it is not particularly important to do so. How can we know about others' motivations when so often (1) they do not know them themselves (rationalization and delusion are well known) and (2) an individual's many actions are subject to multiple motives, sometimes even conflicting ones? The impossibility of parsing out motivations becomes even more evident when we consider that (3) few large-scale policy and institutional designs are the creation of a single individual and few, if any, are implemented by a single individual. That means, of course, that the likelihood is even greater for multiple and mixed values as motivation for the actions taken in pursuit of any design or policy goal.

The fact that individual motivations are essentially unknowable does not imply that the rationales presented for policy and designs are unimportant; indeed, they are enormously important for rallying support, galvanizing supporters, and assessing outcomes against goals. The stuff of leadership is to a large degree the ability to envision rationalizations for action that will resonate with others and will motivate collective action. The purity of leaders' motivations is unknowable and ultimately not so important. Pure motives accompanied by bad outcomes are prized only by the least pragmatic of people.

We turn next to the public values problem that is really the nub of things and the chief obstacle to a public values–based approach to policy and design: the Identification Problem. The good news: we think we have a viable solution (imperfect but viable).

Public Values: Approaches to the
Knowing-Them-When-You-See-Them Problem

We did not want to tell the reader this until now, wishing not to dampen enthusiasm for finding a solution, but resolving this problem is not in any sense a precondition to public values management and leadership. We have, of course, already tipped our hand on this issue. We note, more than once, that public values leaders achieve great things with no apparent knowledge of public values theory and with little apparent questioning of their own ability to identify public values. Still, we have tentative solutions or, better said, approaches to setting aside the problem.

Our proposed approaches to identifying public values include the following:

1. Positing them
2. Inferring them from
   a. relevant literature
   b. historical documents
3. Specifying criteria for assessment
4. Asking people

Each of these approaches has some hazard, but each of them can work just fine. We review them in turn.

Positing Public Values

Operationalization is a wonderful thing. If I think that, say, reducing infant mortality is a public value, why would I need to go into great conceptual agonies to defend the idea that most people, excepting the occasional Malthusian, would think society better off with more live births and fewer dead babies? Relatedly, would we not be willing to suspend discussion about whether this is a fundamental right to which citizens should feel entitled? This, of course, is why public values leaders can get a lot done without the aid of analytical philosophers—they just get at it.

But what about a more difficult case? As we will see below, citizens are split on the issue of whether the ability to own firearms is a public value. Certainly, it is a part of the US Bill of Rights, but in language that is fraught with possibilities for interpretation and disagreements. What does this mean for positing a public value? In the scheme of things, probably not that much. Those opposed to unrestricted gun ownership will believe they are working for a public value, and those who want to guard against any barrier to gun ownership rights will, likewise, be confident they are working to achieve a public value. In either case, lessons about public values leadership and management are obtained (though we confess that we are hoping more people in one group apply those lessons than people in the other group).

The important issues about positing public values are that it needs to be done clearly, people must understand the public value, and it helps to do so without prevarication and with a commitment to living up to the standards and consequences of the public value. One should also expect, as in the gun control case, to engage those who do not agree. You may posit your public value, and you may deeply feel you have tapped a public value, but that does not mean that all will agree—which is true of every other approach to identifying public values.

Inferring Public Values

Two approaches have been used for inferring public values. Jørgensen and Bozeman (2007) undertook an analysis of literature pertaining to public values and identified more than 200 putative public values and then sought to pare them down into constellations of values. Some of the more prominent public values elicited in the study included human dignity, collective choice, majority rule, protection of minorities, accountability, openness, ethical consciousness, integrity, compromise and balancing of interests, legal protection, justice, and citizen involvement, all reflecting a public values literature where what little data have been collected are derived from public officials and public managers.

The other approach to inferring has not often been implemented but has often been suggested by public values scholars: infer public values from the most important political and legal documents in a society, especially founding documents if feasible. This has the merit of identifying values that are demonstrably important but, of course, must recognize changes that occur in values and the emergence of new documents that give evidence of those changes. Below we discuss one study that used this approach.

Asking People

Remarkably, the "asking people" approach to identifying public values has thus far gained relatively little traction. While there are several studies examining public managers' ideas about public values, we know of exactly one (Bozeman 2019) that tried to elicit public values assessments from a set of ordinary citizens. Thus, we review that citizen public value research literature, all one of them.

The study began by developing a list of candidate public values, ones common in literature but also intuitive. Then, the candidate values were set in historical context, rooted in specific foundational documents, including the US Constitution, groundbreaking policy statements or speeches, and landmark Supreme Court decisions.

Bozeman surveyed more than 2,000 US citizens, asking them whether they viewed each nominated value as a public value according to the definition of public value provided them, one quite similar to that used here and in previous publications, but simplified for a diverse set of respondents. Finally, results were examined and classified.[8]

A high bar was set for designation as a public value—90% agreement among the respondents. The task of identifying "candidate values" as possible public values is not in any sense objective. However, the use of a stringent criterion for qualifying as a public value certainly made the task easier. Values not making the 90% threshold but exceeding 50% were classified as "contested values." Presumably, some of these might ultimately evolve into consensual public values.

As reported in Bozeman (2019), the research went on to discuss the attributes of persons supporting particular values as public values, and, importantly, another part of the research examined "enacted public

TABLE 3
Citizen-Assessed Public Values

Consensus Public Values	Contested Public Values
Freedom of speech (97.5%)	Women's right to terminate pregnancy (62.3%)
Liberty (97.2%)	Gun ownership (63.8%)
Civil rights (96.0%)	Racial and ethnic diversity (71.5%)
Political participation (93.8%)	Privacy (82.0%)
Freedom of religion (92.9%)	Economic opportunity (85.0%)
Gender equity (91.4%)	Access to health care (85.0%)
Safety and security (90.1%)	Protection of minority interests (86.1%)

Source: Adapted from Bozeman (2019).

values," ones that required not a rating but a response to a concrete situation. Unsurprisingly, when given a concrete decision to make (such as whether to support free speech even if the speaker is criticizing active duty military), the support for candidate public values diminishes. However, we are interested not in detailed aspects of the article but in the public values that emerged from the research. These are presented in table 3.

Do you find any of these public values surprising? Bozeman did. The fact that 91.4% of respondents agreed that gender equity is a public value, a "prerogative to which all citizens should be entitled," while certainly a laudable sentiment, seems a bit out of step with a society in which so many face gender-based obstacles. Perhaps social policy has not yet caught up with social consensus. One the other side, Bozeman was surprised to find that access to health care did not quite make it as a consensus public value. In all likelihood, the contentious nature of the US debate on health care policy undermined any possibility for greater consensus.

Discussion

The odds are pretty small that any readers were included in the study above, so here is a chance to have your say. Maybe you will wish to answer the questions below and, even better, discuss them with others.

1. Among the list of consensus and contested public values presented above, which meet with your agreement (remember-

ing the definition of public values provided at the beginning
of the chapter)? Which ones do not meet your standard for a
public value, and why?
2. What is missing from the list?
3. To what extent do you feel that the United States (or fill in the
blank with your own country if you are a citizen of a different
nation) has in large measure provided these public values?
4. What have been the vehicles for providing these public values
(to whatever extent provided)? What has been the role of,
respectively, public policy, organic social evolution, citizen
demands, and other historical forces? Can you identify particular individuals who have been most important in either helping
provide the public values or thwarting them?

Knowing One When We See It: What Approach Is Best?

The five approaches to identifying public values are certainly quite different from one another, and they also differ a bit in function and utility. Positing public value has the merit that it is easy to do and, with
care, easy to communicate. If people are going to work hard to achieve
a public value, they probably do not require a massive analysis or de-
construction of the concept, just a good understanding of the public
value to be pursued.

Distilling public values from existing literature seems a useful enterprise only for academics (and we are, and so we have). But it has
limited value for public values management and leadership, and few
people can be induced to join a cause because of its presence in academic journals. "Rally around the Literature!" is just not a powerful clarion cry.

Distilling public values from documents and cultural artifacts probably holds a little more promise for practical public values leadership
and management, but chiefly as an educational function. It may well
have value for public values warriors to know more about the history
and origins of their public values concern and how and why public values have evolved.

The chief value of the criterion approach is that it can require some thought and some clarification of purpose and approach. There is no reason why any set of criteria should be taken as the be-all and end-all, especially given the advantages likely to accrue from people thinking about just what criteria are important to them in their own public values efforts.

Finally, there is the "ask them" approach. While this approach may prove helpful in some circumstances, it is probably most useful in identifying values in which controversy remains. In particular, much can be learned by having respondents choose among public values, perhaps pitting one public value (or contested value) against another. It is likewise potentially useful to consider the difference between talking the talk (evaluating a value as a public value) and walking the walk (applying it in a concrete circumstance).

Where does this leave us? We urge researchers to do more research, theorists to do more theorizing, and public values managers and leaders to do what they always have: change the world and wait for researchers and theorists to catch up.

2

Three Premises of Public Values–Based Management

As academic researchers we have, over the years, picked up many of the habits nonacademics often associate with professors: a focus on abstraction, a fascination with esoterica, and seemingly inexplicable devotion to abstruse theory. Guilty as charged. However, the previous chapter on public values theory notwithstanding, our chief concern here is not with theory but with the achievement of public values, and, ultimately, public values are achieved by leaders and managers. Thus, time to talk about what we mean by public values–based management.

While the term "management" has been defined in innumerable ways, most definitions suggest that management involves the coordination of people and resources to obtain common goals (Pettinger 2012). Public values management has much in common with other approaches to management, but when the most important organizational goals are rooted in public values, some aspects of management differ a bit and others are turned inside out. For example, one of the truisms about almost all organizations is that their first imperative is their own survival (Bennet and Bennet 2004; Lamberg et al. 2009). However, in public values management, the organization's growth, longevity, and survival often are less important to leaders and stakeholders than the public value goals the organization serves. Managing for public values does not require that public values objectives drive out other objectives or even that public values must necessarily be the first priority for the organization. As we see in many places in this book, organizations that are not primarily focused on public values often contribute greatly to achieving public values. Monomania is not required, nor is public values zealotry. Organization leaders and managers often contribute by being part-time public values warriors. Nonetheless, there are instances when the organization and its survival may be less important than the public values served by the organization. Not often, but it happens. For example, if you are a scientist working in a pharmaceutical company and you know that your organization is delaying the distribution of a vaccine that you have helped produce that will save tens of thousands of lives for the reason that its price fixing scheme is not yet fully developed—is the priority the organization or the public value? Yes, this is an extreme example, but not an unrealistic one. To put it another way, one does not have to be a full-time public values warrior to be an excellent leader, but one must keep at least one eye on the prize, the public values prize, not (only) the commonplace objectives of accumulating great personal or corporate wealth, or fame, or power. Public values leaders may in some cases compromise on public values, trade them off against other values, put their achievement on hold until the time is right, or work fervently on other objectives having nothing to do with public values—but public values leadership does not work unless there is always some attention to the need to achieve public values to some degree and at some appropriate time. Any other values framework puts one in the garden-variety self-interested category.

There are many leadership and management books aiming to help people be garden-variety, fully and rationally self-interested "successes." This is not such a book. We are not speaking into the void. We know that public values managers and leaders, current and future, are out there. That is one thing we know from the long-popular "public service motivation" (PSM) research (Perry 1997; Moynihan and Pandey 2007; Perry and Hondeghem 2008; Ritz, Brewer, and Neumann 2016), even with its many occasional flaws and measurement problems (Bozeman and Su 2015). The PSM literature has as its focus just what the name implies, measuring and theorizing about the extent to which people profess or manifest a motivation to serve the public, usually but not always while working in public service organizations.

If we can believe the hundreds of people who have responded to PSM surveys in a great many studies in multiple nations, the force is strong within them, at least a great many of them. Likewise, Bozeman and Crow note that in their experience teaching literally thousands of public policy and administration students the "[motivation] to serve the public" idea, whether measured in PSM or not, is both pervasive and real. Students go into public affairs education with the career objective to "make a difference," a sentiment usually in accord with achieving public values.

In this chapter we posit three "premises" for public values management and leadership. None of these will seem unfamiliar since we discussed them in the introduction and chapter 1, but not in detail and not under the "premise" label. But these ideas are sufficiently important that they warrant further discussion and recognition as core bases of public values management. The premises include a core public value assumption, sector agnosticism, and pragmatism. As is our usual approach in this book, we not only give details about each of these premises but also provide context in cases and examples. The chapter begins with a case all too relevant for our time: the eradication of a worldwide scourge, in this case smallpox. The chapter ends with a much more localized personal case: the continuing transformation of Arizona State University into a public values–focused institution.

Deep Case. A First-Order Public Value: Smallpox Eradication and the Preserving of Human Lives

On October 12, 1977, in Somalia, Ali Maow Maalin, a cook in a local restaurant, was operating a vehicle that contained two small children, both quite ill. Less than two weeks later Ali became ill with a fever, and then a few days he later developed a rash. When he went for medical attention, he was diagnosed with chicken pox and sent home. As symptoms developed further and ugly pustules began to appear on many parts of his body, it became clear that he had contracted the dreaded smallpox, a disease once rampant but now rare. Ali had never been vaccinated for smallpox. Though Ali was legally required to report to an isolation camp, he had no wish to spend his last days—if that was what they proved to be—away from his home and friends. However, one of his friends eventually reported Ali to the authorities, collecting a reward for doing so.

Officials from the World Health Organization (WHO), the lead institution in the worldwide effort to eradicate smallpox, learned that Ali had come into contact with 91 people. They began a frantic but systematic search. Eventually they found all 91 of those whom Ali had been in contact with, including 12 who had not been vaccinated against smallpox. Then, a national search began to identify and observe each of those with whom the 91 had interacted. By December 29, WHO set out to vaccinate as many people as possible, and after having directly observed the hundreds of people just vaccinated, they found that none had already contracted smallpox.[1] By this time, Ali had survived the deadly disease and had the "honor" of being the last person on the planet to contract smallpox from natural exposure to the virus.[2] He went on to use his experience as an unvaccinated smallpox victim as an object lesson in his subsequent decades-long activism in the campaign to promote polio vaccination in Africa. He died in 2013, long after the World Health Assembly had declared that the world was free of smallpox in 1980.

Smallpox, one of the most horrific diseases known to humankind, was eradicated because cooperating citizens and leaders of public values–based institutions succeeded in an ambitious agenda to achieve that most fundamental of public values, saving human lives. However, smallpox had a long run as a scourge on humanity. Well before recorded human history, the variola virus—the virus causing the disease we would later call smallpox—was not only present but also virulent. It killed millions of people. No one knows exactly when the variola virus emerged, but everyone agrees it was certainly many thousands of years ago. Through most of human history, smallpox remained a source of massive mortality, and those spared both feared and dreaded it.

In the eighteenth century, smallpox killed an estimated 400,000 Europeans per year, rich and poor, including five sitting kings and queens (among them, Louis XV of France and Mary II of England). The list of famous smallpox victims includes Samuel Ward (nineteenth-century US Supreme Court justice), Henry Gray (of *Gray's Anatomy* fame), Jonathan Dickenson (renowned minister of the "Great Awakening" and among the first presidents of the university we now know as Princeton), and, like so many of her kin, Pocahontas. Fortunate survivors of smallpox included Abraham Lincoln, Andrew Jackson, George Washington, and (less fortunate for others) Joseph Stalin.

During most of history, about half of those infected died, and many of those who did not were rendered permanently sightless. In the eighteenth century the world population was much smaller than today, and by the beginning of the twentieth century having only 400,000 dead from smallpox would have almost seemed a blessing, as hundreds of thousands turned into millions. By the early 1950s, an estimated 50 million cases of smallpox occurred each year, with many of the most terrible epidemics occurring in Africa.[3]

From 50 million in a year in the 1950s to zero in 1980—unquestionably, the eradication of smallpox serves as one of the greatest health care advances in history, and arguably among the most important public values achievements. The story of smallpox eradication in many ways serves as an exemplar of public values achievement.[4] Smallpox eradication involved interinstitutional cooperation; partnerships among government, businesses, and nonprofit organizations; a pubic value vision; and many kinds of leadership.

In the introduction, we examined Mothers Against Drunk Driving to illustrate the possibilities for designing and implementing an institution aimed at achieving public values, in that instance public safety. MADD grew from a perceived social need. Its early leaders had a strong vision of the social need as a public value, not just a limited or exclusionary social need for a limited social group. The smallpox case we present here is much larger in scope and involves many more people.

WHO (and its many partners) and MADD certainly are not alone in their ability to achieve public values. In this book, we identify, and in some cases document, many successful public values achievements, both contemporary and throughout history. Successful organizations and institutions serving public values are quite varied and include, among many others, efforts focused on promoting public education (e.g., the GI Bill, the land-grant university system), public health (e.g., the interinstitutional effort to eradicate smallpox, clean drinking water initiatives), and sustainability and environmental conservation (e.g., the US National Park System, repopulating endangered species), as well as institutions aimed at protecting free speech (e.g., the American Civil Liberties Union, the National Coalition Against Censorship).

Given our smallpox case and other examples of public values–focused activities and organizations, we see that under the right circumstances the individuals, organizations, and institutions dedicated to achieving public values can quite literally and with no hyperbole change the world. However, we hasten to note that public values achievements more often play out on a smaller stage and with goals that, while generally ambitious, do not dramatically change the course of human history. Public values goals may well focus on an organization's clients or customers or one's neighborhood. The community served may be as large as, literally, the world and as small as a handful of people. Indeed, it is possible to serve public values even when the target is ill-defined.

Let us note further that the term "public values–serving" certainly is not synonymous with "well loved." How does one classify Planned Parenthood? Many citizens feel that Planned Parenthood has offered enormous public value by providing health care to the poor and improving health outcomes for mothers and newborns. Many others feel that Planned Parenthood is their enemy, typically because it sponsors abortions and counsels those contemplating abortion (Huss and Dwight 2018). Is Planned Parenthood a public values–based institution? In our view, the key issue is this: if participants and stakeholders view their work as public values–serving, then the organization and its mission benefit from a public values leadership approach.

We noted in chapter 1 that MADD, while receiving many accolades, has accumulated almost as many critics. What is there not to like about saving lives by reducing drunk driving? Turns out, quite a lot. Some object to the moralistic tone of MADD, one consonant with its Reagan-era morality policy but a tone not in line with a contemporary spirit of pluralistic morality. Some have accused MADD and its leaders of being "neo-prohibitionist" (Longwell 2012), focusing on not only drunk driving but also modest social drinking and promoting "alcohol-free environments." The funding of MADD by the hospitality industry strikes some as, at best, awkward. Our point: organizations need not be controversy-free or "pure" to achieve public values. Public values often clash with other values, including other public values.

To sum up, the beginning point for public values management is quite simple: the desire to achieve public values. That does not imply that public values are the only values embraced by the individual or organization or that all actions taken are focused on serving others. But serving public values, even when it is not a full-time mission, requires a different approach to management, an approach often at odds with the management textbooks.

An Approach to Public Values Management

While much research in management and public policy is relevant to public values management,[5] none is right on point. This is due to the fact that almost all management approaches are tied to their sector base (public, private, nonprofit) or the functional context of management (e.g., health care, social work, research and development).

Our approach flows from the public values focus, and as we have emphasized, public values can be achieved by organizations in any sector (or working together with other organizations from other sectors) and in any functional area. Our views flow from values and normative commitments, and thus the ideas we present are unavoidably tied to our own values. We make no pretense of being value neutral, and sometimes our values influence our views about management, in some cases leading us to assertions that many would view as questionable.

Here is an example of an assumption that might well be disputed by many others: we think that a focus (in whole or part) on public values tends to make organizations stronger and more sustainable. Let's consider an example of a set of organizations that we feel have been weakened by the fact that most of them have abjured public values: private, for-profit colleges and universities.

We and colleagues (Bozeman and Anderson 2014; see also Anderson and Taggart 2016) have argued that almost all for-profit colleges have made the same mistake—trying to serve educational missions while ignoring public values. During the period from 2010 to 2016, many for-profit colleges began to fail, especially as the Obama administration's Department of Education began to investigate some of them owing to concerns that massive student debt was being generated, but with poor graduation and retention outcomes (Angulo 2016). While there are many reasons why for-profit universities ran into difficulties (Wong 2015), one reason is that citizens and consumers expect public value from universities—all universities, including ones that make a profit. These expectations are fueled in part by the extensive advertising of for-profit universities, ads focusing on the student not only making more money but also contributing to society. Most for-profit universities were not prepared to meet these expectations, and others that started with a public values component transmuted into an enhanced shareholder model (Anderson and Taggart 2016). According to John Murphy (2013), one of the founders of the University of Phoenix, the online university was initially founded to broaden public education and make it more accessible. Later, the University of Phoenix changed dramatically once that value moved to the background in favor of maintaining stockholder value. It has subsequently lost not only market share and market value but also enrollment, standing, and many of its early employees.

In our view, public values achievement may be "good business," especially for private firms that have "high publicness" (Bozeman 1987; Moulton 2009; Moulton and Bozeman 2011) organizations that, regardless of their legal status, rely substantially on appropriations, tax subsidies, government contracts, or appropriations. For-profit universities that rely on de facto transfer payments from students' government loans to university tuition are prime examples of high publicness organizations inasmuch as they cannot thrive in the absence of government resources.

While it is true that some businesses have a take-the-money-and-run strategy for profits from public resources, and that they often thrive while doing so, it generally turns out to be a poor long-term strategy. Providing at least some clear-cut public value can prove more effective, especially when receiving public resources and when the organization's product has strong public interest and public values aspects.

Does our view that public values–focused management is generally beneficial to the organization signal that we are cheery optimists? Perhaps. However, we can (and will) document many instances of organizations thriving while working to achieve public values. Nevertheless, our defense of public values management must be attenuated. After considering the caveats below, one sees that ours is a constrained utopianism.

Caveat 1: Partially Public Value Institutions

We are not advocating that Exxon, Microsoft, or the US Department of Defense transform into registered charities. Most organizations that achieve public values have multiple and even conflicting values, and only a minority of organizations are designed primarily to serve public values. Most organizations focus on achieving private values, most often profit and wealth, and seek to achieve value for organization owners, members, and shareholders. Other organizations serve faith-based or spiritual goals. For some organizations, especially older ones that may be near the end of their life cycle, survival and maintenance can become a central goal. Organizations serve multiple missions and multiple values, one of which may be to achieve public values. For example, many faith-based organizations (e.g., Salvation Army and Catholic Charities) are quite successful at providing the public values related to basic human existence, including providing food, clothing, shelter, and a variety of crucial social services. Likewise, an entire field of business management, corporate social responsibility (CSR), focuses on aspects of private firms devoted to social goals (Matten and Moon 2005). This does not, of course, imply that all or most businesses are concerned with CSR, but certainly many do include CSR missions, including ones that contribute to public values. Few private firms exist chiefly to serve public values, but full-time devotion is not required (Siegel and Vitaliano 2007). Indeed, a great many institutions—governments, business, and nonprofit—serve public values in part. The extensive social achievements of Catholic Charities and other faith-based institutions do no undercut, and often support, their primary religious mission.

Caveat 2: Get-In, Get-Out Public Value Institutions

Just as institutions and organizations can contribute greatly to public values while at the same time pursuing other values and missions, they can make vitally important public values contributions during some periods of their life cycle and not others. One conspicuous example is American Telephone and Telegraph Corporation's management of US federal laboratories during World War II. As America raced to develop an atomic bomb, it was critical that the effort in federal laboratories such as Los Alamos, Sandia, Brookhaven, and Oak Ridge be well managed. Managerial expertise was nearly as important as scientific expertise (Bozeman and Wilson 2004). In some labs, and for certain periods, the military performed management functions. However, President Truman, relying on a sense of patriotic duty, asked leaders of American Telephone and Telegraph Corporation, one of the largest and most technologically competent US firms and the owner of the internationally renowned Bell Labs, to agree to managing federal laboratories on a "handshake basis" and at no cost to the federal government. After the war, in 1949, both Los Alamos and Sandia National Laboratories (the largest US federal laboratory, the one tasked during the war with developing bomb casings) were formally designated as government-owned, contractor-operated (GOCO) laboratories. President Harry Truman asked the president of AT&T, Leroy Wilson, to "render an exceptional service in the national interest" by agreeing to manage Sandia. Other technology-centric firms also managed GOCO laboratories, including Martin Marietta (now Lockheed Martin) and the Battelle Corporation. The first GOCO relationship between AT&T and

Sandia continued until 1993, when AT&T, which had become a very different company since its court-ordered monopoly breakup in 1982, decided to no longer participate in the contract.

The case of the war effort and the private management of federal laboratories provides an excellent illustration of the fact that firms can at some points serve public values as part of their mission and then focus on other missions during other periods of their history. The GOCO case itself proved highly changeable because the public service contributions transmuted into profit-seeking contractual contributions. As the relationship changed, the size of contracts for managing federal labs ballooned enormously, due not least to the desire of the federal labs to offload environmental and safety legal liabilities (Valdez 2001). What started as a handshake in the 1940s later evolved into fixed-term contracts for many millions of dollars (US Department of Energy 2004). Today the cost of private management of all the GOCO federal laboratories exceeds $10 billion.

Personal Case (Bozeman). How National Lab Management Contracts Evolved from Public Service, to Profit, to Pariah

For about seven years in the 1990s, my colleagues and I at the Georgia Tech Research Value Mapping (RVM) program were the only social scientists regularly receiving grant funding from the US Department of Energy's (DOE) Office of Basic Energy Science, an office tasked with funding basic and precommercial research and development. To what did we owe this good fortune? I would like to say merit, but in truth it was a match of interest to need. For many years the RVM program focused on evaluating government research and development impacts. Government science agencies are very pleased to have assessments of their research impacts, especially if they have confidence those impacts will be assessed as beneficial.

One fine day in the fall of 1995 (it is always a fine day when one is offered a job), I received a phone call from an official high in the DOE food chain, requesting a meeting. I flew to Washington, DC, that same week and was ushered into this official's office. It all seemed a little hurried and hush-hush—and for good reason. The official (you will see why no name is provided here) said, essentially,[6] this:

Perhaps you know that Bill Richardson [then secretary of the DOE] has been meeting with the Republican leaders in Congress and talking about their new Contract with America[7] idea. Bill is a lifelong Democrat, a good secretary, and a damned good guy but he has gotten it into his head that if we do not toss the Republicans a bone, they will either close down or eviscerate DOE. This is the bone: he wants us to show our commitment to markets by having DOE change its GOCO contracting rules, rebidding all management contracts on a four-year cycle. I guess you know what that means, but I don't want to prejudice you because we would like to give you a consulting contract to interview the national lab leadership and get their take on the idea. Interested?

Even though fully booked at the time, with other grants and the usual teaching and service obligations, I agreed to take the contract. Why? Because I certainly did "know what that means." It was common knowledge at DOE, and even among consultants, that the GOCO concept was beginning to fail because of lack of institutions interested in bidding to become lab managers. Not only were some long-time GOCO managers disappointed in the intellectual property returns from their contract (GOCO managing companies get first dibs on intellectual property), but, more importantly, gigantic lawsuits had been filed against the labs because of hazardous waste and related accidents at lab sites. The legal stakes were literally in the billions of dollars. The most recent GOCO request for bids to run a national lab had received not a single bidder and was rebid. When rebid, DOE attracted one lone bidder, and even this bid was offered only after DOE made it clear that company legal liability would be quite limited. Thus, the idea of having more frequent bids would yield no competitive results during this period, perhaps not any bidders at all, but would certainly entail sizable administrative and opportunity costs.

My research team visited almost all of the major DOE GOCO laboratories and, of course, received a consistent set of findings, which we reported back: that essentially all the officials we interviewed strongly opposed changing the GOCO bidding rules, action they felt would cost a great deal and achieve nothing. Our report went to DOE headquarters and was circulated, and my team and I presented the results. Secretary Richardson received the report but was not in attendance.

The new bidding "reform" never occurred. Because of the report? Probably not. High-level government decisions rarely work that way. However, the fact that leaders in DOE were so bold as to go against their secretary to authorize a research study that would inevitably provide evidence counter to the secretary's plan may itself have been a signal to which the secretary and others paid some heed. More likely, the bidding idea was probably shelved owing to the combination of the usual gnat-like attention span in Washington and the rapidly diminishing influence of the Contract with America.

The public values message? During and shortly after World War II, the large university and corporate institutions that contracted to manage the national labs were uniformly focused on public values, chiefly ones related to winning the war and, then, the Cold War. From the 1950s to early 1980s, GOCO contracts were generally viewed as both a good public values proposition and a good business proposition. Remember, as we have pointed out and will continue to point out, business objectives and public values objectives need not be at odds with one another. But in the 1990s, what had started as a public values contribution and was also, after World War II, motivated by profit transformed into "show me the way out of here"—no war, less clear-cut public values imperatives, and a great deal of corporate risk.

Discussion Questions

Bozeman makes no secret of the fact that he knew that his consulting work in the above case was not initiated either because of his impeccable professional credentials or because Bozeman was considered by the client to be an objective scientist. Bozeman and DOE officials knew each other well, knew each other's views, and had developed a certain level and type of trust.

- Question 1: Would it have even been possible for Bozeman to be objective when he already had knowledge of his interviewees' opinion of the contracting question and had his own established views? Bozeman reports that he would certainly have reported views in opposition to his views and expectations, had there been any to report. Is this enough? Would you have taken on the job knowing that a given result was expected?

- Question 2: Bozeman reports "a certain level and type of trust" in his relationship with the DOE client. Is this generally a positive thing in that it facilitates communication and promotes a good working relationship? Or is it a bad thing because it may prove inimical to conducting good, scientific policy research?

One important element of the above DOE/GOCO contracting case is the contention that business organizations are almost never set up specifically to serve public values (there are some exceptions, as we will see later in the book when we report interviews with the founders of the Sweet Earth food products case). Let us consider the example of a company we all know at least something about—the McDonald's Corporation. McDonald's had no obvious public values basis in its founding.[8] The company is chiefly designed to make money for its owners, franchisees, employees, and stockholders. McDonald's competes in the marketplace, in a highly competitive fast-food market, and most of its decisions focus more on profit and growth than on public value. However, even this international corporate symbol of US capitalism serves public values.

For many years, McDonald's has used a small percentage of its profits, as well as public contributions, to support its Ronald McDonald House, a program set up to serve families with sick children. Is the purpose of the Ronald McDonald House charities to serve the public values, or is it to shore up the public image of the McDonald's Corporation? Does motive matter if social benefit and public value are provided? This is not an easy question to answer. For example, some people working at McDonalds, with its Ronald McDonald services, may be chiefly motivated by the public values it serves, whereas others may care nothing about the program or even wish that it would go away. Corporations are not monoliths, but rather are made up of diverse people with diverse motives. Thus, in our view, it is better to celebrate corporate contributions to public values rather than sneer at them.

Obviously, McDonald's provides substantial contributions to socio-economic benefit. In the regular course of its business, McDonald's pays salaries and stock dividends and creates economic development for the regions in which it operates. In most cases this constitutes positive impacts, but is it a public value? That depends on what one means by "public value." By our concept economic development is not per se a public value.

Caveat 3: Public Values People in Organizations

Our predominant focus is on managing organizations to achieve public values, and we note in various places in this book that the book is written for people who want to achieve public values within the context of organizations. However, that does not mean that everyone who wishes to achieve public values works in public values–focused organizations, or, for that matter, that they even work in a formal, traditional organization of any sort.[9]

Sometimes people who are actively seeking to achieve public values work in an organization that has little if any regard for public values. In cases where people wish to achieve public values within an organization bent on thwarting public values, the only option may be to be a whistleblower. Consider Jeffrey Wigand, formerly vice president of research and development at Brown & Williamson Tobacco Company. Tobacco companies have not often been held up as exemplars of public value, but Wigand may have helped save many lives when he disclosed that the company had intentionally manipulated the level of nicotine in cigarettes in order to make one of the most addictive drugs even more addictive. Wigand was fired from the company. After being attacked by the company in the press and in the courts, Wigand went on to have a successful career as a high school teacher and a consultant, and he was portrayed by Russell Crowe in the critically acclaimed movie *The Insider*.[10]

Not all whistleblowers have long happy lives, not even ones who have movies made about them. Karen Silkwood was an employee of the Kerr-McGee Cimarron Fuel Fabrication Site, which made plutonium pellets for use in reactors. She alleged that she had been contaminated by plutonium, and after being tested, she did prove positive for massive contamination. Alleging negligence on the company's part, she agreed to meet with a *New York Times* reporter and provide evidence that she said documented her claim. On the way to that meeting she had a fatal automobile accident, with evidence indicating she may have been rammed from behind.

People wishing to achieve public values in their organization need not be whistleblowers, nor do they necessarily need to work against the stated interests of their organizations. Indeed, many organizations encourage employees to be socially engaged and sometimes reward them for it. The Points of Light Foundation provides annual awards for the 50 companies that are "most socially engaged." Recent winners include such familiar companies as Adobe Systems, AT&T, FedEx, General Mills, Raytheon, and Southwest Airlines. Among the 50 award-winning companies, half include social and community engagement as a part of the employee performance review and three-quarters provide grants for employee-led engagement activities (Scott 2015). In short, even when working in a large organization that does not include public values as a major part of its mission, it is often possible to achieve a great deal, sometimes with the organization's active encouragement.

Public Values Premises: What We Believe and Why

Anyone who has read our book's preface will know something about the background and experiences of the authors and will perhaps assume, we think correctly, that the public values premises presented here are forged from those experiences. Crow has had a great deal of experience in managing higher education institutions to achieve public value but has also been active in many other public values activities, as is shown with various cases and illustrations throughout the book. Bozeman has had less experience in managing for public values, but neither has he sat on the sidelines, as some of the Bozeman-focused cases and illustrations will show. More of Bozeman's career has been focused on research and teaching, and inevitably these activities affect his views on public values management.

Regarding the subtitle for the section, "What We Believe and Why," it is easy to answer the first part and not at all easy to answer the second part. But surely the why includes formal education, managerial experience, experience consulting with organizations, doing research and evaluation, and being interested observers of the world around us, not only the immediate world but also the world as filtered through knowledge of history, events, and people and, of course, our own values and, yes, biases.

Core Public Values Premise: It is possible and desirable to manage organizations with the express goal of achieving public values.

This is our most important premise, because if we are wrong about this one, then we have wasted a good deal of time writing this book. However, we anticipate that this is likely our least controversial premise; the amount of history one would need to ignore to reject it is truly overwhelming. Even fervent libertarians would likely find this premise acceptable, since even most libertarians seem to have little objection to the organized actions required for national security and public safety.

More controversy emerges in discussion of which particular security actions should be performed by whom. These particulars can prove quite contentious. Before moving along to the more controversial issues, it is useful to at least reflect on and perhaps amplify this beginning premise, and one way to do this is to turn to our public values leaders' thoughts about it.

Why Do People Retreat from Public Values?

Since we do not expect much pushback from our core public values premise, and since we know from research that an enormous number of people embrace public service and public values, but under different flags ("making a difference," "public service," or even "doing what's right"), let's consider instead this question: why do so many people who begin a career sincerely committed to public values, or with some related pro-social motivation, later move away from this initial motivation? One of our public values leaders has an explanation.

Comment: Linda Hunt on Public Values Reluctance

Linda Hunt, in her capacity as CEO of Dignity Health's Arizona service center, has five hospitals in her jurisdiction. She has degrees in nursing and nursing administration and has spent her career working in and managing complex hospitals and health care organizations. She has worked in institutions that one expects to be intimately involved in achieving public values. However, she often finds such institutions rigid and overly conservative in pursuing public values, in some cases completely displacing public values while pursuing others. Here's her explanation:

> Personally, I think [some people in public values organizations] are fearful of change—and all the unknowns that go along with change. Often their biggest fear is fear of making mistakes. All the unknowns. That's one of the worst things that could happen, when people are immobilized by fear. The flip side is that they may also be too comfortable with the status quo. They don't look forward to what the future could bring and the challenge and the excitement of doing things a little bit differently or opening their thinking to approaches that others might challenge. People who may have begun with public service motives become too comfortable and turn away from them. However, if they were less afraid of change, they might find that embracing it could be 3,000 times more satisfying or more successful than if you keep doing the same old thing.

Let's follow up Ms. Hunt's useful observation with a research moment. Her observation certainly seems to be supported by research results. While studies again and again show pro-social motivation in those intending to go into public service jobs, typically at much higher rates than those planning to go into the private sector, this early motivation does not seem to make public sector or nonprofit workers and managers any less prone to experiencing midcareer "burnout" or low levels of job satisfaction (Golembiewski et al. 1998; Machado et al. 2013; Van den Broeck et al. 2017). Having strong PSM, likewise, does not mitigate lower job satisfaction levels in public employees (Bright 2008).

This brings us back to the issues raised by Ms. Hunt. How and why do persons who begin with strong public values and work in what we might think of as public values–serving institutions (e.g., health, hospitals, higher education) find that these early motivations are not much help in staving off lowered job satisfaction or burnout? Research gives multiple answers. Some research (e.g., Patil and Lebel 2019) suggests that public employees' perceptions of the unpopularity of their jobs with the citizens they serve has much to do with burnout and limited job satisfaction. Others suggest that occupying jobs where tasks are not clear-cut, a greater likelihood as one moves up in the organizational hierarchy, can lead to a lack of focus and job dissatisfaction. But doubtless, Ms. Hunt's idea, that people just get accustomed to a rewarding status quo, is a point well-taken.

Discussion Question

- Question 1: What do you think can be done to reduce the likelihood that the pro-social, public values, "make the world a better place" motivations that so many people begin with will turn sour with more time on the job? Hint: there is research on this too, suggesting everything from developing compassionate managers (Eldor 2018), to organizational job rotation (Ho et al. 2009), to programs for addressing stress (Brunges and Foley-Brinza 2014). But what are the other possibilities?

We turn to another public values premise, one that has framed our work for many years—sector agnosticism. The basic elements have been introduced in earlier chapters, but here we consider them in more detail. Unlike the core premise, this one not only represents belief in a value but also has importance for developing public values management strategies and designs.

The Sector Agnosticism Premise: Public values achievement can emerge from organizations in any sector or as intersector partnerships. No sector "owns" public values.

Myths about functions of sectors and organizations badly need to be set aside. In our view, demonstrably false assumptions about the limits of government and the limits of markets have been disproved again and again, and the need to separate markets and government organizations neatly is a myth, but one that dies hard. Perhaps most injurious is the idea that governments should be brought in during—and only during—instances of market failure, that government is a residual category of institution, for which there is no other positive role.

Anyone familiar with the great accomplishments of the twentieth and twenty-first centuries can easily put aside the "no positive government role" idea. As we will show, the government, not the private sector, was the earliest and most effective mover in not only the internet but also the framework for its commercial development. The role of the US Department of Defense's Defense Advanced Research Projects Agency has featured prominently in some of the most important technological breakthroughs in history. The early development of air travel and the later development of the aerospace industry depended crucially on government design, resources, and control. Countless instances of government proving or facilitating public values, social benefit, and even private economic benefit can be provided (and many will be provided here). Perhaps the most sobering point, at least to those who are more interested in empirical evidence than in sustaining sometimes self-interested myths, is that studies of nations' economic strength show again and again that one of the most important common features of a well-functioning economy is a well-functioning government, one that is not simply a last resort but a proactive element in a democratic society's economy.[11]

Even as we challenge the myth of government as problem-solver of last resort, let us remember that agnosticism is the watchword. We do not suggest that government is necessarily effective, only that it can sometimes be effective, even when it is "interfering" in the market. Another myth to set aside is the idea that government is necessarily focused on the public interest or public values. The idea that government institutions always act benevolently to achieve public values purposes is in some cases as far removed from reality as the misguided notion that all business is made up of rapacious capitalists just waiting their chance to prey on consumer-citizens. Extreme instances of government behaving badly can be found throughout history: natives being treated as subhuman obstacles to Manifest Destiny, women being denied the same political rights as men, slavery and the post-Emancipation denial of African Americans' civil rights. If one needs more specificity, there is the history of exploitation with the Tuskegee experiments, the DOE's intentional irradiation of US citizens for purposes of seeing results, the Department of Defense's use of Agent Orange long after knowledge of its harmful effects, and cases of racial profiling by police and unwarranted violence.

The foregoing examples represent only those easily proved and relatively (at this point in history) noncontentious. However, we could create a much longer list of grievances if we include actions still debated, such as the complicity of the US Forest Service in deforestation, the US Army Corps of Engineers' vast damage to the ecology of the Everglades, and the authority of the state lent to the practice of capital punishment.

No, we are not implying that everyone is evil and that a Hobbesian society is unavoidable. Some people in government do great good, some do great harm, and some do very little at all. The same is true of business. Nor should we conclude that nonprofit organizations are entirely benevolent, given clear evidence to the contrary. Many nonprofit organizations are pillars of public value, but at least some are no less self-interested in their motives and behaviors than the most socially unconscious business firm. Basic point: organizations from every sector have the potential to contribute to public value, especially if one does not let sector stereotypes get in the way. Likewise, organizations from every sector have the potential to thwart public values.

In the US political culture, it is most often market myths that systematically prove problematic in solving social problems and developing institutions to contribute to public value. In the United States, even more than in most countries, there is a tendency to lionize markets and private enterprise and to vilify government. In our view, one grounded in historical cases presented in later chapters, there is no good reason to abide by such common ideological clichés as "the best government is the one that governs least," or to assume that governments should be residual institutions, reacting only when markets fail. We believe in positive government. But we also believe in positive markets. Private institutions—not only nonprofit organizations and nongovernmental organizations (NGOs) but also businesses operating in competitive markets—are very much part of seeking and delivering public value. Just as government agencies are not, despite ramped-up rhetoric, sinecures for rent-seeking, nonproductive bureaucrats, private businesses are not replete with predatory cutthroats interested only in maximizing wealth at the expense of the disadvantaged or the everyday worker.

We believe in positive government and positive markets, but we also believe in negative government and negative business. Calling out negatives and ineffectiveness requires no particular cynicism. The world is rife with examples of people and organizations doing bad things. Public values sometimes are riven asunder by market competition and a tunnel-vision focus on private wealth maximization. It is not at all unusual, unfortunately, for some of the largest and most profitable firms in America to plunder consumers with hidden and illegal fees, usurious interest rates, legalized Ponzi schemes, and callous disregard for citizens' health. Likewise, "public sector" does not equate with "public value." In the very worst of cases, agencies charged with public trust have purposefully irradiated US citizens, have locked them in internment camps because of their race, have withheld knowledge and treatment from syphilis patients so as to study their decline, and have killed thousands of innocent noncombatants as "collateral damage."

While we are well aware of the sad history of both government and business victimizing ordinary citizens, we can also cite a great many instances of government and business institutions providing great service to public values, and thus we feel comfortable with our sector agnosticism as a core assumption. In our view, one of the obstacles to institutions working effectively is a general climate of extremism, views that government can never be trusted, that business is always out to get us, or both. Ideological views about the efficacy or villainy of the respective sectors are reflected in book publishing cottage industries of venomous smackdowns of institutions. The titles tell the story: Glenn Beck's *Common Sense: The Case against Out-of-Control Government* (2009), or *Plunder and Deceit* (2015), Mark Levin's rant about civil society being "devoured" by the federal government. Market villain books are almost as common, especially after the Great Recession, the housing crisis, and the Wall Street bailout. Thus, we have such titles as Ted Nace's *Gangs of America: The Rise of Corporate Power and the Disabling of Democracy* (2005) and Erin Arvedlund's *Open Secret: The Global Banking Conspiracy That Swindled Investors Out of Billions* (2014). However, Michelle Malkin wins the award for most audacious title with her *Sold Out: How High-Tech Billionaires and Bipartisan Beltway Crapweasels Are Screwing America's Best and Brightest Workers* (2015). But even beyond the innovation of using the neologism "crapweasels" in a title, the book is noteworthy for its attacking both political and market miscreants—not that it is the only book to lump together evil business with evil politics (see, e.g., Rena Steinzor's *Why Not Jail? Industrial Catastrophes, Corporate Malfeasance, and Government Inaction* [2014]).

In short, public values progress calls for ideological and sector-based agnosticism and, as a corollary, approaches that are more pragmatic than unbending. When we put on ideological blinders, good things rarely happen. Enter the next assumption.

Comment: Anne-Marie Slaughter on Sector Expectations

Among our interviewees, the person who has the most to say about sector agnosticism is Anne-Marie Slaughter, the head of the New America Foundation, and formerly dean of Princeton University's School of Public and International Affairs and director of policy and planning for the US Department of State. It is not surprising that she would have ideas about organizational roles given that she has spent virtually her entire career trying to forge public values partnerships among institutions from different sectors and with different missions. She offered the following:

> I think the thing I have encountered that I didn't expect, but should have, is presumed monopoly on public value of the public and civic sectors. We

think of ourselves as custodians of public value, but government agencies and nonprofits have a lot in common with industry with respect to protecting self-interest. When I was in the State Department, I was stunned to realize that economic development NGOs had trade associations of lobbyists just like corporations did. When I wanted to change, say, the way the State Department and USAID did business, I got lobbied just as much as if I'd wanted to regulate food producers and agribusiness. I think the thing that is critical to understand is that people who think that pursuing public value is their own industry will fight just as hard to preserve their interests as will any for-profit entity, especially when threatened by change.

Government is not enough. Even if government is doing everything you want it to do, it's not going to be able to get you where you want to go. Equally, government is often not doing what you want it to do. You need what Hilary Clinton used to call the three-legged stool—the civic, private, and public sectors.

As far as I'm concerned, there need not be any division among the sectors. It makes more sense to look at different models of how you create public value. If people say "My goal is only profit," even then you'll find that creation of public value and profit are sometimes aligned.

She goes on to draw from her experience working in university administration to provide an observation about the problems of rigid sector boundaries, seeing them as an obstacle to achieving public values:

Our universities need to inculcate the idea of erasing sector boundaries. As dean of the Woodrow Wilson School [School of Public and International Affairs, Princeton University], I would say, "Choose the substantive area you're interested in. It can be environment, or human rights, or poverty reduction, or health. I don't care. Then plan to pursue that in all three sectors. Develop experience with all sectors and then think about different motives and strategies and how they fit different institutions." To do public values right, we've got to get away from this notion of sectors, and that's a big change.

Each of the public values leaders we interviewed emphasized, to one degree or another, the need to recognize that any sector can make substantial contributions to public values, most often when working together. The premise we discuss below is related but more general: the need to embrace pragmatism.

The Pragmatism Premise: The philosophy of pragmatism is the best guide to public values management. Pragmatic public values management involves learning what works and does not, adapting and managing based on observed success.

Pragmatism, "America's only original philosophy" (Rosenthal, Hausman, and Anderson 1999), and John Dewey, its best-known adherent, seem to be coming back in fashion, if, indeed, they ever left (e.g., Koopman 2014; Pring 2014; James 2015; Brennan and Keller 2017). While many have made fundamental contributions to philosophical pragmatism— most notably William James (1907) and C. S. Peirce (1905)—the name most often associated with pragmatism, and perhaps its greatest champion, is John Dewey.

We are not immune to the allure of pragmatic philosophy and, especially, to John Dewey's ideas. Dewey's work aligns closely with our approach to achieving public values, which is not surprising since much of our previous work relies on the Dewey oeuvre. Bozeman's (2007) public values book devotes an entire chapter to the relation of Dewey's work and pragmatism to public values and public interest. As Crow and Dabars (2015, 217) note, "pragmatism is concerned with the resolution of problems," a fitting philosophy for an approach to institutional design that requires cooperation rather than agreement on all points.

Key to the application of pragmatism is the recognition of the need to take into account multiple views and to build support for public values–based policies and actions. Dewey's work shows great respect for participation and democracy and sees fair and legitimate agenda setting and decision processes as key. In Dewey's view, pragmatism necessarily entails accommodating multiple views, and process matters because multiple views must be elicited broadly and fairly. Great care must be taken with process, not least because "modern life . . . has so enormously expanded, multiplied, intensified and complicated the scope of the indirect consequences, has formed such immense and consolidated unions in action, on an impersonal rather than a community basis, that the resultant public cannot identify and distinguish itself. And this discovery is obviously an antecedent condition of any effective organization on its part" (Dewey 1927, 314). Thus, we can infer that, for Dewey, pragmatically achieving public values (he discussed achieving public interest) necessitates recognizing and acting upon the knowledge that true consensus is rare and that a "solution" that excludes major parties to the actions and outcomes is not worth serious consideration. He provides a simple but powerful explanation in his book *Liberalism and Social Action* (Dewey 1935).

Of course, there are conflicting interests; otherwise, there would be no social problems. The problem under discussion is precisely how conflicting claims are to be settled in the interest of the widest possible contribution to the interests of all—or at least of the great majority. The method of democracy—insofar as it is that of organized intelligence—is to bring these conflicts out into the open, where their special claims can be seen and appraised, where they can be discussed and judged in the light of more inclusive interests than are represented by either of them separately (Dewey 1935, 81).

A key insight is that it is in the interest of those with the majority view to take pains to include other views because doing so allows public values consensus to emerge from these dialogues, discussions, and arguments (Festenstein 1997). Even when no consensus emerges, the deliberative process often proves useful. The open and full discussion makes it more difficult for parties to advance private interests in the cloak of public values. Thus, deliberative democracy can be not only desirable from a normative standpoint but also the most pragmatic of approaches, particularly so when parties are contentious but at the same time stakeholders to the outcome of the deliberation. In our view, deliberations about public values and ways to achieve them are in and of themselves useful and productive because such discussions require recognition and acknowledgment of others' views, often an important step to achieving any joint objectives.

Comment: Governor Jeb Bush on Why Pragmatism
Is Important and Not Enough

One expects politicians to be pragmatic, at least until relatively recently when party and ideology lines have hardened to such a degree that pragmatism, at least among politicians, has become more difficult, especially if pragmatism means compromise.

Part of pragmatism is learning-by-doing and making adjustments. The term "adaptive learning" (e.g., Tyre and Von Hippel 1997; Midgley 2014) characterizes this approach, a pragmatic approach discussed by Governor Bush. His following statement is very much consistent with the adaptive learning approach in pragmatism:

> I always started with a premise that whatever we were trying to do, sometimes it would work and sometimes it wouldn't. If it's not working, then you identify different structures, try them, and don't be afraid to discard approaches that have not worked. The challenge, though, is that a lot of businesses get their snout closer to the high-grade slop at the front of the trough. Lobbyists have special sanctuaries to protect what they have. You have to make sure you distinguish between some creative new way of involvement with a not-for-profit, or a for-profit business in government, some new partnership. You have to make sure you're not giving the impression that you're giving a sweetheart deal to somebody that's going to be making money without a real focus on the desired results.
>
> You have to be ready for the fact that not everything succeeds. We had some failures, and they were doozies. The one that was the most frustrating was our inability to create a better procurement system. It turns out the lawyers that the business people hire to defend their interests in procurements are much better or at least more numerous than the lawyers in the government. The procurement laws were so cumbersome that we just never got that right. We didn't plant the seeds right on that one. There are all sorts of things that, just in terms of efficiencies, government should be able to do. But sometimes there are so many [entrenched and powerful interests] that no matter how hard you work at it and how pragmatic you try to be, it is just not possible to reallocate money to public values, to the true needs of the people. . . . If you want to achieve anything at all, you

have to be realistic and realize that there are some land mines along the way. You have to be sensitive to them to get anything done.

This is a nice antidote to the usual Bozeman and Crow sunny optimism. Here is one way to summarize these insights about pragmatism: it is important to realize that public values almost always compete against private values, sometimes with private values having great resources behind them, and the achievement of any degree of public value sometimes requires compromise with these private values. The "half a loaf is better than none" cliché has a good deal of veracity in the world of practical, pragmatic politics.

Michael Crow, ASU, and Public Values Premises

We conclude this chapter with an extended story by one of the authors, one that could hardly be more personal. The case below focuses on the transformation of Arizona State University into a public values–based institution, one referred to as the New American University model. This story touches on many of the themes in this chapter, illustrating not only the idea of the core public values premise but also those of sector agnosticism and pragmatism.

Personal Case (Crow). ASU and Its Charter: Building A Public Values–Focused University Using the Public Values Management Premises

The story of the development of the ASU Charter is really only a part of the larger story of the transformation of ASU into a highly innovative, public values–focused university and also one that is controversial, disruptive, and—despite its clear and official public values mission—not universally loved.

Even before I came to ASU in 2002, I was already giving a good deal of thought as to what a public values–based university might look like and was trying out the term "New American University." I was in part inspired by reading books from college presidents I admired, including Frank Rhodes's (former president of Cornell University) book *Creating the Future*, in which he laid out a powerful vision of what universities should be doing to transform themselves. About the same time, I read Jim Duderstadt's book *A University for the 21st Century*. Duderstadt was president of the University of Michigan, which, like ASU, is a large state university serving diverse students. Those books and others led me to think through some of my then-half-baked notions about university missions and about designing universities to serve those new missions. I knew I wanted to transform ASU into a public values–based university, but I was not at the outset exactly sure what that might look like. However, I did have several threads long before 2002.

Thinking about a public values university, a main driver for me was my early experience as a university administrator. My first leadership-level experience in higher education administration was at Iowa State University (ISU), a very traditional, very successful land-grant university that has deep connections to midwestern farmers and excellent programs in agriculture and agricultural economics. I saw and understood the power of this connection to these farmers. I was an alumnus of Iowa State, and when I was an undergraduate there I worked on something called the Iowa Coal Project, a response to the energy crisis of the mid-1970s. When I was working on that project, I had the opportunity to work not only with farmers but also with miners, environmentalists, and all the many kinds of people who had a vital stake in energy resources. Even then, it was not difficult to see the potential of a university as a transformative institution. In my classes I had read about the Morrill Land-Grant Act and its major impacts on reshaping universities, and, of course, ISU was both a beneficiary and contributor to the outreach and community impact goals of the act. In my graduate studies at Syracuse University's Maxwell School, where I met Bozeman, we worked with some Syracuse engineers, especially Walter Meyer, in developing the university Energy Research Institute and solving real-world problems.

After my time as a faculty member and administrator at ISU, I took a position at Columbia University, where I had another set of experiences and influences, also related to public values institutions. Columbia is not a land-grant university and is greatly different from either ISU or Syracuse, but since it is located in New York City, it has a long history of serving the city and interacting with public officials in accomplishing social and economic objectives.

At the same time as I was experiencing some of the impacts that universities such as ISU and Columbia could have, I also began to be a more systematic student of universities in general and came to the conclusion that something was missing from most universities. Many had become selfishly focused on a kind of competition with one another, and often the competition had the result of diminishing the universities' service roles. Doing work with social impacts and achieving public values were not criteria in university rankings and prestige and so were easily set aside. I also began to think, "Government is not going to fix this." True, there were some important government supports for educational access, especially the Pell Grants, but by and large neither the federal government nor the states had focused much on the creation and development of public values–based, egalitarian universities.

When I was offered the presidency at ASU, one of my motives for taking the job was that it seemed to me that Arizona and the Phoenix area would be hospitable to change. The culture of the West is more open, less locked in. It also helped that ASU had already changed a great deal, beginning as a small teachers college and then, before I arrived, evolving into a large, full-service research institution.

Maybe just a little history is helpful. The transformation of ASU into a chartered, public values–focused university is recent but also rooted in its history. ASU started as the Arizona Territorial Teachers College in 1885, and though its name changed several times along the way, it was until 1945 very much focused on educating teachers and still reported to the superintendent of public instruction. But by 1945 it had expanded its mission with degrees in engineering and mining, as well as traditional liberal arts, and had begun to look like a comprehensive university. It still lagged behind the University of Arizona, at the time the state's only full-fledged state university.

In 1945, the president at what would become ASU was Grady Gammage, who would serve from 1933 to 1959. He was interested in changing and expanding the role of ASU and thought a good first step was getting it removed from the authority of the superintendent and placed under the Board of Regents. That was the first step in a long struggle to become recognized as a state university. This was at the same time as many other universities were on the path to transformation. For example, in 1945 the institution that would become UCLA was still California State Teachers College at Los Angeles. Universities such as UCLA and ASU that emerged relatively late were not part of the land-grant system and thus did not in most cases have a formal charter.

Despite his long service as president of what would at this death be Arizona State College, Grady Gammage was not able to get the college established as a university. Despite widespread support from Arizona citizens, the governor was against doing so, as was the legislature, as was the leadership of the only state university at the time, the University of Arizona. Finally, in 1958 Proposition 200 gets on the ballot, and the question whether ASC will become ASU is taken to the voters. It passes easily.

Now back to the twenty-first-century ASU. After accepting the ASU presidency, I spent from March through October of 2002 working intently on university design, and then, at my presidential inauguration in November 2002, I presented these ideas, outlining eight university "design aspirations." These were sort of first principles for achieving a university focused on innovation and public values, and they remain in place, though they have been augmented by, among other things, the university charter. These eight design elements, still very much in use, are as follows:

1. Leverage Our Place. ASU embraces its culture, socioeconomic, and physical setting.
2. Enable Student Success. ASU is committed to the success of each unique student.
3. Transform Society. ASU catalyzes social change by being connected to social needs.
4. Fuse Intellectual Disciplines. ASU creates knowledge by transcending academic disciplines.
5. Value Entrepreneurship. ASU uses its knowledge and encourages innovation.
6. Be Socially Embedded. ASU connects with communities through mutually beneficial partnerships.
7. Conduct Use-Inspired Research. ASU research has purpose and impact.
8. Engage Globally. ASU engages with people and issues locally, nationally, and internationally.

These ideas on how to think about university transformation did not just come from reading other presidents' books, and they did not just spring one day from my own brain. They were tried out with other people, and other people helped shape them. I talked to a good number of people for whom I have the greatest respect. I brought in Derek Roberts, who was the president of University College London; Malcolm Grant, later president of University College London; and Larry Faulkner, who was the president of the University of Texas. I had been friends for many years with my fellow Maxwell School doctoral student Mark Emmert, then president of University of Washington (now director of the NCAA). They would come and meet, discuss, argue, and almost always conclude, "yes, these are changes universities need and someone needs to start the ball rolling." I brought in many of these colleagues four or five or six times, listened to their advice, and I have met with some of them ever since then. I have always had some set of formal and informal external advisors.

Readers not familiar with the norms, history, and cultures of universities may well view any or all of these design aspirations as common sense and largely unthreatening. Why wouldn't a university value innovation? Of course a university should worry about whether its research is used. But universities often have a logic of their own. For example, there is a long tradition in many fields of focusing chiefly on curiosity-driven research, the assumption being that use and application will sort itself out after the fact. This notion works better in some fields than others.

Perhaps most controversial for the 2002 ASU faculty was the idea of fusing and transcending disciplines. My assumption was that problems, social and intellectual, rarely come wrapped in nice disciplinary packages. I think many people agree, including most faculty members. However, that does not mean that faculty want to abandon organization according to traditional disciplines. Faculty are usually more comfortable with disciplines because of their familiarity. Disciplines have their own norms, known to those who affiliate with the disciplines and their respective professional societies, and these norms differ from one discipline to the next. Things can really get messy when people from different disciplines come together in an effort to solve problems that transcend disciplines. People have to work with those who may not have the same worldview or the same training or skills. On the one hand, that is exactly why they need to come together. On the other hand, it takes many people outside their comfort zone, at least initially.

The people that were most positive about my ideas for a public values–focused university were community leaders, many of whom had been longing for a different kind of university, one that would not be walled off. However, there was faculty opposition, including among some faculty leaders. Typical comments among the opposition: "Who does he think he is!" "What's wrong with the way we are now?" And, in many cases, "No worries, we can wait him out. This is just a stepping stone and in two or three years he will be back to some place like Columbia."

I had been involved in higher education long enough to know that you can't bake a cake, even a very tasty one, without breaking some eggs. I realized at the outset that this vision I was advancing, and which was ultimately legitimated as the ASU charter, was not going to be immediately embraced by all parties. I turned first to the faculty centrism of the university's culture. There were people who believed that I did not have the authority to advance a new vision for the university, that doing so was the job of the faculty, and that I should just administer their will, a will that was highly likely not to be much changed from one president to the next.

This is not to say that faculty were anything less than crucial to the development of a public values university. They have to do most of the heavy lifting, and if they cannot be won over, the transformation will not succeed. ASU, like most state universities, was "faculty-centric" in that most of its mission and objectives aligned very closely with the aspirations of individual faculty—but paid little attention to much else. In my view, universities have to be "student-centric." The faculty roles and objectives are vital, but in some cases those goals, especially the common goal of "more research and less teaching," come at the expense of students. Likewise, the role of the community is absolutely vital, especially for a truly public values–focused university. Not only should the university serve the community in a thousand different ways, but in doing so it can more likely count on community support for the universities' innovations and initiatives.

As is typically the case, some of the opposition was not well informed on exactly what we were trying to achieve and, of course, rumors ran rampant, with few having a sound basis for sorting rumors from fact. There was one faculty group that was extremely upset with the organizational changes that we had already begun implementing, and they wanted to get together and start a vote of no confidence. Get rid of the troublemaker early, before he has a chance to change much of anything. My tactic, a direct one, was to call up the leader of that group and say, "I hear you guys are getting together; why don't you invite me to the meeting?" And so they did. I asked, "What do you want to know?" and tried to replace the rumors with fact, but I also gave them direct answers on some developments that really were occurring and that they were not so keen about, such as the shakeup of traditional disciplinary departments. I spend most of my time, not just with this group but with many others, in direct engagement, responding to concerns and trying to convince people that the mission change was sincere, serving good causes, and that they could be a vital part of it, all without radical changes to their research, teaching, or professional lives. Some people never came around, and many of these left ASU. Others embraced the idea of a public values–based university, some as early adopters, some later. Now we are at the point where the mission itself is exactly what attracts some of those wishing to work at ASU.

There had been no new buildings constructed at ASU between 1990 and 2001, and certainly no new research buildings had been built for a long time. Now, seemingly all of a sudden, we are building multiple research buildings and we are building whole new campuses, not only the downtown campus but the polytechnic campus and a campus in east Mesa. I think many people concluded, "Well, he might be crazy, but he is delivering." It helped that a couple of local foundations gave more than $10 million to be used for advancing the ASU mission as a New American University. We received more than $170 million from the Fulton Family Foundation, and entrepreneur Bill Carey gave us several million dollars for what became the W. P. Carey School of Management. The Piper Charitable Trust, a local foundation, gave us $10 million to get going, and ultimately $75 million. Many well-known and public-interested Arizona families played a major role in providing the investments needed to transform ASU. They really stepped up. Many of the donors were responding enthusiastically to the public values vision that was ultimately validated and formalized in the ASU charter. So, we get to the climax of the story—the development of the charter.

Local political support was vital, a necessary ingredient for many of our objectives, especially those involving serving the community. So, we went to the legislature and won on some issues that had never been won before, the building of new major research facilities. We went to the city of Phoenix, including people standing for election, and worked hard to develop joint visions for ASU. The idea for a downtown Phoenix campus was an idea developed in discussions with Phil Gordon, a candidate for mayor, later elected. We started out talking about how ASU could help reinvigorate downtown Phoenix. My idea was not to have the university in just a single place, not just on our historic Tempe campus, but disbursed and embedded in the community.

The downtown campus had economic development aspects that appealed to the city and citizens, but for us it also had implications for a more egalitarian and accessible campus. Among other things, we wanted to have greater appeal to the people who lived downtown or nearby, in most cases lower-income families, many of them Latino.

The initial plan was to move four of the ASU colleges downtown. We started leasing or buying downtown buildings, moving as quickly as possible to renovate them and set them up as academic buildings with faculty offices and classrooms. Most local politicians and citizens were excited about the prospect of change in an economically declining part of the city. However, the ASU faculty had a different view, and none of the four deans of the affected colleges was on board with the move. I replaced all of the deans. I worked closely with the increasing number of faculty and administrators who had begun to embrace university reformation and, in some instances, the downtown campus.

Especially helpful were the faculty who were very committed to social action—this included a large number of people. Many ASU faculty wanted a more definitive social purpose, they wanted a deeper impact on the community, and they realized that the university could do more. I spent a lot of time with faculty, meeting with faculty, individual faculty members, groups of faculty members. They thought it was strange because I would walk around, seemingly randomly, going from one faculty office to another.

The change from traditional departments to multidisciplinary units was taking shape and took some care. Let's consider an example. We had a Department of Anthropology, a well-rated and high-quality department. In the spirit of modernization of the university, we took Anthropology as a base, added faculty from some other disciplines, including Sociology, and created the School for Human Evolution and Social Change. Many faculty, not all, were supportive. It helped that we brought in Sander van der Leeuw, a person who is a genius and thinks in many dimensions. He was the one who came up with the basic design for the school. When created, about 80% of the school was in alignment, another 10% didn't care, and the other 10% hated the idea and hated me. One of the people who hated me was probably the most distinguished faculty member in the school. So, he actually had orchestrated a public campaign against me, calling me a corporatist and, now famously, "a thug in a suit." Early on, many faculty had the view that I was, indeed, just a money guy, interested in bringing in money to the university, but money for its own sake. Not many rejected the ideas behind a public values university; instead, they were cynical about it, assuming that it was all talk.

We had to find people able to create new funds from new sources. Faculty and staff helped enormously in writing new proposals, not just the familiar National Science Foundation or National Institutes of Health research proposals but also many proposals to other foundations. Many of these were successful and helped provide resources to fuel the transformation of the university.

This is just one example of the several major redesign efforts that were going on simultaneously. We constructed a School of Life Sciences out of three departments, as well as a School of Earth and Space Exploration. By most indicators, these were very positive changes. But not everything worked right away. For example, we tried to bring together history, philosophy, and religious studies into an integrated unit, and that did not work well, at least not initially. We had to try several structural changes before landing on one that was acceptable from the standpoint of both acceptance and performance. And, of course, there were many units that were not redesigned. Nothing was done merely for the sake of change, not just to shake things up, but for the sake of improving performance. Redesign is not the only thing. It is also important to know when to leave things alone.

After a great deal of positive disruption, structural change, new programs, and new funds, we focused unrelentingly on developing support for an ASU charter. We wanted to win people over to the idea of the charter, not only people at ASU but also political and community leaders. We saw the charter as both the legitimation of the New American University and the best chance for ensuring ASU's perpetual commitment to public values.

Could we get the electorate to vote for the candidate? A central element of the campaign was enrollment. Could you get people to embrace the idea that the central role of a research university was to provide a quality education to a great many people, to be inclusive rather than seeking to refuse a higher and higher percentage of people so as to seem more elite and prestigious? That campaign continues even now, but the realization of the charter was a key step.

One way we realize the mission in the ASU charter is that we hire administrative leaders who are excited about our goals. Everyone at the dean's level or above must be on board with ASU's distinctive mission. So, there is Chris Callahan. He was the associate dean of journalism at the University of Maryland when we were interviewing him. We had pulled journalism out of what was the old College of Public Programs (now the Watts College of Public Service and Community Solutions).

Chris comes in and reads the charter, reads the design aspirations, and then presents a proposal about how to do this. The same thing happened with Sander van der Leeuw, who designed the College of Human Evolution and Social Change. If people respond to the mission, they succeed at ASU. We try not to hire people who are generic administrators, as happy to work one place as another. In fact, I find that some of our best administrators are people who were accomplished scholars and never particularly aspiring to be administrators. None of our deans at the Watts College or in the law school or in engineering came from the usual dean career ladder; rather, all are distinguished, award-winning academic researchers and teachers. We found that the charter is a galvanizing force, a lure for the kinds of people who want to come to ASU.

One of the things that would build the university was the development and implementation of the charter and the values it represented. After we made clear just how different the ASU design could be from what I called, somewhat derisively, the "generic state universities," the ones that seemed to have little distinctiveness and sense of purpose, we began to get a good deal of support. People inside and outside the university were beginning to tell me, "This is a good vision; we like it." But they were also beginning to tell me, "And it has to outlast you." That was the idea of developing the charter, ensuring that this creation, the public values–based university, would extend well beyond my tenure.

Developing the charter was not one of these heroic leadership things. A great many people helped, and it could not have been achieved without them. For example, Craig Weatherup, an ASU graduate and the former CEO of PepsiCo, and Rick Shangraw, president of the ASU Foundation and a friend for more than 30 years, helped shape the charter vision and bring it into being. By 2011, we had survived the recession and the spending cuts, had become more autonomous in our vision, and were really focusing on the finalization and acceptance of the charter. I spent two years working with the ASU faculty and the Arizona Board of Regents developing support for the charter. We developed consensus for what I called a derived charter, one that was transformational but at the same time contained the good ideas of many different people. I was able to go to the Board of Regents and say, "This is a set of ideas that ASU is committed to, not just its president." We had the support of the ASU academic senate, which had voted overwhelmingly to support the charter.

Then, in 2013, I went to the Board of Regents, and they approved the charter. ASU will continue to evolve, and it has changed enormously over the years, but the public values mission has been solidified and broadly accepted. The idea that the university can be egalitarian and at the same time a high-quality university doing high-quality research and fulfilling an expansive teaching mission that reaches a huge number of incredibly diverse and talented students has become part of the university's DNA.

Foundation president Rick Shangraw, also a Syracuse University Maxwell School graduate, said at the time the charter was approved, "Now that is done, you better make sure you put in in stone." Taking his advice, the ASU charter is now literally written in stone (see fig. 1). The charter explicitly uses the language of public values and focuses directly on public values missions. We are planning to put similar granite statements on every ASU campus. We are a democratically derived university with a democratically derived charter.

The student body reflects the commitments in the charter. In 1987, the ASU student body was 98% white, 2% nonwhite. It was 1% Pell Grant eligible. It had a 12% graduation rate. And it had little funded research. Now, the student body is completely representative of the socioeconomic diversity of the state. In-state students are almost 50% Pell Grant eligible. The majority of the most recent 14,000-member freshman class is nonwhite. The graduation rate is the highest of any large university that still admits B students. ASU is a very different place, and its charter reflects these differences.

Figure 1. ASU charter carved in granite, across the street from the Fulton Building, ASU's primary administrative offices, including the president's office.

As we have already mentioned more than once, our book is self-consciously personalistic and based in experience, ours' and others'. The story of the ASU charter touches on and demonstrates a belief in each of the premises presented here—the core public values premise, the sector agnosticism premise, and certainly the pragmatism premise. The case above is nothing if not pragmatic, and it also demonstrates the possibilities of thinking about a traditional government institution, the state-government-established universities, in new ways that transcend sectors. But let us also reflect on a few points pertaining to the possibilities of adapting the ASU experience to other institutions.

Discussion Questions

- Question 1: To what extent do you think the ASU experience can be replicated in other universities or even other large nonedu-cational organizations? What are the adaptable lessons, and what parts of the ASU experience are due to such factors as timing, geography, and the historical trajectory of ASU?

- Question 2: Crow provides a detailed and candid story about the steps toward making ASU into a public values–focused institution, and who better to do so given that so much of this was his vision? Still, as he mentioned above, not everyone thought (or thinks) that the mega-university in the desert is a good idea. While Crow has garnered some credit and even a few accolades along the way, the "thug in a suit" has been roundly criticized by one or another interested party each year of his presidency. What are the limits, if any, of the insults, criticisms, and attacks a public values leader should be willing to accept in pursuit of a good cause?

- Question 3: Let's try a mind-meld thought experiment. Put yourself in Crow's role and take on his mission: wishing to lead a university toward public value. What might you have done differently, if anything?

Conclusion

This chapter and the next compose a set. Here we provided what we refer to as public values premises, the basic assumptions on which the book is based. They are presented with the temerity of near-lawlike, "this is what we believe" statements.

In the next chapter, we present public values propositions. We have carefully chosen the term "proposition"—not guidelines or principles, but propositions. By one definition a proposition is essentially an opinion.[12] But a very different definition of a proposition is a "tentative and conjectural relationship between constructs that is stated in a declarative form" (Bhattacherjee 2012). In the next chapter we both declare and opine, but fully aware that our propositions do not fit all circumstances and that, even if they conform closely to our own experiences, others' experiences may contradict them. We are calling for that engaged reader mentioned in the preface.

3

Public Values
Management Propositions I

The defeat of the Greek Army in the Peloponnesian War (431–404 BC) and, nearly 2,000 years later, the temporary madness of King George III, the English king who presided over the losing side of the American Revolution—what could these events possibly have to do with one another? Well, perhaps nothing. We cannot be sure. Nobody practiced microbiology during the 1700s or earlier. But according to one contemporary forensic microbiologist and expert on food contamination (Satin 2007), microbes may have caused both the Greek Army's defeat and the king's madness. Cereal grains may have caused the Greeks to lose many previously able soldiers to sickness and caused King George's arsenic poisoning. Prefer more solid evidence of celebrity death by foodborne illness? The Argonne National Laboratory conducted a survey that provided strong evidence that food containing arsenic shortened Beethoven's life (Stevens, Jacobsen, and Crofts 2013).

Throughout history, up until the present day, human beings have died as a result of contaminants in the food they ingest. But that is not to say that life (or its termination) goes on without change. In the past 100 years or so, we have witnessed enormous progress in our ability to maintain food safety, to track sources of contamination, to provide information about unsafe foods, and to quickly remove unsafe foods from the market. As is the case with so many elements of human progress against hazard, geography makes all the difference. In some countries food safety measures have not progressed much since the time of King George III. In other countries, the chances of serious illness from foodborne disease have been reduced to a minuscule fraction of the threat level of just a few decades ago. The story of how this has happened is a good touchstone for understanding how public values–based institutions and leaders achieve public values objectives.

Here is a clear-cut instance of human intent to address food safety: In 1795 the French government established a reward of 12,000 francs for anyone who developed a practical means of preserving food.[1] And they had a winner. Nicholas Appert, a French confectioner, demonstrated that meat cold be preserved by placing it in glass bottles, boiling it, and securely enclosing it. He discovered what later came to be referred to as canning (Brody et al. 2008).

The person who invented most of what we know about the relationship of microbes to food safety is, of course, Louis Pasteur. Building on Anton van Leeuwenhoek's discovery of bacteria and, in general, the microbial world, Pasteur was the first to provide a truly causal explanation for the relationship of microbial organisms to all manner of chemical changes in foods, including not only fermentation processes but also foodborne illness. He demonstrated in 1857 the effects of microbes on milk spoilage and three years later the role of microbes in contaminating beer and wine. With Pasteur's findings, those seeking to address food poisoning and food safety finally had a valid set of causes and effects to focus on. Even so, progress was not rapid: food safety required so much more than the knowledge of the science of food degradation; it also required social mechanisms for rapidly identifying problems and addressing them.

Public Value Propositions

In the previous chapter we presented three "public values premises," each of which can be viewed as a fundamental assumption about public values management and leadership—assumptions that we do not spend much more time articulating or defending. We posit these premises, we feel they are correct, they guide our work. They are essentially articles of faith.

In this chapter and the next we present for the reader's consideration a number of *propositions* about public values. Why two chapters? We provide some evidence for each of these propositions in the form of cases, anecdotes, or interview data, and some of these are extensive.

As mentioned in chapter 1, the notion of "proposition" we use here is very much aligned with the root of the word—"propose." We have thoughts about how leaders can achieve public values, and we propose these ideas not as "how-to" guidelines but as suggestions for others, and especially the reader, to compare against their own ideas and experiences. Not only are we not certain of the unvarying potency of these ideas; we *know* they sometimes do not work. Different circumstances require different strategies, resources, and actions. Rather, we feel that the propositions reflect factors that are *usually* important in achieving public values.

The public values propositions are presented in table 4. The table simply provides our propositions and a description of their claims. In the remainder of the chapter (and throughout the rest of the book) we expand on these relatively simply propositions, hoping not only to describe them in more detail but also to see how they relate to a variety of circumstances (and also determine when they do not seem to relate at all). In this chapter we also provide comments from the public values leaders we interviewed, and we continue with our food safety base case.

Food safety serves as an excellent illustration of many of the requirements for achieving public values and relates well to all, if not most, of our propositions. In the first place, public safety, including food safety, is among the least contentious public values. Less obvious, the arc of progress in food safety is long and winding and, especially relevant, has occurred because of the contributions of a great many institutions, often working together. Despite the long-term, evolutionary change, the actions taken have for the most part been the residue of human de-

TABLE 4
Public Values Propositions

Proposition	Claim
Articulate a vision	A coherent vision is required, one that is unambiguous and legitimated by participants in the vision's formation. The vision transcends any individual and focuses on the aspirational self of the collective or community participating in the vision.
Develop multilateral institutional interactions	In contrast to pursuit of private values, public value achievement almost always entails working with other institutions in processes requiring participation, at least some direct interaction, mutual learning and accommodation, and joint commitment to change.
Inclusiveness and accommodation of minority interests	Public value pertains to the rights and obligations of all citizens, and thus it is vital actively to seek out participants from diverse cultures, socioeconomic groups, regions, and political allegiances and to elicit the views of minority interests.
Engender trust	During a period of eroding public trust in institutions, public values leaders must strive to promote trust in the public value objectives promoted and the institution and people pursuing the public value.
Embrace mutable leadership	Changes in time and circumstance require not only change-oriented, adaptable leaders but also the emergence of new leaders with different talents relevant to different needs.

sign, not just the sort of trial-and-error progress that sometimes occurs with modest human intention.

Public Value Proposition: Articulate a Vision

Throughout this book we steadfastly reject the notion of the heroic leader and maintain that little of importance in public values achievement is accomplished by the driven, solitary genius working alone. The articulation of a vision is in some cases and in some respects the exception. Here the charismatic individual visionary plays a role, at least at the beginning of the public values trajectory. However, even here the vision ultimately is a collective work. Even when individuals provide a vision, others must legitimate it. As Victor Hugo said, "there is nothing so powerful as an idea whose time has come." But others, not the visionary, determine whether the time has come. The time has come when others sign on to the idea. History is littered with poorly received good ideas that were embraced later.

Equally important, it is often the case that public values are achieved as visions of individuals come together, sometimes over a considerable period of time, to help achieve public values. In most cases where the achievement of public values involves many institutions working over an extended period of time, it is not the sole vision that triumphs, but the multiple visions that come together. Think of, for example, the development of the internet, a case we will spend some time with later. We shall see many visions coming together: packet switching, protocols, interfaces, policies for commercialization, the creation of a worldwide web.

There are several reasons why one must begin with the vision and why one cannot succeed in attaining public values without it having been articulated early on. The most important reason is that public values are almost never obvious, universal, or tangible. If one's vision is to maximize wealth or elevate kill ratios or build a movie studio that wins the most awards, then the vision is easy to understand and easy to communicate. But if the vision is a public values vision, it may be fuzzy. Whereas most private values are crystal clear to all, many public values are broad and even amorphous. Thus, if one's vision is to greatly expand opportunity for citizens, then it will be easy to obtain agreement on that goal. However, it will not be at all easy to develop a consensus on just what "expanded opportunity" means, nor will it be easy to point out steps one, two, and three in pursuit of that public value. The public values vision gives specificity to values; it suggests exactly what is to be accomplished and possible paths for getting from problem to solution.

Achieving public values requires cooperation, but it is imperative that people know what it is they will obtain from that cooperation. Rhetoric, no matter how well crafted, cannot sustain. It is certainly possible to motivate people with rhetoric and generalities. And hollow rhetoric can be enough to motivate episodic engagement (e.g., casting a vote). But cooperative institutional design requires sustained activity, and in almost every case sustained activity requires a shared vision of the values achieved at the end of the hard work. The vision may change along the way, and the specification of values may change. Sustained activities need not require constant attentiveness and activity. Nonetheless, absent the vision, institutional design for public values cannot succeed. If there is any indispensable leadership role, it is the role of the visionary and communicator.

Deep Case. Food Safety

Food safety—so, what was the vision and how was it articulated? In the first place, we note that the history of food safety is centuries long and includes many visionaries. For example, Louis Pasteur and Parisian chef Nicholas Appert, inventor of air-tight containers, long ago had achieved remarkable visions about public safety in food consumption. As an excellent example of businesses' contributions to public values, the firm Donkin, Hall, and Gamble contributed by direct action. In 1818 they provided the British Admiralty with 30,000 cans of safe food products (Satin 2007). As is often the case, the public values vision is not spelled out, but rather reflected in actions, actions that can be accepted and replicated by other individuals and institutions. When public value pursuit occurs over many decades or even centuries, it is helpful to set some boundaries for analysis. Thus, for the sake of convenience let us focus on the relatively recent US context, starting with one landmark visionary, a professor no less.

Dr. Harvey Wiley, from Professor to Food Safety Czar

In 1883, Dr. Harvey Wiley left his position as chair of the Purdue University chemistry department to become the chief chemist in the US Department of Agriculture's Bureau of Chemistry. Before Wiley's appointment, the bureau's chief activities pertained to soil samples and fertilizers. But Wiley was interested in "food adulteration," which entailed any chemical process, human-induced or natural, where the purity of food was compromised. Not all food adulteration is harmful. In some cases, it is simply a matter of wishing to combine flavors or increase shelf life of foods or use more economical materials. But in most cases, some undesirable form of adulteration is at the bottom of harmful foods. Thus, harmful bacteria may be the culprit, or chemicals introduced for processing may be at fault. In a sense, Dr. Wiley was a natural foods advocate before natural foods was a meaningful term to most people. Dr. Wiley worked tirelessly on issues related to pure food, developing research evidence and political support for legislative action.

In 1906, the US Congress passed the Pure Food and Drug Act, a landmark establishing the first federal policy statement on food (Coppin and High 1999). The legislation is often referred to as the Wiley Act. It was written almost entirely by Dr. Wiley and his staff. But Wiley's work only began with the vision. The writing of the legislation was vitally important, but not more so than his campaigning for it, developing a network of supporters and advocates in both the government and the private sector. He had a powerful and unambiguous vision, articulated clearly and forcefully, and he committed years to it, including developing what we would now call evidence-based policy. Fortuitously, he also had the political acumen and common sense to bring others along to participate in the vision (Coppin and High 1999).

Muckraking in the Jungle

We can contrast Dr. Wiley with another important historical figure and food safety visionary, muckraking journalist and novelist Upton Sinclair. The contrast features not only different kinds of visions but also different kinds of public values leaders. Sinclair galvanized support for food safety reforms by calling public attention to an issue that was not yet at the forefront of most people's concerns. His novel *The Jungle* was based on his 1904 journalistic research visiting many of Chicago's stockyards and meatpacking plants, taking notes about sundry practices, both repugnant and unhealthy, practices largely unknown to the general public. His descriptions of rancid meat, food trimmed and falling onto a sawdust floor and then packed along with the sawdust residue, a lack of care about insect parts and rodent infestations—all of this captured the public imagination (as it probably captures the contemporary reader).

The impact of the book was not exactly what Sinclair expected. He was an ardent socialist, and his socialist newsletter *Appeal to Reason* originally published a serialized version of the book in 1905. Sinclair's social realism novel focuses on the squalid and unhealthy living conditions of persons, largely immigrants, working in the meatpacking industry. It recounts the trials of the fictional Jurgis Rudkus, a Lithuanian immigrant, and his family, including incidences of unsanitary and overcrowded housing, heartless employers, unimaginably bad working conditions, and rampant harassment at work, both mental and physical. The novel is dedicated "to the workingmen of America."

The readership, even those who did not identify or register much concern about poor immigrants, were themselves meat consumers, and they could not avoid imagining the work practices described in the book. One of these disgusted readers was none other than President Theodore Roosevelt, who turned his attention to advocating legislation and easing the path of the 1906 Wiley Act, despite widespread industry opposition (Hilts 2003).[2]

What was included in the act President Roosevelt signed in 1906? It prohibited the adulteration of food products, banned the use of misleading branding of livestock, and prohibited the use of unsafe modifications of meats. For the first time, it provided regulations about how animals intended for food could be slaughtered and for the inspection of meat before it was to be marketed (US Food and Drug Administration 2017).

By contrasting the contributions and styles of two persons contributing to the public value vision for food safety, we can begin to understand the very different paths that visions and visionaries can take. In some respects, Upton Sinclair was an "accidental visionary." While there is little evidence that he was able to engender much support for the poor immigrants working in the meatpacking industry, he did, almost by accident, help develop a groundswell of support for food safety reforms and, ultimately, policies. Indeed, Sinclair himself was well aware of the fact that his food crusader legacy was unintended. As he wrote in a 1906 *Cosmopolitan Magazine* commentary, "I aimed at the public's heart, and by accident I hit it in the stomach" (Schlosser 2006). His literary legacy provides evidence of "the accident." Books focusing on the ills of capitalism dominated his career before and after *The Jungle*, taking on such industry titans as J. P. Morgan, John D. Rockefeller, and Henry Ford. But the food industry was never again a focus of his work.

In the inimitable words of Bruce Springsteen, "you can't start a fire without a spark."[3] Yes, fires are not always started with just a spark, and, indeed, after the fire starts, one interested in a continued flame must accelerate and preserve the fire. Still, often it is the spark that is missing and that matters most. Even if Sinclair did not intend to contribute monumentally to food safety, can we really say that the contribution was purely an accident? We think not. In the first place, Sinclair's professional life up to the point of *The Jungle*, and well thereafter, was devoted to impassioned, reform-focused writing, and he clearly exhibited talents for getting the readers' attention and for galvanizing opinion. One could say he had a sense for public values failures.

Second, while his primary contributions were as a writer, he was a long-time political activist, at one point even mounting a campaign to be the governor of California, one that did not succeed but was nonetheless quite credible for someone running as a known socialist. He had political skills and savvy and thus was well equipped to light a public value spark, even if he did quickly thereafter turn his attention to entirely different public value concerns, most often the plight of the poor. Accident? As Sinclair's antisocialist nemesis Thomas Edison remarked famously, "good fortune often happens when opportunity meets preparation."

Discussion Question

We suggest that contributing to public values does not always occur in a straight fashion where one has an objective, a plan, and pursues the plan with a set of linear actions. Often public values leaders are in the right place at the right time with the right idea. We suggested above that Upton Sinclair had a "sense for public values failures." We did not mean that literally; if the world needs a true sixth sense, we vote for ESP. What we mean is that it is possible to cultivate attitudes and behaviors that make one ready when opportunity meets the vision. But why do some people have this "attitude" or sense for public values and identifying public values failure? Is it innate, a matter of early-instilled family and personal values, or is it the result of education and training, or hanging out with the right people, or life experiences, or any of these in the right combustible (the "spark") combination? If you wished to develop a nascent public values sense, what are the best ways to enhance it? We certainly hope that "Reading this book" is your response! But, seriously, to what extent is being a public values visionary amenable to formal education of any sort?

Contrasting Public Values Visionaries: Sinclair and Wiley

When we think of public values visionaries, there are "insiders" and "outsiders," those working with others in institutions and those who are more solitary. Both are important, but for our purposes, focused as we are on public values *management*, the insider is more relevant if not necessarily more important.

Upton Sinclair's vision is at one end of a continuum, the one representing time-delimited, unintended consequence of great import; the Wiley vision is at the other. Wiley was in the food safety business for most of his adult life, fashioning a single-minded vision. Wiley's vision, like Sinclair's, was based on research (but sustained research rather than narrow-frame journalistic research) and rooted in scientific observation rather than the amalgamation of fact, fiction, and passion. Wiley followed through with his vision to an extent and in a manner that Sinclair never did. Wiley actually developed the public value reforms and championed them, ultimately playing a major role in both the drafting and the passage of the Pure Food and Drug Act.

Dr. Wiley and Upton Sinclair are arguably the two most important persons shaping a vision and galvanizing support for food safety. Sinclair started a spark that spread quickly and flourished after he had moved on to other things. By contrast, Dr. Wiley was a developer, sustainer, and implementer of a vision. Dr. Wiley helped legitimate his vision by working directly with others for a long period of time. Upton Sinclair legitimated his vision indirectly, but effectively, by capturing the attention and commitment of tens of thousands of readers that he never otherwise met. Both provided foundational visions related to the public value of food safety and security.

The contrast between Upton Sinclair and Harvey Wiley provides an excellent illustration of the difference between a visionary and an institutional public values manager and leader. Undeniably, Sinclair helped galvanize public knowledge about, and interest in, food safety, and his contribution to advancing food safety is considerable. However, his contribution had nothing *directly* to do with the design and management of institutions charged with bringing about change. This is not to say that Sinclair was uninvolved in establishing institutions and working to develop them. In particular, he founded the California branch of the American Civil Liberties Union (ACLU), he worked with and promoted the Industrial Workers of the World, and, of course, no one can run for governor or Congress, as he did on several occasions, without attending to institutions. But his institutional contributions were episodic and, moreover, not in any way directed to the public value issue of food safety. Visionary? Unquestionably. Institutional public values leader? No.

By contrast, Dr. Wiley easily meets criteria for public values management and leadership. He systematically set forth a vision for public value, and he worked to develop an institution to deliver that public value. He helped sustain his vision with bureaucratic infighting. Not only was his agency constantly involved in industry-initiated lawsuits, some of which the agency won and others it did not, but he also spent much of his career fighting a rearguard action against the powerful Secretary of Agriculture James Wilson, a staunch industry advocate who rarely sided with Dr. Wiley in any dispute. Indeed, their battles generated such acrimony that in 1912 Dr. Wiley resigned his position in government, leaving behind him a rebuilt and formidable Bureau of Chemistry that would evolve into the Food and Drug Administration (FDA). His commitment to the public value of food safety never waned. He spent most of the remainder of his professional career as a pioneer consumer advocate.

Table 5 provides a contrast in the public values contributions of these two individuals most responsible for enhancing food safety in the United States and creating a pathway for much of the rest of the world.

TABLE 5
Visionaries and Public Value–Based Design Visionaries

Articulating the Vision	Upton Sinclair	Dr. Harvey Wiley
Provide public value vision	Provided case evidence on need for food safety, but it was coincidental to the primary focus on immigrant living conditions.	Provided research and advocacy relevant to a clear, unambiguous public value of ensuring food safety.
Gather support for public value vision	His novel raised awareness of the issue.	His research provided evidence raising others' awareness; he joined an institution, the Bureau of Chemistry, thus including others attracted to his vision, and he worked with policy makers to pursue the vision.
Sustained commitment to the public value vision	He had sustained commitment to public value visions, but *not* public value related to food safety—his contribution was one-off.	Devoted his career to developing the vision, obtaining support, and implementing policies and actions advancing the vision.

Public Value Proposition: Multilateral Institutional Interaction

Single organizations have, on some occasions, been able to achieve a great deal working largely on their own. But usually the achievement is of *private* values, including sometimes private values that have implications for broad publics (e.g., massive job growth). However, we can identify few instances of clear-cut public values achievement where an organization is largely working on its own, using resources it has generated, to achieve outcomes that other organizations and individuals have contributed little to accomplishing. In the introduction we discussed Mothers Against Drunk Driving, which at first blush seems to have "owned" the public values associated with sharply decreased drunk driving and attendant deaths and injuries. However, notwithstanding MADD's accomplishments, it is useful to remember that many of these accomplishments required public policy changes and a great many allies in a variety of policy-making bodies, especially state legislatures. In fact, the role of MADD in improving automobile and pedestrian safety is in some ways an exemplar of the idea of multilateralism.

MADD officials worked tirelessly and for many years developing allies, both committed individual activists and institutions. Their partners were not only government institutions. MADD developed support and resources from alliances with both nonprofit organizations and businesses. These partners are diverse but include some that are intimately involved in automobile safety, for example, the insurance firm Nationwide and the General Motors Foundation. Other partnering groups range from the National Parent Teacher Association to the National Football League. Organizational partners have been instrumental not only in providing funds but also in bringing the organization's message to an extremely broad audience.

Comment: Anne-Marie Slaughter on the Relation of Leadership Vision to Multilateral Institutional Interaction

Dr. Anne-Marie Slaughter, president and CEO of New America, had this to say: "Vision is really about building networks. You start by articulating goals, using research, and by convening people and organizations. You also need to think about matching the organization to the issue. You don't partner with both Coca-Cola and Pepsi on an obesity project, but you work together with them on a water project. Both of them have a real stake in clean water." Dr. Slaughter's bio can be found at https://www.newamerica.org/our-people/anne-marie-slaughter/.

One definition of multilateral is "involving or participated in by more than two . . . parties."[4] But the key to our public value proposition is the nature of the interaction. First, note that we use the word "interaction," not "collaboration" or "partnership." The reason is that "collaboration" and, especially, "partnership" provide too high a bar. Both terms suggest a level of coordination not required to achieve public values. Institutions can interact, with positive results, while not having close partnerships (more on that later). Sometimes multilateral interactions can be managed strategically even though the organizations are not in contact with one another; management can involve anticipation, monitoring, planning, and incentives or, in current parlance, nudge behavior.

To qualify as multilateral institutional interaction, there are some minimal requirements. The interaction must be activity based rather than symbolic or ceremonial; the interaction must entail commitments to the same public value goals, or at least components of the same goals (but not necessarily agreement on the means to ends); the interaction must involve some degree of cooperation, but the cooperation may alternate with or occur at the same time as competition; and the interaction requires good faith communication and learning from one another, though not necessarily completely open communication on broad-scale sharing of information.

In many cases, institutions develop groups of individual supporters, sometimes loosely organized and sometimes not really organized at all. Often these individual supporters (think of, e.g., individual donors of small amounts to a political party or nonprofit organization) can be vital, even a prerequisite to the institution achieving its goals. We are not diminishing those ties; it is simply not what we are talking about here. We are talking about institutions working with other institutions. The relationship may be just one institution working with another, or with many different institutions. In large organizational sets there is no requirement that all institutions work directly with one another, only that those focused on the same public value work with at least some others focused on that public value. Nor do all of the institutions focused on the same value necessarily have to communicate directly with one another; sometimes one institution may be in the lead, either in general or just with respect to coordination and communication. But there must be some direct communication and mutual learning and accommodation within the public value institutional set. As one might assume from our sector agnosticism design principle, the participating institutions may be a mix of government, nonprofit, business firms, universities, and "hybrids" such as public authorities.

We certainly do not see competition as the enemy, and, of course, market competition often has very beneficial results. But market competition is decidedly different from multilateral institutional interaction. Let us consider a simple example. Let us assume that a computer software firm is interested in developing a powerful, commercially dominant new operating system. The firm knows that code underlying software is easily copied; it is very close to pure knowledge-based intellectual property requiring no extensive technological refashioning or manufacturing. It is all about the knowledge that is embedded in the code, and it is, at least theoretically, possible to cheaply copy or "reengineer." The last thing a company wishes to do in such a circumstance is to share information openly and broadly. Doing so could result in disaster—competitors either pirating or, more likely, modifying the code and cutting into a projected huge and profitable market.

This does not mean that business firms do not cooperate, only that they do not cooperate much when they are pursuing the same specific objective. They may cooperate on precommercial knowledge, they may cooperate in developing human capital, they may cooperate on setting industry standards, and they most certainly will cooperate with suppliers and venders and customers. But the exclusiveness of the profit-based value and the interest in maximizing profits and shareholder value essentially prohibit cooperation in some circumstances. In some cases socially beneficial interaction is not beneficial to the firm and could imperil its very existence.

By contrast, let's consider briefly a public values outcome familiar to nearly everyone—the development of the internet and the World Wide Web. Our contemporary concept of the internet could not have occurred in the same manner as the development of a market-focused computer operating system occurs. In the case of the web, there are simply too many purposes and too many moving parts, and the (ultimate) level of cooperation required could never have been brought together by any single firm, no matter how powerful and regardless of its international reach. Issues of regulation required government action, issues of *self-regulation* required nonprofit interaction (e.g., ICANN),[5] and the sharing of research and scientific and technical knowledge required an openness common to basic research but not often found among business firms. This is not to say, of course, that firms did not contribute to the development of the internet. They contributed enormously, not only in competitive mode and product development but also in multilateral partnership. But they could not have unilaterally achieved the public values embedded in the internet.

Let's return to our base case, food safety, and within that context consider multilateral institutional interaction. It is a long and winding road.

Food Safety Policy Making as an Example of Multilateral Institutional Interaction

The case of food safety as a public value not only provides a good example of the importance of multilateral interaction among institutions but also illuminates the ensuing difficulties when institutions that have the same broad values work against one another.

To illustrate the importance of multilateral institutional interaction, let us move our food safety historical perspective from the early twentieth century to 2017. On January 4, 2017, President Obama signed legislation that was among the last major initiatives of his administration, the Food Safety Modernization Act (FSMA). After the progress made nearly 100 years ago with the FDA food testing and certification programs, one might well ask, what is still required to protect the public from foodborne illnesses? Actually, quite a bit. More than 100 years ago it was possible for tens of thousands of people to quickly become extremely ill or die before anyone could determine the cause or the remedy. What is different today is the speed of remedy. According to the Centers for Disease Control and Prevention, 3,000 Americans die each year from foodborne diseases, a prodigious drop (especially on a per capita basis) from the bad old days of 100 years ago and earlier, but still eye-catching. Moreover, a great many more (128,000) are hospitalized from foodborne illnesses, but, as a result of better medical care, earlier discovery, and better food tracking, most survive. Still, anyone who has been in the hospital with food poisoning certainly wants to see improvement in public food safety. Likewise, the corporations that lose millions of dollars when disaffected customers stay away because of food safety concerns are understandably interested in doing what they can to make sure that customers stay safe. How much does it matter economically? Since 2015, the Chipotle chain has unfortunately had a great many highly publicized food poisoning cases traced back to their food, including 120 illnesses in Massachusetts (mostly college students at one restaurant), 64 in Minnesota, and 98 in California (Shumaker 2015). Highly publicized, but many fewer, Chipotle-based illnesses continued in 2016. In February 2016, the chain closed all of its 1,971 stores across the country for one day in order to give employees a refresher class and, doubtless, to try to give their customers a reason to believe they were taking the illnesses seriously and making changes. The chain also announced a $10 million program to work with farmers and suppliers to enhance food safety and develop more stringent food handling protocols. Later, it was determined that Chipotle, once one of the fastest-growing, most profitable, and best-reviewed food chains (in terms of quality and safety), had declined by more than 44%. The chain's slogan, "Food with Integrity," has been widely mocked. Some even questioned whether Chipotle would survive.

In short, despite the enormous progress that has been made in the United States in food safety (as attested to by the fact that none of the Chipotle poisonings resulted in death, most being confined to relatively mild sicknesses), it is clear that problems remain and that the public value and the economic consequences are substantial.

Now, with that dose of contemporary reality, let us return to the FSMA. The act includes a number of important initiatives, including (1) food illness prevention plans presented by food facilities; (2) mandatory produce safety standards related to hygiene, packaging, and food care; (3) doubling the number of government food inspections of food facilities; and (4) a program of accreditation for food testing laboratories.

Our concern, however, is not with traditional regulation, a major aspect of the act, but with multilateral institutional interaction. The FSMA is based on such interactions, both in the formulation of the act and in its implementation. The institutions in question are government institutions, but we should not assume that there is a history of happy and fruitful interactions among government entities. True, all government agencies and levels profess to share a focus on public interest (a term in more widespread use than public values), but government organizations often have very different conceptions of the public interest and, of course, are as likely as most organization types to compete with one another (Nicholson-Crotty 2005; Volden 2005) and jealously guard their respective resources and prerogatives (Kenyon 1991; Radaelli 2004).

The history of a great many policy and regulatory domains, including pollution control, transportation, and (especially recently) health care and immigration policy, shows that federal and state governments sometimes have very different ideas about the public interest and that the states can thwart the best-laid plans of federal lawmakers. Food safety is another policy domain in which the multilateral interactions often have proved neither pleasant nor effective (Sharkey 2009).

In the food safety domain, there is plenty of responsibility for both state and federal governments. The federal government is in most respects the "primary," having broader responsibility and the power to develop regulations binding for the states. The federal food policy includes not only the safety and inspection policies of the FDA but also a wide array of related policies that are the responsibility of autonomous agencies. These include, for example, the farm bills and Temporary Assistance for Needy Families / food stamps programs of the Department of Agriculture, the Supplemental Nutrition Assistance Program (also known as "SNAP"), farm and commodities subsidies, crop insurance, marketing regulations, export and import policies, and labor laws affecting all those involved in the development and delivery of food. But this leaves a good deal of responsibility for the states. State governments share responsibility for public health regulation, food-related environmental regulation, support and regulation of agriculture, and implementing most of the social welfare programs that deliver food and food services to the needy. The states regulate policies related to the homeless and, particularly relevant, food banks. In short, if the federal government and state governments are at odds with one another, the ability to achieve broad goals and improvements in food safety is much diminished.

Provisions of the FSMA focus explicitly on "enhanced partnerships" between state and federal government agencies sharing responsibility for food safety and also coordination with other nations' governments. The act requires the FDA to develop strategies to help assist state and local governments in improving defenses against the delivery of unsafe food, including a multiyear grant program to encourage state governments to expand their food safety programs. Another component of the act facilitates teamwork in inspections and decentralizes inspections and their administration, including providing more money to state and local government for inspection resources. The FSMA expands the ability of the FDA to work with foreign governments and other nations' firms developing and delivering training of US food production requirements and food safety. This is certainly timely given the internationalization of the food supply, as any shopper knows who buys farmed tilapia from Vietnam, winter peaches from Chile, or korma rice from Italy, not to mention the millions of prepackaged foods from all over the world. Since we do not have an up-close-and-personal history of the "enhanced partnerships" provisions of the FSMA, we cannot say anything from this case about the processes of forging multilateral institutional interactions in pursuit of public values. However, we do feel that the case has implications worth reviewing. The first point to bear in mind for any multiorganizational objective is the need to be hardheaded in asking this question: "What does my fellow actor gain by working with me?" While there are certain realms where command and control can be viable, alignment of incentives usually presents a better long-term approach. Thus, in the case of the FSMA, the act clearly expands the role and responsibilities of state and local government but also provides targeted funding aimed at helping with those responsibilities. Funding is often a good answer to our question about gain.

Perhaps even more important is a second implication, one related to the breadth of activity sometimes required to achieve public values. In today's world, one characterized by internationalization and both economic and political interdependence, not to mention environmental interdependency, the achievement of public values often requires a much higher degree of interaction among far-flung and diverse institutions. It also requires an ability to think strategically about "butterfly effects." Thus, a change in the political climate, or a drought, or even a change in consumer appetites in one nation can have major effects on the world supply of food staples. Similarly, as we know well from the recent history of climate change policy, some values depend on standards agreed on by nations. Food standards are no different.

As we see, food safety is a team enterprise. Little can be accomplished working alone. Below, we present a personal case of a different complex public values undertaking that, likewise, could not have been effective in the absence of close collaboration.

Personal Case (Crow). The University Innovation Alliance as a Multi-institutional Interaction

Having been president of Arizona State University for nearly 20 years, I am sometimes asked, perhaps in hopes that I will retire soon, "What would you still like to achieve?" A very general answer would be the creation of more public values–focused universities. If we could, especially, have more universities embrace the notion of inclusiveness and access for all qualified students, regardless of race, gender, ethnicity, age, or income, then we would have taken a giant step toward public values universities.

This chapter talks about the importance of institutional actors working together. That is not always easy to do, especially in universities. Some universities are Byzantine and cannot even get the units to work together. Often universities' departments are powerful and independent actors that work on the basis of informal treaties that have been developed over many years of struggling with one another. Universities themselves are natural competitors; they compete for students, faculty, research money, and donations, not to mention the more visible competition through sports.

Still, multi-institutional partnerships are not impossible and can even thrive. One such case is the University Innovation Alliance, a partnership aimed at forging ties among like-minded universities, ones that are especially focused, whether or not they use the same concepts and language, on what we call public values–based leadership. Working with a number of forward-looking partners, not all of them universities, we managed to find common objectives, to share information, and, to some extent, to set aside the usual competitive compulsion.

For quite some time, ASU has been recognized as an innovative university, with dramatic changes in student performance and outcomes. In discussions with foundations, chiefly the Bill and Melinda Gates Foundation, we began to exchange ideas about possibilities for diffusing some of the work at ASU, with its focus on inclusiveness, learning technology, and public values. The Gates Foundation is essentially a public values–focused foundation. Much of their thinking seems to have converged with what was happening at ASU. Knowing this, we sent some ideas to the foundation, suggesting some possibilities for funding and joint work.

As luck would have it, Melina Gates was visiting Phoenix one day in 2013, and, based on the materials we sent her, she decided she wanted to meet with me. So, I go to this hotel in Scottsdale (a suburb of Phoenix), and we sit down and talk about what we're doing, and we agree that we share values and that I should meet with the president of the foundation. ASU hired a visionary woman from the Gates Foundation, Hilary Pennington. Hilary is the founder of Jobs for the Future and a fantastic program designer and implementer, and we knew she would work well at a public values–focused university such as ours. What I was after with hiring Hilary was her brainpower. We hired her as an advisor to help us think about how we might advance the project on multi-university innovation. She had retained her contacts at the Gates Foundation, and she introduced us to Dan Greenstein, who at that time was director of postsecondary strategy for the foundation.

So, we started talking with Dan. He visited ASU a couple of times. I went to the Gates Foundation a couple of times, and our team went a couple of times. Dan had this very elaborate, highly analytical, highly systemic plan and a set of specific goals about how to help transform higher education. Ultimately the Gates people said, "We're interested in getting some proposals from you but not for you. We want you to facilitate the building of a group of institutions." They figured, and we agreed, that there was not much chance of changing all or most institutions, at least not quickly, but that it might be possible to change at least a few institutions, ones willing to work together. So we took on the task of developing a coalition of universities, ones not just focused on innovation but also concerned about public values and inclusiveness.

So, I then went out and started meeting with university presidents that I felt I could convince to sign up for an alliance, for our proposal. First, I visited some universities I was already working with, ones where we had good relations and shared goals. I started with the University of Central Florida, and then I started building a stronger relationship with Georgia State University. We then got some seed money and did some research on "research universities of the next generation," identifying not only ASU, UCF, and GSU but also such places as SUNY Buffalo and University of California, Riverside. Hillary ran this study for us.

Next, enter a new partner. The Aspen Institute knew about the Gates Foundation interest and wanted to help facilitate. There were two meetings at Aspen in which we asked certain universities to come to the meetings to talk about how we might innovate together. Then, based on those meetings, we sorted through which were the best universities that we could work with. We had developed some rules of engagement. Participating universities had to be committed to producing more graduates (and particularly more graduates from low-income families), they had to be committed to innovating together, and they had to be willing to think about things like how to lower costs. We found other universities that were receptive to partnerships, including Oregon State and Iowa State University, both with presidents committed to egalitarian access. We reached out to Purdue, and while the Purdue faculty were not initially "all in," its president, Mitch Daniels, was excited about the alliance and kept working to build enthusiasm with his faculty. Ultimately, we brought together 11 universities. We then developed a proposal and sent it to the Gates Foundation. They liked the ideas but said we needed participation from more foundations.

Serendipitously, Bridget Burns joined ASU as an American Council on Education fellow that year. Bridget had just arrived from the Oregon University system. She had been chief of staff of the Oregon University system, at least until the state did away with that system. So, I said, "Okay, why don't you stay a while at ASU and help us advance this alliance initiative." With Bridget's help and that of others, we met with six or seven foundations interested in contributing to the alliance, including, for example, Lumina in Indianapolis and Kresge, among others. With their help, the University Innovation Alliance was born in 2014. Bridget Burns became our executive director.

The net outcome is that we had found a way to innovate together and share innovations, ultimately leading to the creation of this University Innovation Network now connected to the University Innovation Alliance. In five years, we have increased the number of Pell-eligible graduates by more than 30%, which means an increase of tens of thousands of students. Basically, these 11 universities' increase in Pell-eligible graduates is more sizable than the total number of graduates from all the universities in the Ivy League.

Not all the shared innovations relate to students. A requirement of the Alliance was that all universities would be willing to open up their hoods and let others look at their engines and how they performed. One example is Alliance member Michigan State University. Michigan State is an egalitarian-access, public values–focused, large-scale research university, similar in many respects to ASU. They were at one point having retention problems and even attendance problems among some of the lower-income minority students in their freshman class. So they were trying to figure out why. Ultimately they realized that every Michigan State student was getting overwhelmed by the number of communications received from the university. Freshmen were receiving as many as 400 email messages from the time of admission to the time of arrival as a freshman. Most families were probably not eager to deal with information overload, but it was often most difficult for relatively poor families where the student would be the first one attending college. Some of these families, even after admission and acceptance, were saying, "Forget it, you're not going there." The forms and emails were intimidating, both in number and in scope. After some investigation, MSU found that this was common and was a big deal. So, then the innovation was that Michigan State learned a lesson about how to enhance communication. All the other universities in the Alliance learned from this lesson, and all of us modified our approaches to dealing with incoming freshmen.

Another shared innovation case began with ASU. This innovation involves using big data analytics to predict student academic risk. Working with Alliance universities and an innovation cluster of all the financial aid officers at all 11 schools, we wanted to cut the red tape and barriers to financial aid. We won funding from the Department of Education to build big analytic data systems to help with student loan processing. Just recently we received about $1 million from the Eric Schmidt Foundation. Our project focuses on a technology tool to enhance people's abilities to fill out FAFSA (Free Application for Federal Student Aid) forms. FAFSA is complicated, and there is no 1040-EZ version. It is so complicated that a large number of families that are eligible for federal financial aid simply refuse to fill out the forms, or they do not succeed in filling out the forms properly.

Our idea was to take this large grant and come up with a remedy and then share it with other universities in the Alliance. Now you might say, "Why don't you make it available to everyone?" It doesn't work that way. Most universities are inherently self-focused and want to solve all their own problems rather than share others' innovations. But we do have a ready market for sharing in the Alliance. We appointed a liaison at each university, as well as an innovation fellow. These people are part of Bridget Burns's team, working closely with the provosts and presidents of Alliance universities. This resulted in more sharing, such as Georgia State University's program that provides last-minute financial aid to seniors who may have to drop out for some financial reason. It is actually quite common, especially with Pell-eligible students. They almost get to the finish line, and then some emergency happens, or they simply exhaust their resources and can't finish. With this emergency relief the problem is greatly diminished.

The Alliance is still evolving, but we have learned some lessons. Particularly relevant, we have done quite well using the Alliance to get the attention of foundations that want to make awards beyond any single university but have few institutions they can look to for common effort. We have also learned to pick our spots; it is easier to share innovations in some domains than others. But starting with a set of universities that have some affinity, some of the same fundamental goals, it becomes much easier to plan, coordinate, and work toward commonly held public values.

Discussion Question

Crow mentions that it is often remarkably difficult to get universities to work together. Most major universities are either public or private, nonprofit. We expect businesses to compete, but how do you explain the fact that universities, which have no pressure to generate shareholder value or to see their stock prices rise, often compete just as fiercely? How does this sometimes-vigorous competitiveness relate to achieving public values? Is it possible that competition serves to sharpen the vision of public values–focused institutions? Or is competition among public and nonprofit organizations more likely to have bad effects for all involved?

Scheduled Work Break

Yes, we have many public values propositions, but we see no reason to throw them all into one gigantic chapter. A meal, especially a rich one, is best served in multiple courses. So, we will attend to other public values propositions in the next chapter.

Recommendation: During face-to-face classes, we at some point say to our students, "Get up, stretch, then come back. It will help you get your head back in the game." Or, for present purposes, how many public values propositions should one expect to digest in one setting? There is more to come in the next chapter, but take an active break. Then come back. Sitting down is the health curse of the academic writer and many office workers,[6] so don't let it be yours! Walk around the block, feed your cat, or tend the lawn. We will be here when you come back.

4

Public Values
Management Propositions II

Now that we are refreshed and energized to continue with public values management propositions, let's get right to it. We continue with a proposition that presents unique challenges, especially in light of fractured and generally divisive contemporary politics.

Public Values Proposition: Inclusiveness and Accommodation of Minority Interests

Inclusiveness is not about working relations among *organizations*, but rather more focused on individuals and groups, including groups that may not be formally organized. Nor does inclusiveness necessarily involve cooperation, partnership, collaboration, or even working together at all. Rather, it requires, as a minimum, that various stakeholders' views and needs will be taken into account. Naturally, when direct interaction is feasible and practical, it is best.

The fact that inclusiveness enhances long-term prospects of achieving public values does not mean that it is always the most *efficient* approach. In some cases, being inclusive hampers efficiency and can slow down processes for getting things done. Just ask members of the majority party, whether Democratic or Republican, in the US Congress—majority parties routinely run roughshod over minority parties (Disch 2002). Public values–focused programs and projects, by their very nature, must be more than highly specialized activity focused on longer-term interests and cannot represent only the interests of a few; they must also represent more than simple majorities. The notion of public values is that they are in the public or collective interest. Unlike private values that may benefit only individual or group interests, public values benefit society and the public as a whole.

A practical justification for the inclusiveness proposition is that it almost always gives rise to superior decision-making. Considerable research shows the value of multiple perspectives and multiple sources of knowledge in order to improve planning and decision-making (Surowiecki 2005; Golub and Jackson 2010), not least because having more people involved almost always ensures insights gained from differing opinions.

An especially difficult aspect of public values–focused activities is that they generally require engaging with "the enemy." The opposition needs to be accommodated, co-opted, convinced, or in some cases beaten back. But unlike the aforementioned congressional strategy of running roughshod over the opposition, public value pursuit simply cannot work that way. Numerical muscle may work in the short term, but not in the long term. In fact, it would not work in the long term in Congress either, except that with a two-year election cycle in the House of Representatives, "long-term" has a different meaning.

One might surmise that pursuit of public values would require no great effort to build supportive coalitions. After all, if one is focused on a *consensus* public value, does that not imply that all or almost all would cooperate? Such is not the case. In the first place, in almost every case, public values are pitted against private ones and often include private interests that are well entrenched and powerful. Second, even when people agree on public values ends, they may disagree on means to achieve those ends. Third, one public value may conflict with another, and many do.

Let us consider an example. In a recent study, described in part in an earlier chapter, Bozeman (2019) set out to identify truly consensual public values, meaning that more than 90% of a sample of American citizens agree that a value is a consensus *public* value. One of the consensus public values is citizen political participation. More than 93% of respondents agreed that free and open public political participation, which includes electoral participation, is a public value that benefits all of society.

How does this public value consensus square with a US history of denying the vote to women and minorities and, initially, citizens who were not landowners? Well, perhaps values change, but not always in the direction of public values achievement. Today, one of the most contentious partisan issues is "protection against voter fraud"—at least that is the issue's rhetorical labeling. With many states passing or advancing legislation to require more stringent evidence of eligibility in order have the right to vote, the result is a tilt in elections.

To be sure, no one is advocating voter fraud, but just how much of a problem is voter fraud? A study reported in 2014 by the *Washington Post* (Levitt 2014) examined evidence from elections between 2000 and 2014. The study found that out of more than 1 billion ballots cast, there were a total of 31 *possibly* credible instances of voter fraud. Other studies have found similarly low numbers. State legislatures' efforts to save our democracy from the perils of voter fraud—0.0000031% of the total votes cast—have chiefly had the effect intended: tilting election outcomes away from the people deterred by these restrictive laws, typically poor people, naturalized citizens, underrepresented minorities, and those with limited transportation. The chances of being struck by lightning are nearly 35 times higher than the chances of voter fraud—unless one counts as "voter fraud" efforts of incumbents and political parties to cling to power by making changes to electoral requirements that will benefit them.

We are not the first to observe that underrepresented minorities in many districts tend to vote disproportionately for Democratic Party candidates and that Republican lawmakers are disproportionality in favor of voter fraud legislation. Indeed, every recent instance of a stronger voter identification measure passed in the states has been passed in a Republican-majority legislature. We are decidedly *not* suggesting that Democrats serve public values and Republicans do not. Rather, we are suggesting that elected officials and public servants often act in their own self-interest, even in cases where self-interests seem to be counter to public values or public interest. In some cases, such behaviors are simply crass disregard for the public interest. More often, in our view, they are a reflection of the values trade-offs that politicians must make almost constantly, especially ones relevant to this question: "How will I be able to pass policies I strongly believe are in the public interest if I am turned out of office?" This is the moral crucible of electoral politics, one that has always been present in our democracy, the point at which one trades a policy issue for an electoral issue. It is not a straightforward choice for any elected official. Moreover, the example shows the powerful forces that can work to undermine any public values issue.

So, let us assume for the moment that (1) the vast majority of studies of voting fraud are correct and there is remarkably little voter fraud; (2) many US states have avidly pursued legislation that requires greater documentation and, arguably, diminishes voter convenience; (3) the result of increased anti-fraud measures is in most instances reduced turnout; and, finally; (4) the reduced turnout is greater among minorities and the poor of all ethnicities.[1] If, when all is said and done, the major outcome of measures to decrease voter fraud is actually reducing voter participation among those legally entitled to vote, then why would anyone be enthusiastic about such measures? Since political participation is a consensus public value, and since those who are passing voter fraud legislation are elected officials supposedly charged with representing the public interest, what is going on here?

The support for voter fraud legislation, at least if one believes most of the evidence on the topic, cannot be easily explained only by a fervent desire to prevent the 31 instances of fraud per 1 billion votes. The case illustrates, perfectly and sadly, just why consensus on public values does not equate to a generalized commitment to pursuing public values. Public values compete with private values and perceived self-interest, and in this contest they often lose.

In many cases the opposition aligned against public values efforts has nothing to do with moral reasoning. In some instances, people oppose public values not for the "greater long-run good," but simply because they have personal stakes that are important to them and that are at odds with public values activities. In such cases, the inclusiveness injunction provides a special challenge. In such cases, evidence is beside the point, and convincing is not an option.

We have focused on the food safety and security issue in the previous chapter, and we return to it here. Yes, we like food safety and security because it is so fundamental and, of course, tied directly to sustaining human life, a public value about which there is considerable consensus. Thus, let's consider an illustration relevant to food safety and then return to the question of what steps to take when powerful private interests are steadfastly in opposition to steps taken to serve public values.

Back to Food Safety Policy: The Challenges to Inclusiveness

Food safety policy has not been a paragon of inclusiveness, despite the fact that it affects literally everyone. While there are a few activist citizens' groups focusing on such topics as regulating and promoting organic farming or parental groups focused on nutrition labeling issues, the more common role of the public has been to lie dormant until a major adverse event happens and then become activated for a short period of time.

There are a number of reasons why it is not easy to activate the general public or even to grow and sustain public interest lobbies for food policy. In the first place, many of the issues are complex and require a level of scientific understanding that not many people are prepared to deal with. It is not easy to put a spotlight on some issues because they are "system issues," related to an intricate set of growers, manufacturers, suppliers, and retailers that are increasingly internationalized. This can lead to a sense of citizen inefficacy and frustration. If there are problems with Japan overfishing for tuna or with misleading labels and food products coming from Indonesian fish farms, one might well begin to feel that the likelihood of effective action is minimal.

One recent instance of the limited ability to catalyze the public in food safety is the 2017 US federal government budget proposal, on the heels of the bipartisan passage of the Food Safety Modernization Act in 2011, to reduce the Food and Drug Administration's food safety program budget by $83 million—more than double the increase in funding provided with FSMA implementation in 2012 (Coukell 2017). The public outcry was modest, certainly not in proportion to the level of continued threat with foodborne illnesses.

Perhaps one problem with galvanizing the public on food safety issues is ubiquity. There is a saying in intellectual property studies that "if it belongs to everyone, it belongs to no one"—meaning that companies have little interest in public domain issues that cannot easily and directly provide exclusive benefit to them. Relatedly, policies that focus on *not* having something happen, prevention rather than accomplishment of new results, seem to draw attention only in the direst circumstances, such as civil disasters. The best parallel in food safety is genetic engineering of food. When people imagine food sources forever being destroyed or radically altered by "Frankenfoods" or crop contamination, the perceived stakes are sufficient to motivate action. But for topics such as preserving seed variety, an important issue as crops become increasingly homogenous and more vulnerable to specific parasites or to regional climate disasters, the vision is less apocalyptic.

Another reason why inclusiveness of large swaths of the public has not been as common in the quest for food safety relates to the litigious nature of public policy. Modern food safety policy has, time and again, been characterized by fights between regulators and industry, often giving rise to courtroom battles. This has not been a battle between evil industry and good government. In some cases, history is on the side of industry. Thus, for example, much of food safety champion Harvey Wiley's activity in ardent defense of "purity" had little or nothing to do with the harm entailed in products. In large enough doses, purity can kill you. For example, while pure, USDA-labeled "Choice" beef is marbled with fat and laden with cholesterol, and the old soda pop with six tablespoons of pure, unadulterated cane sugar was not exactly healthy. Thus, Wiley's legal skirmishes on adulteration and purity often came to nothing from the standpoint of improved public health (Coppin and High 1999). The basic point is not that industry challenges to regulation are bad or misguided. Likewise, despite occasional missteps, we certainly should not conclude that government regulation of food is undesirable. Quite the contrary. But when much of public values–related policy is a struggle between institutional titans and expert witnesses, the room in the public sphere may seem crowded out, and ordinary citizens may have a difficult time sorting out differences in evidence and opinion provided by various authoritative parties. Difficulties are exacerbated when citizens are only casually interested in the dispute. Thus, below we consider strategies for energizing the inattentive or even disaffected.

Inclusiveness Strategies for Public Values Leaders

From the history of food safety, we see that inclusiveness is not always as easy as it might seem. Sometimes people do not want to be included, and sometimes they do not have any idea about how to be included. So, what can the public values leader do to increase inclusiveness and to have someone other than the arrayed set of well-resourced institutional actors have a stake in policy formulation and choice? One strategy is to "pick your victories" (not "pick your battles"). The battles will go on, and they should. The dialectic about food regulation involves a great many issues, changing rapidly, with new information sometimes accompanying the changes. Food safety is likely to remain a dynamic public values domain, and the battles will and should continue well into the future. What we mean by "pick your victories" is to emphasize issue types that give rise to citizen concerns and activation and stand ready to take advantage of and even nourish activation, even if it is short-lived or sporadic.

A second strategy that could be useful in being inclusive with a reluctant, or simply inattentive, public is what we refer to as "inclusion marketing." Many of the same strategies used in business to develop consumer interest in a new product that most people know little or nothing about can succeed in drawing citizens' interest in public values–focused initiatives. Companies spend a good deal of time on market research and understanding market segments before launching a product. When Amazon launched its Echo series of smart speakers, they well understood that certain potential customers would find appealing the ability to use a device to regulate home appliances and utilities. But they also understood that others would find home regulation boring or useless (especially those living in a dorm) but would be attracted to Amazon's music services, or the ability to place instant Amazon orders on their Echo, or the ability to use the device as a ready information resource or perhaps as good company (e.g., "Alexa, tell me a joke"). They knew both their markets and their market segments.

Much the same is true about broad, multifaceted "public values products." Going back to food safety, we might expect very different elements to energize the public according to, among other factors, their political views on corporate food suppliers, their status as vegetarians, whether they are city dwellers or farm dwellers, whether they have allergies or celiac disease, or whether they eat out regularly. This type of marketing / market segment strategy is often used by charities. For example, organizations such as Catholic Charities and the Salvation Army understand that some of their donors are motivated by religious faith, but many others are not faithful at all, or perhaps are from a different faith tradition, but are interested in supporting the charities' social outreach mission.

A third strategy, again one used regularly in business, is "media tailoring." The old-school idea of encouraging inclusiveness by holding a public meeting continues to work well for some citizens. But for others, a Facebook or Twitter or Instagram campaign might be much more effective, or a worksite or school-site presentation, or both. In short, inclusiveness is not as easy as it seems, and it is the public values designer's responsibility to design inclusiveness rather than engage in head-scratching over the question "Why don't people act in their own interest?"

Inclusiveness and the Big Tent

One can think of many examples where disparate individuals and groups have pursued the same outcomes but for very different values. Having a "big tent," welcoming people who may not be entirely like-minded, may be extremely important to addressing public values. In many cases, people might agree on end values but maybe disagree on the means to obtain the end values, or sometimes disagree on the instrumental values leading to the final desired outcomes. It is even possible for people to value the same outcome but for very different reasons.

Let's consider an example of a public values–focused big-tent strategy, one that brought together a set of people who were not always ideologically or personally aligned but who nonetheless came together, albeit for different reasons. In late 2003, the state of Utah set for itself an extremely ambitious goal: ending chronic homelessness in Utah (McCoy 2015). While this is a formidable goal, it is not an insane or impossible one. In the first place, there were only an estimated 14,000 homeless people in Utah, a small number by national per capita standards. For example, the city of New York had an estimated 60,000 or so homeless people in October 2015. In *relative* terms, the Utah homelessness issue seemed tractable. Still, as one of the more conservative states in America, Utah does not seem to be the most likely jurisdiction to take on the eradication of homelessness as a core policy goal. However, according to one analyst, the project was not about ideology, nor was it "stripped from the bleeding-heart manual" (McCoy 2015).

In 2005, Utah had nearly 2,000 chronically homeless. The number dropped to 539 in 2014, a 72% decline. How did this happen? Not by any conventional approach. In the first place, most policies for homelessness do not focus on the chronic homeless—the traumatized war veterans, drug addicts, or the severely mentally ill. The majority of homeless individuals and families are transitory homeless, typically experiencing a relatively small number of days or weeks on the street, and often searching regularly and ardently for housing or jobs. It is easier to help them. Why would you waste time trying to find houses for people who have been on the streets for years? But that is what Utah did.

Well, not exactly. Actually, they gave them houses, *new houses*. As Gordon Walker, then director of the state Housing and Community Development Division, explained, "If you want to end homelessness, you put people in housing. This is relatively simple." Rather than starting with the "low hanging fruit," Utah officials began by identifying the chronic homeless, the ones who had been on the street for more than a year, the ones who, when they are not outside, are likely to be found in jails and hospitals. They are also the ones who regularly frequent homeless shelters, sometimes relying on shelters more often than not.

One of the motivating factors in the Utah homelessness program was much the same as could be found in any city or state program—help people who badly need help (the "bleeding heart manual," chapter one). People who volunteer to help the homeless, people who contribute money to helping the homeless, and people who work for nonprofits helping the homeless almost always report that they simply want to do the right thing and help people who seem to be greatly in need of help. But it is also notable that Utah is, indeed, a very conservative state. When studying the problem of homelessness, researchers found that Utah was spending, on average, $20,000 per year on each chronically homeless person, with a large proportion coming from government funds supported by taxes.

The attentive reader already sees the "big-tent" strategy in Utah, the bringing together of the typical homeless advocacy coalitions with those who wanted chiefly to save money and solve a problem that is in part economic. In that spirit, the state made the difficult, but economically rational, choice to set up nearly all homeless people, including the chronically homeless, in their own house. They also provided extensive contact with counselors who would help them become accustomed to the modern aspects of life and the day-to-day requirements involved in living in a home. The pilot program was in 2004. The state housed 17 people in metropolitan Salt Lake City, and after one year 14 were still in their homes and seemed to be functioning well. The success rate of more than 80% is rare for any social program. The program was expanded and has, according to Director Walker, "saved millions."

Our point does not relate to the ease or effectiveness of ending homelessness. Circumstances and need are quite different from one city to the next. Rather, the lesson is that a big tent can sometimes solve problems, certainly more often than acrimonious charges and countercharges between social activists and fiscal conservatives. The big tent does, of course, require at least a modicum of trust, as we discuss in the next section.

Comment: Steve Zabilski on Maintaining the Big Tent

Steve Zabilski, executive director of St. Vincent de Paul, had this to say:

> For an organization like St. Vincent de Paul, the big-tent question often relates to balancing the secular and the religious. For example, if we send out an Easter card, 100 people will say, "Are you crazy, an Easter card with a bunny on it? But if we send out a religious card, this will offend 100 people who volunteer to help but are not Catholics or even religious. We can't please everybody all the time, but we can listen all the time. When I am dealing with people, I never want to come across as being arrogant or having all the answers. It's the society of St. Vincent de Paul, not the society of Steve Zabilski.

Steve Zabilski's bio can be found at https://www.catholicsun.org /2017/01/22/steve-zabilski-20-years-of-serving-the-common-man -at-st-vincent-de-paul/.

Public Values Proposition: Engendering Trust

Many of the public values propositions we present relate closely to one another, especially our proposition about engendering trust. Thus, achieving effective multilateral institutional interaction requires some minimal trust, being inclusive and working with minority interests assumes some modest level of trust to promote relationships, and promoting a vision and having people actually take it seriously and "sign on" to the vision usually requires a deep level of trust. Engendering trust is a precondition of many public values management and leadership strategies.

While it is nearly impossible to overestimate the importance of trust for those seeking to have their institutions work with others to achieve public value objectives, it is possible to have too high a bar for trust, to wrap requirements into trust that need not be integral to a trust relationship. For example, in some cases scholars imply that having a personal affinity or liking for someone is important in a trust relationship. It certainly does not hurt. However, there are many instances, throughout history, of people working together closely and to great positive effect, despite not much liking one another. One conspicuous example is the alliance forged between Martin Luther King Jr., as well as the Southern Christian Leadership Conference, and President Lyndon Johnson. Each trusted the other to act in a predictable and ultimately mutually beneficial manner, in large measure owing to a perceived mutuality of goals. There was never much evidence of personal affinity or friendship between King and Johnson, but there is reason to believe they trusted one another to achieve an outcome that would advance the nation.

As King wrote in "Why We Can't Wait," an article published in 1964 in *Life* magazine, "His [Johnson's] approach to the problem of civil rights was not identical with mine—nor had I expected it to be. Yet his careful practicality was, nonetheless, clearly no mask to conceal indifference. His emotional and intellectual involvement was genuine and devoid of adornment. It was conspicuous that he was searching for a solution to a problem he knew to be a major shortcoming in American life" (King 1964, 98).

One often finds strange bedfellows in common causes, but not always public values causes. Indeed, trust relationships can be forged that undermine public values. For example, one public values–thwarting effort was based on a long-standing, trust-based partnership between the US tobacco industry and the Massachusetts Restaurant Association (MRA). Today, the MRA includes programs to ensure that restaurant employees do not work excessive hours, have adequate pay, and have health care benefits. The MRA has programs focusing on preventing the spread of disease to restaurant customers because of either sick restaurant employees or contaminated food. They have allergy awareness programs. They deliver consumer advocacy, such as promoting menu warnings about the risks of raw shellfish or undercooked meats. What could this organization have in common with the tobacco industry? One study (Ritch and Begay 2001) shows that the MRA worked for more than 20 years with the tobacco industry to defeat state and local laws that would restrict smoking in public places, but especially in restaurants and bars. The tobacco industry, not often a friend of the restaurant associations, was able to easily set aside any antagonism and work closely with the MRA in opposition to state and local smoke-free restaurant, bar, and workplace laws in Massachusetts, according to the records and documents Ritch and Begay (2001) analyzed.

While most people understand the importance of trust for joint work, whether public values–focused or public values–thwarting, it is less easy to know how to go about engendering trust, especially when one is dealing with diverse people and institutions with little or no common history. We have already seen that trust does not depend on personal affinity. What does it depend on?

Trust and Temporality

Often, those seeking to engender trust spend a good deal of time and effort trying to convince those with whom they have common cause that their motivations are the "right" ones and that their respective objectives are in alignment. In many cases this is time poorly spent. Who has not had some dishonest person try to sway one based on a profession of purity of motives? Most people learn quickly to be skeptical, sometimes even extending skepticism too far. What does impress people, even extreme skeptics, is accomplishment. Thus, if one can approach a desired public values partner or collaborator and say, essentially, "I understand that having cleaner water [or reducing discrimination, or expanding economic opportunity, and such] is important to you. Please consider my organization's [specific] accomplishments thus far." An implication is that trust, much like any other resource, operates on a timeline. In particular, it is a good idea to try to engender trust immediately after accomplishing a major public value objective, preferably after not only accomplishing it but also being able to demonstrate or measure it. Only profit-making new start-ups get to say, with any hope of success, trust me now, trust my concept, even though we have accomplished nothing and are losing money hand over fist. The investor in a new market-based start-up realizes the risk, even enormous risk, but seeks outsized personal reward and thus, sometimes, takes the risk. When the appeal is for common, nonfinancial objectives, taking more to the table is usually required.

Trust and Rational Calculation

Trust is also related to people's calculation ability. In many cases the fact that people are not so good at rational thinking, especially with respect to probabilities, affects their trust. In particular, they sometimes trust high risk and do not trust lower risk. Thus, many of the same people who fear taking a trip in a commercial airline (odds of death: 1 in 3.5 million) think nothing of driving their car to work (odds of death: 1 in 36,000; lifetime odds of 1 in 80) (*Economist* 2015). Of course, this is not a straightforward comparison, and, indeed, it illustrates a few points about trust. First, we are more likely to be less trusting of air travel than automobiles if we have experience with one and not the other. Much the same is true with people and organizations. Second, we are less likely to trust people, organizations, and technology when they are highly publicized and have big impact, no matter how infrequent. The "lesson" is that if you screw up, do so quietly and incrementally, not all at once (something successful embezzlers have known for a long time). Relatedly, social psychology research has long confirmed that almost everyone is more affected by their knowledge of negative outcomes and adverse events. This implies that a great deal of good is required to even begin to offset organizational or personal negative outcomes, suggesting that trust is hard to win and easy to lose.

Trust and Constancy

Individuals who are designing public values institutions are more likely to engender more trust if they have a consistent message. Two types of consistency are important. In the first place, it is important to have a trusted brand. If your organization is to be the "go-to" place for environmental action, then it may not help the cause, or the trust, to develop a set of activities focused on, say, health care for the elderly at the same time. This is not to say that organizations, public, nonprofit, or private, are destined to be a "one-note" organization forever, only that they usually do well to master that one note before moving to the next. It is not simply about being careful with financial resources. Trust is also a resource, and moving too quickly in too many directions can undercut trust in core values and previous accomplishments.

Consistency is also important in dealing with diverse stakeholders and partners. It is often the case, quite understandably, that organizations tailor the message to the audience. While that can make sense—no need talking to people at great length about topics they care little about—it can greatly undermine trust if there is a perception (much less a reality) that the organization's representatives are "talking out of both sides of their mouth." If the messages are consistent, there is less danger of tailored messaging undermining trust. However, if there is a perception of inconsistency or, especially, contradiction, then hard-won trust can be quickly lost.

Trust and Third-Party Validation

In a great many cases, trust, that most virtuous of organizational characteristics, is not likely to be within the power of the public values–based organization. There are a variety of reasons why this might be the case, including both simple ones, such as the organization being new or a new actor in the public values domain of interest, and complex ones, such as those having to do with other organizations' calculation about the possible crowding out of even nonprofit actors working in the same public values domain.

In some cases, trust is simply too important to leave hostage to competition. One resolution that has worked well in a great many sectors is third-party validation. This can take many forms. One of the most important aspects of third-party validation in the private sector is the setting of technical standards for new technologies. In the United States, the primary actor on technical standards is the US National Institute of Standards and Technology. One might well ask, "Why would any private firm with a superior product wish to support outside parties' imposition of standards?" The best answer to that question is "Have you heard of the Sony Betamax?" or "What ever happened to the Apple Lisa computer?" These questions are another way of saying that the superior technology does not always carry the day. The success of a new technology depends on not only functionality, price, and marketing but also, at least in many cases, interoperability. For complex technologies, such as computers or automobiles, suppliers must not only consider their own technological attributes but also ensure that those attributes work with technologies others supply. Thus, if you invent a computer using compact disc, but no one supplies compact discs, it is not likely to succeed. Or, if your computer requires a really high compression disc that, unfortunately, has not been invented, the same problem arises. Relatedly, the earlier barrier to electrical cars was less technological than the absence of "fueling stations."

Third-party verifying organizations may be from any sector. Thus, the "verifying organization" familiar to most academic researchers is the Institutional Review Board (IRB), which has a set of standards, at least some of which are accepted throughout the active research world, about required ethical behavior when dealing with human subjects. If a researcher submits a study and the IRB approves it, then the research can proceed, government agencies can fund it, and the researchers can publish it. Thus, even though universities compete for research funds, having a third-party verification system is generally viewed as in their joint interest and, with some conspicuous exceptions, designed to engender trust not only in researchers but also in the research enterprise.

Since we noted a not-so-savory activity above involving restaurant associations, let us be evenhanded and note that restaurants and restaurant associations have often promoted third-party verification and most know well that they share the value of avoiding the fallout from customers sickened by foodborne illnesses. One study (Golan et al. 2004) has shown that many of the innovations in safety in the meat industry are related to the restaurant industry and associations' strong support of third-party verification of the health and safety of meat products they serve.

Another public value domain where universities are, in general, very much engaged with third-party validation is in accreditation. Universities seek to meet accreditation standards in a wide variety of educational areas (e.g., master of business administration degrees, medical schools, public affairs programs), as well as for the entire university. While accreditation is not a guarantee of quality education, it does at least say to the consumer that this program (or college or university) has been evaluated, usually by peers, and found to meet minimum standards.

Three Mini-cases. Perspectives on Trust and Leadership

Trust is essentially a precondition for many public values leadership management strategies. The mini-cases provide three public values leaders' perspectives on engendering trust. Since each of these perspectives was provided during interviews with the authors, in some cases below we retain, for the sake of clarification, the questions posed by Bozeman and Crow (B&C).

Jeb Bush, Former Florida Governor and Presidential Candidate

Governor Bush shows how personalization and displaying "your heart" can help engender trust. Here he talks about the importance of showing one's humanity and genuineness.

B&C: Some people think it's getting more and more difficult these days for leaders to engender trust. Do you agree?

Bush: Yes, I definitely think it's harder today [to develop trust]. We're living in this time where there's so much "fake news" and so much misinformation out there. Compared to when I was governor of Florida [1999–2007], it is harder today to get anyone to trust you. But there is a way to do it, you have to show your heart. You have to humanize. I wasn't great at this, but you have to put everything that you do in a human perspective, whether it's a school choice program or first-generation scholarships for higher education. You just have to be all in to convince people of your sincere interest in whatever the subject is. I was never that popular because I was doing a lot of stuff and angering people along the way. I was pretty controversial. I think at the end of eight years they were probably exhausted and happy I left. But I showed my heart and people knew what I believed in. [After I served as governor], the most rewarding compliment was, "I didn't like much of what you did, but I knew where you stood," or "Your heart was in the right place." That connection is what is so essential in a public leadership position, particularly where you have all these constituents and you have all the cynicism. They are less interested in your ideology or your five-point plan. They want to know that you care first, and that you listen to them a little bit. I did that in a bunch of ways that now might be harder. For example, I answered all my emails personally. I got into arguments on the internet with people. They would say, "Damn, that really is you. I thought it was some FSU intern that was using your name." But once I proved that it was me, they'd say, "Well, dang, you're taking the time to deal with my issue?" And I did. It made me real in the eyes of a lot of people that otherwise wouldn't have had that chance.

Brian and Kelly Swette, Founders of Sweet Earth Inc.

Brian and Kelly Swette have succeeded in developing a thriving company that is self-consciously public values centered in the highly competitive food industry, an industry not always known for having the consumers' interests at the top of its list of priorities but that suffers anytime consumer trust vanishes. If consumers believe that the food they are eating is unhealthy or that the purveyors of the food are not trustworthy, any food business is in trouble. While the food industry in general depends to some extent on trust, in the vegetarian food industry, the segment that Sweet Earth is in, trust is even more crucial. People buy vegetarian foods for a number of reasons, but two of the most important are a commitment to not harming animals and a commitment to the presumed health benefits of vegetarian food. If they believe that either of those values is compromised, then the business may not survive.

B&C: I would think that with all the dubious advertising and labeling going on in the food business, with terms like "natural" being used with ambiguous meanings, consumers must be confused and mistrustful. How have you dealt with this?

Brian Swette: We had a lot of inquiries early on [when people were tasting our vegetarian food], with some saying, "Well this can't be just vegetarian, not with this taste, it has to be egg, or it has to be meat." So, we did have a lot of inquiries, and we still do even today, mainly from people who aren't familiar with what seitan is, or what you could do with tofu, and how turmeric and natural spices and ingredients can enhance colors and flavors. In general, though, I think that they—whether they're looking at our website or looking at the way we talk about our products—I think they find a consistent thread. And once we explain things like seitan is made from wheat, I think we're able to overcome those doubts. These are positive conversations because we love to engage with people on those questions.

Kelly Swette: Our business has always been about authenticity, and so we kind of intentionally avoided the flavor of the moment in terms of what was "selling." We were always about what we put in versus what we took out. You never saw "low this," "free of that." We never put a low-sodium claim or a low-fat claim or a "free of this" claim. No claims. We would just put the numbers, let them read the ingredients, and let the nutritional numbers and the ingredients speak for themselves.

Deborah Wince-Smith, President and CEO of the Competitiveness Council
Deborah Wince-Smith faces trust issues that are quite a bit different from those Jeb Bush and Brian and Kelly Swette describe above. She strives to promote trust among persons who are trying to cooperate in a public values mission but, at the same time, may be long-time competitors or even antagonists. We asked her about how she approaches creating trust among members of the Council, especially those who are competitors.

Wince-Smith: With competitors, the most important thing is creating the right environment for the free flow of ideas and discussion. We try to make sure that the Council is a safe place that exudes respect and careful listening. It has to be a place where people can present thoughts and openly expose ideas without expecting they will be rejected or dismissed by other participants. I think participants understand the need for this environment and try to help create it.

B&C: Can you think of particular programs or projects that you have been involved with that provide good examples of the ways the Council works to develop trust while accomplishing its public values missions?

Wince-Smith: I can tell you about one project that really strained trust but worked out well in the end and achieved common values. We were working on an energy and sustainability project that many viewed as a major competitiveness driver. However, one of the labor leaders from the United Brotherhood of Carpenters and Joiners, the major union in the US for carpenters, was in the middle of a huge battle with Walmart when the vice chair of Walmart was just joining the Council. An uproar ensued. I had already received a call from the head of the carpenters' union, and she told me that if any Walmart executives were brought into our meetings that she would not only resign, but that she would work with all the major labor unions in the US to make sure they would have nothing to do with the Council. I worked with her to build a case focused on the issues, chiefly sustainability, and ultimately convinced her to just come to the meeting and give it a chance. She could keep her options open but come to the meeting before doing anything else. She did come, and I intentionally sat her next to the Walmart executive. As usual, the meeting forum brought people into a safe place where mutual respect was expected. Joining the meeting allowed us the ability to work out an approach that involved focusing on shared interests and a shared path and business, labor, and environmental case for sustainability, a case that could appeal to all parties. The key is just getting people to the table and ensuring that they have a view and that it will be listened to with respect.

Discussion Question

In our interviews with public values leaders, no issue came up more often than trust, and this was not due to any particular prodding or questioning on our part. Nearly all our interviewees spoke to trust issues without us needing to ask. So here are some questions our readers might wish to reflect on. It is probably not that difficult for you to consider a number of people you interact with closely in personal or business life and to give a broad assessment of whom you trust most and least and why. But let's turn things around. Focusing on business associates or clients or customers who are major actors in your life, who trusts you? Why do they trust you? Most importantly, if there are people who do not trust you, why don't they trust you? Is there anything that you can do, that you would wish to do, to cultivate the trust of those people who either do not trust you or perhaps are "on the fence" about whether you are trustworthy? Finally, which of the points made by the public values leaders' observations above are ones you might wish to act on?

Sometimes we simply forget to think self-consciously about such basic issues, and often just reflecting on them gives us new insights. The person who centuries ago inscribed "Know Thyself" on the ancient Greek temple at Delphi perhaps was onto something. Or perhaps you prefer more recent wisdom or gravitate, as we do, to shopworn clichés? We have always liked this one: "Denial ain't just a river in Egypt." And especially this one: "It is hard to lead others unless one can lead oneself."[2] These reflections provide a nice segue into the following chapter, "Mutable Leadership," which includes a kernel of wisdom that has been embedded in a great many leadership studies—that when it comes to leadership it is a good idea to reflect on context because there is never "one best way."

5

Mutable Leadership

Public values leadership differs from other types of leadership and, for that reason, requires a different approach. How does it differ? Typically, the public values goals are more complex and multifaceted than goals faced by typical organizations, and relatedly, most public values goals are not achievable by a single organization working by itself, not even a very large organization with many resources. Another difference is that public values leadership cannot depend entirely on others' perceived rational self-interest as a motivator. In most organizations, workers have motives other than self-interest goals such as making money or personal career advancement, but in public values–focused organizations these "other" motives, such as public service and hoping to change the world for the better, are at the forefront for most people truly invested in the organization's mission. Public values leadership cannot be command-and-control leadership. Since public values–focused organizations actually rely on employees' and other stakeholders' trust and goodwill, they require leaders who can inspire and motivate through the mission more than with the allure of power, money, or status. Public values leadership is not unique, as it shares many elements with leadership in other realms, but it has a distinctive combination of elements. We contend that the leadership approach that best fits the needs of most public values–focused organizations is the approach we refer to as mutable leadership.

What Is Mutable Leadership?

The core idea of mutable leadership is that different circumstances and different times require different talents and, thus, either changes in leadership or changes in the leader's emphasis and needed skills. Mutable leadership is antithetical to much of the literature on leadership, especially the popular literature, with its emphasis on the heroic, all-occasions leader. The mythological leader, the leader-as-hero, wrestles problems into submission by dint of great personal skills and unmatched talent. A great many books have been written on the subject, usually providing guidelines to mere mortals about how to transmogrify into a charismatic, heroic leader. In some cases these books have been written as self-myths, the heroic leader as autobiographer. More often, leadership books lionize historical figures, ones we all know about and who have, indeed, managed great feats, people on the order of George Washington, Martin Luther King Jr., or Winston Churchill. We are skeptical of the heroic autobiographer, but we are also a little skeptical of the great leaders of history, because leadership is mutable, and those who cannot change often are cast aside or, worse, sometimes undo the good they have accomplished. Today's superstar is tomorrow's bench sitter, and often for good reason. Case in point: Winston Churchill, undeniably one of the most important figures of the twentieth century, was a heroic leader but decidedly not a mutable leader.

Winston Churchill as Heroic Leader (But Not a Mutable Leader)

Winston Churchill may be the perfect exemplar of a truly heroic leader, but he was not a mutable leader, and not one who was consistently a great leader, one who could adapt to changed circumstances. His career illustrates why even heroic leaders are so rarely men or women for all seasons. Who could deny that Churchill, the great British wartime prime minister, was an inspiring, courageous, and effective bulwark against Nazi aggression in World War II? Nevertheless, he knew the value of change and its inevitability, even if he did not accede to it. One of his best-known quotations is this: "To improve is to change; to be perfect is to change often." Indeed, there is ample evidence that he took his own advice and that his leadership style evolved over the decades. Yet there is another important lesson from a very different Churchill bon mot: "There is nothing wrong with change, if it is in the right direction." That seems to have been his guiding dictum, and, of course, directions often fail to go where we wish.

The day Great Britain entered World War II by declaring war on Germany, September 3, 1939, Churchill was appointed First Lord of the Admiralty, notably the same position he held during much of World War I. During the Great War, he was a major force for innovation, including, among other farsighted notions, being an advocate for an air force and moving navy fuel from coal, an abundant British resource but not a particularly robust one, to oil, a much better fuel and one, due to Churchill's own prewar maneuvering, of which Britain now had an ample international supply. He was also instrumental in advocating the development of the tank and helping finance it with navy funds. However, despite these many innovations, Churchill's first stint as Lord Admiral did not have the glorious ending he would have preferred. Those familiar with military history will perhaps know something of the Dardanelles campaign and, particularly, the infamous Battle of Gallipoli (a peninsula in Turkey). Gallipoli was the only major victory of the Ottoman Turks during World War I, and for the Allies it was a deadly strategic miscalculation. The Allies expected Gallipoli to yield a relatively easy and final victory over of the Turks. When the smoke had cleared, more than 115,000 British and dominion troops, as well as 25,000 French soldiers, had been killed or wounded. The New Zealand army was literally decimated, having a casualty rate of 87%. While it is estimated that Turkish and Ottoman Empire troops had more than twice as many causalities, they were defending their homeland and ultimately caused sufficient Allied casualties to force the Allied troops to withdraw.

Very soon after the Gallipoli smoke cleared, the blame game began. Even today, it is not easy to sort out culpability given widespread incompetence on the part of a number of Allied military leaders executing strategies that in hindsight were high risk or even delusional (see Haythornthwaite 1991), but Churchill definitely was the "fall guy." It is clearly the case that Churchill was one of the major advocates and designers of the campaign, though not one of the implementers. The combination of Churchill's Gallipoli advocacy and the election of a new Conservative government was sufficient to warrant his dismissal, despite Churchill's many previous accomplishments with the Admiralty. In the face of what could only be viewed as professional disgrace, Churchill enlisted in the army, first at the rank of major, and went on to have a credible military service, serving several months on the western front (but retaining his seat in Parliament). The military service served as a sort of professional rehabilitation. Coming home and serving in Parliament, he was in 1917 appointed secretary for munitions and later secretary for war. The fog of war clouds memories of deeds good and foul.

By the time World War II came along, Churchill had rebuilt his reputation to such an extent that he was again chosen as Lord Admiral. After Prime Minister Neville Chamberlain's pact with Hitler and his now-infamous "Peace in Our Time" speech, the British Parliament was desperately interested in a prime minister who would prove a good war minister rather than the historical apotheosis of appeasement. We need say nothing of Churchill's inspirational leadership during the war or of the esteem, even love, that he enjoyed not only among many British citizens but among other Allied nations' citizens as well. There is some considerable consensus among historians about his role in literally saving his country during World War II (e.g., Weinberg 1995; Kimball 1997; Reynolds 2007).

Now the punchline (though a surprise to almost no history buff): in 1945, the British electorate had no difficulty whatsoever turning out Churchill's Conservative Party and their beloved, heroic leader along with it. True, he later had another term as prime minister (1951–55), but the verdict of history is clear—this great wartime leader has not been viewed, either by the British people or by historians, as a great peacetime leader. The same boldness, rhetorical rallying cries, and uncompromising steadfastness that served so well during world war often proved a liability in times of peace, with their very different postwar needs and priorities. As Ralph Ingersoll reported in 1940, a notable wartime visitor to England remarked, "Everywhere I went in London people admired [Churchill's] energy, his courage, his singleness of purpose. People said they didn't know what Britain would do without him. He was obviously respected. But no one felt he would be Prime Minister after the war. He was simply the right man in the right job at the right time. That time being the time of a desperate war with Britain's enemies" (Ingersoll 1940, 127).

If such a genius as Churchill is something less than an all-purpose leader, why should we expect leaders of public value–based institutions to be suited for all challenges and changes? Well, in part because we are concerned less with leaders tasked with keeping the free world free than with leaders who have a long and stable career contributing to a wide range of public values. The lions of history are often admirable, almost always astonishing, but not often the best exemplars for one trying to lead an organization or a social movement.

In this chapter we elaborate on our mutable leadership concept, explaining why we feel that it represents an improvement over conventional heroic concepts of leadership and providing more details about the concept and what it entails. We also provide a typology of mutable leadership, based on organizational or issue agenda stages and attendant leadership needs. In reflecting on the nature of mutable leadership, we draw from the comments of our public values leaders.

Comment: Deborah Wince-Smith on "Born Leaders"

Deborah Wince-Smith, president and CEO of the Council on Competitiveness, had this to say:

> No one is a "born leader." People have to be nurtured and groomed to be leaders. We don't hear enough about "ethical leadership." Sometimes people even ridicule the idea, suggesting maybe the idea of ethical

leadership is naive. But decisions must be driven by ethics. Our service academies have a great mission to build strong ethical leaders [note: Wince-Smith is on the Advisory Board of the US Naval Academy]. To become a leader, you must first be a follower because leadership can't be developed overnight. You have to watch others lead and then learn from them. Once you are a leader, you still have to be a follower, you have to learn from others even as you lead.

Deborah Wince-Smith's bio can be found at https://www.com pete.org/about/senior-staff/3182.

A Problem of Leadership Studies: Presumptions of Simplicity

In some respects, our idea of mutable leadership is a clear reaction against what we see in many popular, and all-too-influential, treatments of leadership, those books on sale at airport bookstalls (okay, we confess that is one of our aims as well, but still . . .). Of the many objections we have to the "five keys to being a great leader" style of the popular leadership book, our most heartfelt objection is banality. Diet books, cookbooks, and leadership books have much in common. First, they are abundant; rarely does one see a top 100 book sales list that does not include them. Second, they vary tremendously in the quality and utility of their advice. Third, typically they do not provide the result the buyer seeks: the diet is short-lived, or the cookbook is consulted for only one or two meals. The leadership book has an especial disadvantage. With the exception of "one-minute leader" sort of books, the leadership book often requires a full reading rather than a quick perusal for a snippet here and there. This does not always fit the reader's inclination, and thus the leadership book is scanned for the big points and is soon to be displaced by a trendy leadership book of more recent vintage.

We leave it to others to explain the brief half-lives of diet books and cookbooks, but we have some ideas about why so many leadership books record great sales and less-than-great change or even use. To be sure, this is not a one-explanation-fits-all question, but this is part of the problem: everyone wants the leadership messiah, but one's better judgment sits at the back of one's mind. Most people, when thinking about major accomplishments in their organizations, or even for that matter major disasters, find that their own narrative has little to do with the heroic leader. The most basic concept of leadership that one finds in popular press and practitioner-focused leadership books does not coincide with our working life experiences.[1] The heroic leader, the star of many books and articles on leadership, darling of the popular press, often found holding forth during political campaigns, is for the most part a figment of our collective imaginations, a caricature we have built from our desires rather than our experiences.

Designing institutions and realizing the objectives of design are never solitary processes. No matter how skilled, determined, or heroic they may be, *leaders must ultimately rely on and work with others.* Necessarily, institutional design is a social enterprise requiring participation of leaders but also groups, organizations, networks, and followers, especially follower-leaders (those who follow on some issues and lead on others).

Without agreeing with all his points of view and criticisms, we nonetheless find inspiration in Jeffrey Pfeffer's (2015) provocatively titled book *Leadership BS.* Pfeffer, an organizational sociologist of some renown, contends that leadership is overrated and, worse, that people tend to select narcissistic, self-serving persons as leaders instead of individuals who are highly competent but not as focused on self-promotion and hogging credit. More effective leaders, when they get a chance to lead, are those who work through persuasion, consultation, and steady determination. *In short, they are not vastly different from good followers.*

While we do not go quite so far as to subscribe fully to Pfeffer's leadership-as-BS,[2] we do feel that the concept of leadership most often embraced—the charismatic, heroic, all-purpose leader—is greatly overemphasized and may even be damaging. *Public values achievement requires multiple leaders working well with followers and with one another.* Indeed, role switching may be necessary, with an individual being a "leader" for certain purposes and at certain times and a "follower" for other purposes and at other times. That is what we mean by the follower-leader, an invaluable asset in any thriving organization.

The Mutable Leadership Concept

Mutable leadership emphasizes that different sorts of leadership are required for different contexts and as events unfurl. This is not a novel idea. Long ago leadership researchers (e.g., Hersey, Blanchard, and Natemeyer 1979; Vecchio 1987; Vroom 1988) pressed upon us the idea of "situational" or "contingency" leadership, and most leadership scholars have long ago embraced the notion of "different times require different talents." Mutable leadership is not exactly the same as situational leadership, but they are conceptual first cousins. Not only do we focus on the situation determining or mitigating leadership effectiveness, but we also contend that very different sorts of leader roles are required according to the organization's life cycle or the strategic or policy issue, a point given only limited attention in situational leadership.

At the beginning of a public values–focused effort, the greatest leadership need is for someone who is good at articulating the public values vision and convincing others of its power and inducing their commitment to it.[3] But other leadership assets, and perhaps other leadership types, are subsequently needed. After interested parties buy into the vision, the most acute needs are to make the vision more concrete, build support, negotiate with others, develop resources, and implement the vision, often a vision different from the one offered initially. The need for diverse leadership skills does not end when the institution begins to accomplish its public values objectives and solidify the mission and the work of the institution. Almost all institutions find that one of their greatest threats is self-satisfaction with early successes and the hardening and inflexibility that often accompany success. Thus, at later stages of an institution's life cycle, there often is a need for revisionary leaders and even "blow-it-up-and-start-over" leaders.

The term "mutable" means "prone to change," and, of course, change is at the core of our leadership concept. But mutability is not the only component. Others are discussed below.

Permeable Leadership

Permeable leadership is an important element of mutable leadership, with permeable leadership simply suggesting the need for access and communication between those viewed as leaders and other organization members. In our view, the widespread tendency to distinguish sharply between leaders and those led is both misguided and sometimes harmful. This is not to say that there are rarely sharp boundaries between leader and the led—organizations and the people at the top of them do love hierarchy—only that sharp boundaries are almost always a bad idea.[4]

With permeable leadership the leader is available, is open, and makes it relatively easy for others to provide opinions, suggestions, or criticisms. We are not suggesting a literal "open-door" policy, but rather a leadership style and an accompanying organizational structure that not only permits but also facilitates alternative views.

Under mutable leadership it is not a good idea to be perceived as aloof and unapproachable. One need not be a populist, or even particularly outgoing, just approachable. But permeable leadership is more than personal approachability. The structuring of leadership must promote some degree of open access. Even if organizational leaders are approachable in terms of their personalities and willingness to consider others' views, there must still be an organizational framework that permits this to happen. If just a handful of advisors stringently filter access to leaders, then the organization is impermeable and, thus, the leader is unapproachable, sometimes without even much awareness of the extent to which others are closed off.

We are not suggesting that permeable, open leadership is an attribute of all successful leaders. One can easily think of leaders who emphasized the majestic aspects of their leadership, ones who had no inclination to be "one of the people" or even to promote two-way communication. In some cases, there is something to be said for this sort of leadership. It can work, but maybe in ways that are culturally dependent. One thinks of Charles de Gaulle.

Mini-case. The Magisterial Leader: The Exception That Proves the Rule?
When French war hero and ardent nationalist Charles de Gaulle became
president in 1959, he led a country that had still not fully recovered from
World War II, one whose colonial ambitions had taken a blow with the
Algerian War and that had lost its role as a military superpower in a
bipolar world dominated by the United States and the USSR. This man,
who during World War II had declared without irony "Je suis la France"
(I am France), was by nature aloof and distant (Williams 1993). Franklin
Roosevelt, not an admirer, told Winston Churchill, "De Gaulle may be a
good man, but he has a messianic complex." Moreover, de Gaulle's
demeanor was not simply an extension of his personality but rather a
studied plan. Consider the following quotes: "It is essential that the plan
on which the leader has concentrated all his faculties shall bear the mark
of grandeur," and "First and foremost, there can be no prestige without
mystery, for familiarity breeds contempt."

Despite these views, perhaps even because of them, de Gaulle was
revered by most of the French people. He served as head of the French
provisional government in World War II and then as the elected president of France from 1959 to 1969. He was not turned out of office but
rather resigned in 1969 when a decentralization referendum he supported failed to pass. When he died the next year, the intensity of
national mourning was perhaps unparalleled. The point is that there is
more than one way to be a leader, and that de Gaulle certainly defied the
idea of the mutable leader, perhaps being one of the least mutable
major political figures of the twentieth century.

A de Gaulle–style leader gives little thought to being approachable, so
why do we place currency in permeability? A basic assumption of
mutable leadership is that leaders will be more suited to some tasks than
to others and, relatedly, that different leadership talents and, sometimes, different leaders will need to emerge as requirements change. De
Gaulle certainly seems not to have envisioned any changing conditions
that would require a different set of talents, probably an understandable
view given his *Je Suis la France* view of the world. But mutability requires
approachability. Without approachability and organizational permeability,

the leader hazards being desperately and dangerously out of touch, perhaps even being resigned to obtaining news and current events from just a few agreeably compatible television sources and close-at-hand advisors and family, perhaps reacting to the world via social media rather than direct, two-way human interaction. *Noblesse oblige por* Tweet?

Leadership Succession

Some leadership books and, for that matter, many leaders seem to forget or ignore the fact that all leaders are mortal, both literally and metaphorically. Having sound plans and procedures for leadership succession is always important (for an overview of the literature on that topic see Kesner and Sebora 1994), but especially so with mutable leadership, an approach that assumes that leaders should change or, at least, that while remaining leaders they change with the times and the circumstances. Thus, another twist with the mutable leadership approach is that considerable attention should be devoted to planning for the public value–based institution's use of the former leader after that person has retired, stepped aside temporarily, refocused his or her attention, or even been sacked. Any reasonably good leader has developed a wealth of knowledge potentially useful for the organization. True, the succeeding leader may not be anxious to accommodate the hovering ghost of the previous leader, or even the corporeal embodiment of the previous leader, perhaps hanging around and either second-guessing or smugly observing, "We already tried that, and it didn't work." But that is part of the planning; we do not claim that it is easy tapping the knowledge of a former leader, only that it is important to do so.

The processes for executive succession are important in any organization, but there is no single approach that works best (Dyck et al. 2002). About the only thing on which all observers agree is that the process should be put in place well in advance of change rather than being cobbled together hastily at the last minute. When the processes are ad hoc, a great many problems can arise, not least the ability of clever and politically astute participants to use the process to tilt the outcome in their favor. But a more common and usually worse problem is resultant chaos and confusion. Assuming that there is a process in place, then many different approaches may work, including ones that are more or less centralized, ones that are more or less formal, and ones that have measurable criteria or are based on intuition.

One process that is increasingly common these days will likely not work so well for the public values–focused institution. Many of today's institutions have extremely closed executive choice and succession processes, secretive ones involving as few people as possible (Greer and Virick 2008; Gothard and Austin 2013). The lack of transparency and limited participation are often ascribed to the job candidates' preference for confidentiality. Understandably, job candidates in many cases are concerned about their current organization being negatively affected by the news that he or she may imminently depart. But in many other cases, the closed system may be more related to a small group's wish to maximize its decision-making power, also an understandable motive, albeit less beneficial.

In the case of public values–based institutions it is almost always desirable to have executive succession processes and decisions as transparent and participative as possible. In the first place, many such organizations are nonprofit or governmental and, unlike the modal large corporation, have no long history of closed decision-making to which organizational members and stakeholders have become accustomed. Second, more than most organizations, public values–focused organizations are especially likely, in terms of not only mission but also empirical fact, to have concerns about inclusiveness of women and underrepresented minorities. A lack of transparency and a focus on minority or female inclusiveness are factors that do not go well together (Gares and Delco 1991; Konrad and Pfeffer 1991; Gothard and Austin 2013).

Finally, we note that one interesting approach to executive succession and leadership transition is to change not the particular leader but the leadership team. One research study (Virany, Tushman, and Romanelli 1992) of executive succession showed that one of the most effective, though uncommon, approaches to promoting positive organizational change and learning was to ensure a regular process of strategic reorientation of the entire leadership team, including some periodic switching of members, even in cases where the top leader stays in place.

Mutable Leadership Roles

No public values leader, even the most sagacious and adaptable, is well prepared to occupy all the leadership roles vital to the effectiveness of an institution that are required during its full life cycle. This explains much about why so many institutions hit a wall—the old leadership styles and needs are no longer adaptive, but the institution understandably has difficulty in moving away from leaders and leadership styles proven effective for most of its history. The notion of mutable leadership entails ensuring that the right skills are available from the right people at the right time. That act of ensuring is itself likely a collective effort that requires some cooperation and even negotiation.

In this section we discuss leadership roles that may be required at different points as the public values–based institution evolves. These roles are, of course, archetypes and do not always have hard-and-fast boundaries. However, reflecting on these roles gives some insight into the meaning of mutable leadership, especially as contrasted to more static models of leadership.

During the earliest stages of the public value–based institution, a particularly important leadership role is the *Visionary*. As the institution begins to establish itself and to flourish, roles coming into prominence include *Assemblers and Coalition Builders*, *Negotiators and Peacemakers*, *Implementation Leaders*, and, as the institution matures, *Conservers*. As the institution nears the late stages of its life cycle, *Revisionary* leaders are required, ones who are the architects of repair and renovation. Finally, the *Creative Destroyers* come to the fore, leaders who are among the first to notice that the institution no longer serves its public value function effectively or that the environment has changed, reducing the need for servicing the particular public values by this particular institution. We note that most institutions do not think of leadership in this highly segmented way, and, of course, few institutions are explicitly designed to accommodate the natural leadership mutations that occur as institutions change over extended periods of time. Nor can we learn much about the longer-term leadership requirements of institutions by studying single heroic leaders.

We discuss each of the leadership roles in turn, in many cases providing instances of such leadership. Table 6 provides a list of the leader roles, along with a brief description.

Public Value Visionaries

In the previous chapter, we offered the public value proposition "articulating the vision," noting that, when the institution is in the early stages of its public values mission, few things are as important as a coherent public values vision, one that can be embraced by others and motivates others to invest. At that time, we discussed attributes of the vision but devoted only a little attention to the visionary.

First, not all Public Value Visionaries are good leaders, or even leaders at all. For example, one can well have a superb vision but not have any notion of the institutional framework it requires or know what is needed to get others interested in the vision. One example from history of a visionary with no discernible leadership skills is the great inventor Nikola Tesla. Perhaps best known as the developer of AC electricity, he was also a major contributor to such technologies as radar, remote control, and X-rays. Despite his brilliance, he was largely solitary throughout his life, and when working within an organizational framework he generally failed to thrive. His visions were abundant, but they were about science and technology, with little if any concern about exactly how these visions would or could be developed into the practical and world-changing technologies that his visions enabled. There is much evidence that Tesla (Seifer 1996), as is the case for many scientists and engineers, was interested more in the beauty of science than in the social and economic applications to which it gives rise.

By contrast, Tesla's long-time enemy and competitor (and one-time employer), Thomas Edison, is reputed by modern historians to have lagged far behind Tesla in scientific and inventive genius (Hughes 1979;

TABLE 6
Leadership Roles

Leadership Role	Description	Life Cycle Stage
Public value visionaries	Develops ideas as to what is the public value and the social instrumentalities needed to realize it.	Vital at the beginning but also needed later for renewal.
Assemblers and coalition builders	Builds the team of individuals, groups, or organizations that can make the vision a reality.	Especially important at early stage but always extremely valuable.
Implementation leaders	Once the vision is set and resources are in place, facilitates coordination, implementation, and performance evaluation. In other words, implementation requires good management. But good managers cannot be as effective without a leader's communication of the tasks and ensuring their feasibility.	Important from early stages, throughout the life cycle.
Negotiators and peacemakers	Negotiates with stakeholders to "keep the peace" as disagreements and challenges emerge.	Useful just as soon as there is something to fight about, that is, at the very beginning, until there no longer is, that is, the very end.
Conservers and maintainers	Institutions have life spans, some very short, some spanning several human lifetimes. Those in this leadership role conserve values and the mix of activities and resources that have achieved those values.	Useful once there is something available to conserve.
Revisionaries	Revisionaries stir the pot. They are change agents, including sometimes-radical opponents and "troublemakers," but vital as institutions almost inevitably become ossified and weakened.	Can occur at almost any time except the beginning of the organization, depending on the continuing vitality of the original mission and approach.
Creative destroyers	When the useful life of the institution is beginning to end, the leaders in this role recognize that the end is near and help lead the organization as it closes operations and redistributes resources.	End stage of useful organizational life.

O'Neill 2006), but Edison was able to promote and develop his visions (and sometimes Tesla's visions) and to marshal interest and support for them in a way that defied Tesla (Stross 2008).

In the case of the public values leader, the Public Value Visionary must have not simply a strong and attractive vision but one that relates directly to the achievement of public values through institutional mechanisms. After answering the question "What needs to be done in connection with this public value?" the Public Value Visionary must supply an answer that has to do with working directly with other people to build organizations and institutions that will achieve the public values of interest. This does *not* mean that the ideas about institutional mechanisms need to be well developed—that is the role for the Assemblers and Coalition Builders discussed below—but the vision must at least have some notion of being implemented within an organizational or institutional framework. Absent an institution upon which to hang the vision, the visionary may be a thought leader or an advocate but not a public values manager or leader.

In many cases, the organizational framework for the public values leader's vision is easily determined: it is the organization that employs him or her. In some cases, public values visions are developed after long periods of service as an executive in the organization. Perhaps more often the public values vision is attendant on the taking of a new job. Often the leader is hired because of a specific public values vision that has been articulated, making the individual an attractive candidate for the position either because the vision is in line with the mission of the organization or because the organization wishes to go in a different direction than in the past and is looking for a reorienting vision. In other cases, a leader is recruited to an organization not because of any specific public values vision that has been articulated but because the individual has a reputation for being a visionary or has successfully articulated and implemented public values visions in other organizations. Most importantly, it is common knowledge that just about any CEO or director or president of an organization will have greatest leverage, both over resources and in engaging people, at the beginning of service (Shen 2003; Cartwright and Cooper 2014), the so-called honeymoon period.

Once the leader is ensconced in the organization and is actively articulating the public values vision, what are some of the leadership characteristics that will increase the likelihood that the vision will be embraced by others? Obviously, the utility of the leader's vision depends to a large extent on the particular content and attributes of the vision, apart from personal characteristics or behaviors of the leader. For example, the vision must be one that can be understood and promotes shared understanding. If the vision is largely symbolic, more tone than content, it may be quite popular, but stakeholders and organizational members may be enthusiastic about their own distinctive interpretations of the vision, overlaying their own dreams, aspirations, and desired objectives onto an amorphous vision that actually has little content. This is not always an entirely bad development. Visionary ideas, like visionary leaders, need a degree of mutability and adaptability. However, when the actual work proceeds in developing and implementing the vision, agreement is required as to exactly what public values are being pursued. The longer this consensus building is delayed, the more likely that forging it will be difficult and, at least for some, disappointing in result.

Assemblers and Coalition Builders

Some people might view the Assembler and Coalition Builder role as not being leadership at all but rather evidence of good followership. That is not our view. There are few tasks more important to leadership than selecting the team that will be chiefly responsible for shaping the vision and making sure that stakeholders who participate in carrying it out are mobilized and working toward the same overall set of public values objectives.

Historians know the importance of leaders' team selection. Different approaches work for different leaders. For example, Doris Kearns Goodwin (2005) tells us in her justifiably famous book *Team of Rivals* about President Abraham Lincoln's unorthodox approach to building his cabinet, choosing several of his defeated rivals or opponents. While this did not work out in every respect, in many cases the selections were inspired, with some, such as William Seward, becoming lifelong friends and allies and able advisors and implementers of the Lincoln vision.

Similarly, another classic work of political history, James McGregor Burns's (1956) *Roosevelt: The Lion and the Fox* (taking its subtitle from one of Machiavelli's aphorisms), tells us of President Roosevelt's tendency to select cabinet members with quite different views and then play one off the other, collecting diverse information and points of view along the way.

Most public values leaders are working with particular institutions rather than heading a government, and they have team-building styles that are perhaps less idiosyncratic than those of either Roosevelt or Lincoln and, just as importantly, are less constrained in building their teams, usually owing little or nothing in payment-due-on-demand political debts. This is not to say that they are without constraint. One of the most obvious constraints is that public values leaders in many cases do not have the resources or organizational leverage to freely recruit. When one comes into a government agency or a nonprofit or a firm, one may have the ability to bring along or recruit a few key team members, but in most cases the teams will be composed of people who are already there. So, a major part of Assembler and Coalition Builder leadership pertains to human resources assessment, and especially assessing team members for relevant talents, including leadership. Most people would prefer to take their time, get to know people, obtain firsthand evidence of strengths and weaknesses, and come to deliberate, well-thought-out decisions about which team members to deploy and in what manner and, just as important, who is likely to work well with whom. Doing so may be a luxury one cannot afford. If the leader develops effective teams but the honeymoon period has long lapsed, then the teams may have less ability to maneuver, gather resources, and accomplish objectives than it might have had with an earlier start. What this means is that, unfortunately, slow-moving leader deliberation in some cases has it costs. Let's consider what this implies. One implication is that having good first-encounter judgment can be quite valuable

(Cafaro et al. 2012). But few people actually have the ability to make valid snap judgments about others, and, worse, our snap judgments often relate to (usually unconscious) stereotypes and bias (Payne 2006). Moreover, there is no reason to believe that the ability to make good judgments from first impressions relates particularly well to any other leadership attributes.

So let's consider a realistic question: What can a new executive, a presumed leader, do to build effective public values–focused teams if we assume that (1) choices are constrained such that most of the team must be composed of existing organization members, (2) the teams must be built and deployed relatively quickly in order to accomplish as much as possible during the brief honeymoon period, and (3) the executive has no particular talent for sizing up people from brief first impressions?

A good start would be to make optimal use of any recruiting ability that one comes in with. While it is generally true that most new executives cannot manage to negotiate for an army of new employees, it is not at all uncommon to arrange to bring along one or two trusted coworkers or to have free rein in recruiting for one or a few positions. Sometimes these few are more than sufficient. When a new executive arrives, it is invariably the case that he or she receives a great deal of scrutiny by everyone in the organization, as well as by many of the organization's external stakeholders. But much the same is true with regard to the executive's "chosen," those who are joining the organization at the behest of the executive. The characteristics, accomplishments, work styles, and, most importantly, values of the chosen provide strong signals to existing employees (Armbrüster 2004), signals embodied in persons and actions and that are in some cases even more powerful than new formal strategic objectives or speeches and documents provided by the new executive.

In most cases, it is a good idea to put together a diverse team and to draw upon new recruits that have different complementary skills (Barrick et al. 1998). Homogeneity, often overly prized by executives (especially when correlated with loyalty), is by most accounts the best way to kill team creativity (Leonard and Straus 1997; Amabile 1998).

Thus, if the executive has a chance to bring with him or her two or three personally chosen team members, it is best if these individuals manifest different attributes, not only modeling the characteristics the leader hopes to see in others but also providing sufficient diversity of characteristics that current employees will likely see at least some of themselves in the new employees.

In many cases, the new executive does not have the ability to import new employees and, thus, signal desired worker attributes. Such a situation makes first impression management skills even more important but, unfortunately, no more prevalent. There are, however, many standard approaches and heuristics for quickly assessing incumbent employees and their talents. One of the most useful approaches is to obtain assessments from those who are outside the organization (and thus may speak more freely) about organizational members with whom they have frequently interacted. In terms of employee assessments of one another, this is a more difficult proposition, but management researchers have developed some approaches that are useful. We are not fans of 360-degree employee evaluations of one another (e.g., Beehr et al. 2001), as there are too often hard feelings and recriminations (Van der Heijden and Nijhof 2004), but there are well-established approaches (Magjuka and Baldwin 1991), for example, developing a task inventory and asking employees who would most likely be effective in accomplishing the task. Being recognized as effective alienates no one. True, not being on the list may offend some, but in many instances there is no need to make the list public.

In most respects, team building in the public values–focused organization is not much different in its requirements or approaches than for any organization. But there is at least one advantage. In most organizations it is simply assumed that the people who work there are chiefly motivated by either personal economic rewards or professional and career recognition. If you are the executive of, say, a tobacco company, it is not reasonable to expect that your employees are highly motivated by an intrinsic need to make sure that more people smoke. Yes, that is an extreme example, but in less extreme cases it is nonetheless true that for many people in many jobs the work is not a mission but a source of income (Rynes, Gerhart, and Minette 2004). True, many people, even when working for an organization that provides a good or service that is not in itself highly motivating, still have pride in their work or professional commitment, but that may not be sufficient for public values organizations and their difficult missions, which often provide fewer rewards than does most of the corporate world. Fortunately, there is good reason to believe that intrinsic motivation, which is correlated with work in government and nonprofit organizations (Borzaga and Tortia 2006; Lee and Wilkins 2011), many of which serve missions that do not provide much in the way of direct economic benefit to workers and managers, will serve well in any public values–focused organization in any sector. This intrinsic motivation can be a crucial asset in building teams and managing coalitions in public values–focused organizations. A public values leader, one playing out his or her role as team and coalition builder, does well to understand the nature of intrinsic motivation and to use it wisely (rather than merely exploit it).

Comment: Anne-Marie Slaughter Gives the Secret to "Accomplishing Anything"
Anne-Marie Slaughter, executive director and CEO of New America, offers the following: "Especially in traditional Washington politics, you can accomplish anything as long as you don't want credit for it."

Implementation Leaders

Implementation Leader? "Implementation" sounds liked routine management, not leadership. In our view, implementation *always* involves management and *sometimes* involves leadership. In many cases, leaders, even effective leaders, stay out of implementation, delegating implementation to trusted subordinates. Nonetheless, we feel there is a leadership role to be played, albeit a role that may not be a prerequisite to overall effective leadership. The chief requirements for the Implementation Leader role involve ensuring that those to whom frontline implementation authority is delegated have an adequate sense of requirements and standards.

One of the hazards for executives is the relative ease with which they can inadvertently and sometimes unknowingly create red tape and waste others' time and resources (see Bozeman 2000; Bozeman and Feeney 2011). Most good executives have gotten the message—"delegate!" However, the message should perhaps be expanded to "delegate—but only after you (1) have communicated a clear idea of the tasks required of those who are implementing; (2) are confident that the implementers not only understand the tasks but also have a strong commitment to the tasks and the skills and resources needed to perform them, and (3) have at least a rough sense of how to evaluate the tasks and, most importantly, the ability to gauge when and the extent to which the tasks have been accomplished." To put it another way, good management requires good leadership.

It is unfortunate but perhaps not surprising how many executives feel like they have been undercut by their subordinates, people who just cannot seem to accomplish the tasks set for them. True, subordinates are sometimes wanting, but it is good for the leader, especially in the role of Implementation Leader, to recall just who empowered the subordinates and assigned the tasks. Good managers typically thrive when authority is delegated and they have some autonomy about just how to implement the task, but no manager is a "good manager" when the tasks are unclear or the goals murky and ambiguous. Indeed, research on goal clarity shows that it is a major factor in quality performance (Rainey 1993; Chun and Rainey 2005; Anderson and Stritch 2015).

Goal ambiguity is a major element in organizational red tape (Pandey and Kingsley 2000), defined here as rules and procedures requiring compliance and, thus, the use of organizational resources, but having no positive effect on the objectives the rules are designed to achieve. It is easy to see how someone could waste a good deal of time pursuing required tasks but without any real accomplishment, owing to the fact that no one is entirely sure what is supposed to be accomplished. However, executives' culpability may be less obvious and, sometimes, not easy to pinpoint. From red tape theory and research, we know that there are multiple causes of red tape, including not only executives' failure adequately to communicate tasks and performance standards but also sources external to the organization (Bozeman 2000; Brewer et al. 2012).

For a great many organizations, the vast majority of requirements that turn out to be red tape do not originate within the organization but rather are designed by others. Rules designed remotely and not fit to the needs of the specific context can easily prove ineffective. If the rules allow little or no discretion in their implementation, organizational leaders and the managers may find themselves compelled to abide by rules that damage the organization or its clients. However, even in such constrained cases, leaders may still have recourse (Moynihan 2012; Van den Bekerom, Torenvlied, and Akkerman 2017). Possible actions in highly constrained, rule-bound contexts may include petitioning for exceptions, developing a greater understanding of compliance alternatives, or simply maintaining effective relations with the external authorities requiring the implementation of particular rules and procedures.

Negotiators and Peacemakers

The Negotiator and Peacemaker role involves "keeping the peace" and making sure that conflict and diverging interests and perspectives do not get in the way of accomplishing public values. It is here that the leadership role may diverge from formal authority. Why? In many cases it is the executive that is the focus of conflict or, at least, the lightning rod for it. In some cases, the executive is a scapegoat, a convenient answer to the question "How can I summarize all that I do not like about this organization?" Aside from whether the executive is highly effective, scapegoated, truly lacking, or just plain wrong on some points, the truth of the matter is that the role of Negotiators and Peacemakers is generally best lodged elsewhere.

In a public value–based institution, what are some of the likely characteristics of one effective in the Negotiator and Peacemaker role? In most cases it is someone who has considerable tenure in the organization and is known to all parties, especially the disputants. The reason is simple: whatever else is required for trust, mutual experience is a prerequisite (Jones and George 1998). Interestingly, this time-trust relationship seems to hold even for computer-mediated groups (Wilson, Straus, and McEvily 2006). In short, while some leadership attributes are "portable," trust is not one of them. Thus, a reputation earned elsewhere as, say, an innovator, or a hard worker, or as one who is calm in a crisis will sometimes carry to the new organization, but not trust. The fact that persons in the previous organization seem to have trusted the new leader will have little effect on those in the leader's current organization.

In most cases, the Negotiator and Peacemaker role requires someone who is neither an ideologue nor inflexible. Obviously, it is difficult to preside over disputants when one has strong views that are well known and constantly acted upon (Robbins 1974; Schlaerth, Ensari, and Christian 2013). However, there is one difference between the public values–focused organization and most other organizations. If there is consensus on the legitimacy and the organization's framing of the core public values it is pursuing, but perhaps not on means or subsidiary objectives, then having a reputation as the strongest and most indomitable advocate for the consensus public value not only is unlikely to prove damaging but can be a major asset for the person seeking trust as a Negotiator and Peacemaker.

Comment: Tony Penn on Trusting Competitors
Tony Penn, president and CEO at United Way of Tucson and Southern Arizona, offers the following: "In leadership developing trust is extremely important. This is especially the case when you're working with people who are competitors with one another, who, even if they're not direct economic competitors they have different interests." Tony Penn's bio can be found at https://biztucson.com/2018/03/16/tony-penn/.

Conservers and Maintainers

Typically, organizational conservation is not a major element of leadership, but it is sometimes a small, important element. When we speak of conservation, we do *not* mean standing in the way of needed change. From a leadership perspective, the role of Conserver and Maintainer involves the important function of guarding the most central values and assets of the organization or institution. A first step is knowing what these are. In many cases, values, norms, and operating practices are viewed as important just because they are familiar and even comfortable. Conserver and Maintainer leaders will be good at separating the comfortable from the truly beneficial. This is particularly important in public values–based organizations because it is sometimes easy, even easier than in most other types of organizations, to confuse means and ends. In a market-based organization focusing chiefly on profit, it is easy enough to ask the question (and sometimes to answer it) "How does this contribute to the bottom line?" In the public value–based organization, the goals being pursued, however important they may be, are not always easy to gauge and measure. A classic example of goal displacement, substituting means for ends, is in higher education. Every credible university has as a foremost goal improving students' knowledge, learning, and skills. However, having good "raw material" (i.e., top students), highly reputed and well-rated faculty, high performance on peer ratings—none of these actually ensure that students are learning much. Learning is internal, only sometimes manifested externally, and measuring it is not easy. It is much easier to quantify grades, peer ratings, faculty evaluation, and other surrogate indicators or possible inputs into learning. In this case, it may take some leadership to conserve and maintain the principal value: student learning. In universities, good leaders "keep their eye on the prize" even as others may be looking at secondary indicators of core values, even at the expense of core values.

Another role for Conserver and Maintainer leaders is analogous to the well-known role of presidents and other national leaders as "chief of state." While this term has taken on many meanings, one of its early uses was defined by presidential scholar Clinton Rossiter, who described chief of state as one of the seven major roles of presidents. Under this role, the president becomes the embodiment of the nation, symbolically representing the core values of the nation, sometimes in grand and formalized ways, such as receiving foreign dignitaries in traditional ceremonies, and other times in folksy but historically meaningful ways, such as the annual traditions of "pardoning" a turkey on Thanksgiving, lighting the White House Christmas tree, or throwing out the first pitch at the beginning of the baseball season. In the case of the public values leader, the role is much more circumscribed—it involves understanding and representing the symbols, rituals, and historical events that organizational members and stakeholders recognize in common and that represent the public values vested in the organization. Not only is this conserving "chief of state" role important because of its emotional and socially binding effects on organizational members, but it also has the effect of legitimizing and empowering the leader who is charged with achieving public values (Beetham 2013).

Revisionaries

Now the pendulum swings. Even more important than the Conserve and Maintain leadership role is the Revisionary. It is not that change is always more important, but rather that the forces for conservatism are "built in" and reflexive for any organization, especially a public value–based organization. It is change that more often proves difficult (Bryson, Gibbons, and Shaye 2001). There are many reasons for the conservative bias of institutions, including inertia, vested interest in the status quo, and an appreciation of the risks of making things worse even while trying to do better ("if it ain't broke, don't fix it" sometimes is apt, even if hackneyed). In public values–based organizations, the core mission rarely focuses on innovation, but rather on accomplishment by any means. Public values–based organizations are not rewarded by innovation for its own sake (Sharp and Brock 2012) and may be punished for taking risks. By contrast, some private, wealth-focused firms can develop a remarkable amount of leverage, and often a greatly increased share or market valuation, simply by having a reputation for innovativeness, even while not making a profit or accomplishing much other than innovation. This is not usually true for public values–based organizations, and not just because they typically have no market valuation or shareholders. In short, it is very easy for persons leading public value–based organizations, especially effective ones, to be self-congratulatory and to recognize the need to change only after it is too late to do so.

A leader who is a Revisionary stirs the pot. This leader may be the chief executive or not, but the role involves receptivity to change, good judgment about when and why change is needed, and an ability to advocate for change. While sometimes related, each of these requirements is to some extent different, but leadership requires the whole package. It helps if the change agent is also well regarded and a trusted central figure in the organization.

Comment: *Antonia Hernández on Reasoned Risk*

Antonia Hernández, CEO and president of the California Community Foundation, offers the following: "Yes, you have to take risks and, yes, they have to be informed. If there's no risk, there's no gain. They have to be intelligent risks, but there's no gain without risk." Antonia Hernández's bio can be found at https://www.calfund.org /about-ccf/ccfstaff/presidents-office/.

Mini-case. Revisionary Leadership: The Case of the March of Dimes Redirection

One of the best examples of Revisionary leadership is the nonprofit organization March of Dimes, a familiar case study in strategic management of nonprofit organizations (e.g., Salipante and Golden-Biddle 1995; Baghdady and Maddock 2008). Founded by President Franklin Roosevelt in 1938, the March of Dimes was originally known as the National Foundation for Infantile Paralysis (NFIP) and was focused on developing research and treatment for polio, a widespread threat to health during the time, one that had also affected President Roosevelt and would ultimately take his life. The foundation ultimately changed its name to the March of Dimes after one of their major fundraisers, actor and singer Eddie Cantor, began to use the term, a reference to the fact that the charity relied on so many small contributors, including schoolchildren, but also a play on *The March of Time*, which was a newsreel series that was played in nearly every US motion picture theater for many years (Larsen 2012).

President Roosevelt appointed as the initial director of the NFIP his former law partner and trusted confidante Basil O'Connor, who would lead the organization for many years. The NFIP proved remarkably adept at raising funds, not least because it had a single-mindedness in its focus and, in polio, a terrifying disease that chiefly struck children, usually leading to lifelong paralysis and eventually death (Helfand, Lazarus, and Theerman 2001). Each year the organization would develop a new literal poster boy who would be a rallying symbol for such events as the Mothers March.

Ultimately, the March of Dimes would prove to be so effective as to make itself obsolete. One of the recipients of March of Dimes funds was Dr. Jonas Salk, who, along with others, developed the vaccine that would essentially wipe out polio in the 1950s (Oshinsky 2005).

However, after the early discovery, time was required to test and receive approval for the vaccine, to produce it in large quantities and administer it. These months gave O'Connor and other March of Dimes leaders time to consider this question: "What, if anything, do we do next?" Should they close up shop and declare victory, reveling in the fact that they would be credited as the first foundation in history to have essentially cured a focal disease through its own fundraising and research efforts (Larsen 2012)? As O'Connor observed, "I am the head of General Motors and my automobile is going to be declared obsolete" (Baghdady and Maddock 2008, 61).

O'Connor and other leaders of the March of Dimes, including Raymond Barrows and Melvin Glasser, decided not only to engage in a strategic planning effort to redirect the organization but also to employ what was then cutting-edge social science research on public opinion to help them determine a future course. The NFIP contracted with the

Gallup opinion organization and the Columbia University Bureau of Applied Social Research to develop a survey of more than 2,000 people in order to determine their level of knowledge about NFIP, assess the possibility that they would provide support to purposes other than polio, and develop a list of priorities that could be the focus of a new, refashioned March of Dimes. At the same time, the researchers interviewed more than 200 NFIP chapter leaders and 1,000 members of the general public to determine in depth their views about NFIP and the chances they would support a new direction. The resultant study showed that the public would continue to support polio efforts (it had not yet been completely eradicated) and that NFIP should refocus on a different health issue, but there was no consensus as to just what it should be.

Glasser, who was chiefly tasked with developing a plan for redirection, set 28 criteria for judging proposals for a new mission. Among these, the new mission should be health related, as close to polio eradication as feasible; the problem should be one that potentially affected every region of the country; and the new initiative should continue to rely extensively on a network of volunteers and a fundraising strategy focused on small contributions. Finalist candidates included arthritis, juvenile delinquency, alcoholism, and birth defects. After fully five years of planning, O'Connor in July 1958 presided over a press conference in New York to announce that the new foundation (now called the National Foundation rather than the NFIP) would focus on all major forms of paralysis that are in part virus based, including polio, rheumatoid arthritis, and congenital birth defects. The focus would be on crippling diseases, not a particular disease.

Despite the planning, they did not quite get it right. After a few months, it was discovered that they would have a sticky domain fight with the existing Arthritis and Rheumatism Foundation, finding that a proposed merger would not work owing to differences in organization cultures and approaches. They were also met with a confused public. Most people identified arthritis with old people and did not understand why an organization that had so long included poster children and mothers' marches was now focused on the elderly. Further, although the polio mission was not yet successfully concluded, it was perceived to be.

Due to all these factors, donations began to shrink precipitously, by 1965 decreasing to about a third of the peak donations in 1955. Nearly half the chapters were in debt, owing money to hospitals and for patient care.

This second reboot worked. In 1964, O'Connor announced that the foundation was shedding its arthritis mission and, since polio was by this time well under control, that the new focus would be solely on problems related to birth defects. Just as important, the new March of Dimes, taking a page from its previous success, would be chiefly a research-focused organization, developing many more workers in several new regional research centers. In 1958, the foundation had 80,000 volunteers; by 2008, the number of volunteers had increased to more than 3 million (Baghdady and Maddock 2008, 65). In 2015, the foundation had reached more than $153 million in contribution-based assets; had forged partnerships with such industrial leaders as Kmart, United Airlines, Publix, General Electric, and Cigna; and had launched its first Perinatal Data Centers. In all, this was quite a revision.

Creative Destroyers

Usually we think of leaders as people who create, not destroy, but leaders can and sometimes should be Creative Destroyers. As we know from years of research, nonmarket organizations tend to be "immortal" (Kaufman 1976), or at least sometimes outlive their usefulness (Kimberly and Miles 1980; James et al. 2016; Corbett and Howard 2017). There are many reasons—some obvious, some not—why so many organizations go on and on despite widespread analysis that the need for their goods and services has sharply diminished. In almost every case there are people in the organizations who have devoted many years of their lives to it; it is their world, not to mention their livelihood. Some of these people have alternative employment, but many do not, and thus they act as a force for preservation. In many cases, the organization has developed a clientele or customers it supports, and even if the need for the organization has been reduced, these external groups may have a stake in helping keep it alive. In government, one of the most important, but not as obvious, reasons for the difficulty of terminating agencies has to do with the legal and statutory authority upon which they are based. Those agencies that are founded on the basis of an act of Congress often require another act of Congress for their dissolution. In addition to normal forces of inertia acting against an act of Congress, especially for a small agency with a small budget, there is also the disjunction between political need and social need. Often agencies that have only a modest social or economic function are located in the district of a powerful member of Congress who has a stake in the agency's perpetuation. In short, it is almost never easy for any executive in a government organization (or any type of organization that is not literally bankrupt) to call a meeting and announce, "We have outlived our institutional usefulness." Doing so requires a rare form of leadership.

We hasten to note that we do not include under the Creative Destroyer category leadership undermining an organization that is deemed by a great many stakeholders and organization members to be providing substantial public value or social and economic benefit. For decades, we have witnessed the curiosity of political appointees given the reins of an agency or even a cabinet department with the express intent of either sharply cutting back its activities or presiding over its demise. The reason is simple enough to understand. When presidents (and this also happens with state governors) are elected, they are sometimes elected as "outsiders" who have campaigned on the promise of reducing government in general and, less often, reducing specific functions of government, including familiar targets such as tax agencies and regulatory agencies. Truth be told, these efforts have, for a variety of reasons, largely been unsuccessful, but not for a lack of effort by executives who are enemies of their own organization or institution. These are not Creative Destroyers.

What motivates the genuine Creative Destroyers? In some cases, they are concerned about conserving or redeploying resources in a more useful fashion, but in other cases they see that their organization is actually a barrier to change. In yet other cases, there is a widespread recognition that the agency or organization has simply not done a very good job of attacking the problems it was designed to address (Lawton and Macaulay 2017). In rare cases, leaders know that their organizations are toxic, either corrupt or completely dysfunctional (Cuervo-Cazurra 2014).

What are the characteristics of Creative Destroyer leaders? We cannot provide much insight here. This particular leadership activity is extremely rare, much rarer even than is the death of nonmarket organizations, and no one has systematically studied such behavior.

Reality Check and Ideas Crucible

In this chapter we have provided our take on leadership, with a particular message being that public values leadership differs from leadership in most types of bureaucracies, owing to the nature of the mission and the distinctive prerequisites to achieving public values. To a large extent our views have been taken from our own experience and only to a lesser extent from research on leadership (in part because there is so little scholarship directly relevant to *public values* leadership).

Experience is by its very nature valid, but only for the individual. It may or may not pertain to others. We have noted previously that our book aims to actively engage the reader as a public value theorist and critic; thus, the five leadership cases presented in the next chapter are not "tests" of our leadership theories but rather reports of experiences that may or may not comport with those of the readers. We challenge the reader, as we challenge ourselves, to grapple with these many and diverse ideas, some mutually compatible and some not, and come to his or her own nascent public values leadership theory (and maybe report back to us!). Just as so much of philosophy ultimately boils down to the personal, so is the case with leadership.

6

Case Studies in Public Values Leadership

This chapter presents some modest relief from the authors' voice (though we do not exactly exit stage left and head outside for a cappuccino). Here we provide case studies of public values leadership, reported in the words of the leaders we interviewed. Our only intrusions include some editorial abridgement and, in a few cases, some modest paraphrasing when needed to provide clarification. We do provide comments at the end of each case, and we invite the reader to reflect and "comment" as well, comparing his or her own experiences. The only conspicuous exception to the lapse in the authors' voice is a mini-case from coauthor Crow.

Most of our public values leaders have a relatively low political profile, and only one of them has significant experience as an elected official. But we begin with a case that shows that elected officials, mixed agendas notwithstanding, can in some cases provide public values leadership. The discussion below focuses on Governor Jeb Bush's work on mental health programs in Florida. As we shall see below, this is to some extent a Bush family legacy, with both Presidents George H. W. Bush and George W. Bush also having been very much concerned with mental health policies and goals.

The other four leadership cases in this chapter include Freeman Hrabowski (UMBC and the Choice Program), Brian and Kelly Swette (founders of Sweet Earth foods), Steve Zabilski (St. Vincent de Paul and the development of a downtown Phoenix Human Resources Campus), and Ed Zuercher (Phoenix city manager who presided over the city's light-rail public transit initiative).[1] After each of the cases, we present a few discussion questions and then conclude with some overall observations about the similarities and dissimilarities among the leadership styles and approaches in the respective cases.

Leadership Case. Jeb Bush and Florida Policies for Disabilities

One of President George H. W. Bush's proudest accomplishments was his role in developing and signing into law the Americans with Disabilities Act of 1990 (Berkowitz 2017). Likewise, the second Bush president, George W. Bush, was active in legislation for physical and mental disabilities, including his "New Freedom Initiative" in 2001, featuring a variety of community-based service programs for individuals with disabilities. Governor Jeb Bush's legacy in disability policies is based on his leadership as governor of Florida, beginning his work at the onset of his first term in 1999. The case below describes the shambles of disabilities policy that greeted him and the steps he took to achieve public values–based policies.

Bush: Let me tell you about what greeted me my first week in [the Florida governor's] office. I was summoned from Tallahassee to Judge Ferguson's court in Miami.[2] Judge Ferguson had started to take over the program for the developmentally disabled in our state, which was under federal court review because public officials had chronically mismanaged it. At that time, I didn't know that the federal judiciary could take over a state program. But Judge Ferguson had threatened to do it because there were about 30,000 families whose loved ones were not receiving any services—services the state was duty bound to provide. Certainly, for me at least, it's a public value that the most vulnerable in our society should be in the front of the line, not the back. Yes, there are many people that don't need help of government, and they should patiently wait their turn. But there are others, including adults with mental and physical disabilities, who cannot live a life of dignity without assistance. In the case of the developmentally disabled, it's easy to argue that someone who cannot take care of themselves should be institutionalized, but the cost is high (it could be up to $120,000, depending on the severity of the person's challenges). In many cases, institutionalizing them means putting them in a warehouse somewhere and letting them languish.

Yet, we had families who wanted to care for their loved ones and could do it at a lower cost. What's the value of human dignity? It is high. I acted on that belief and convinced the judge not to take over the program.

I went to the legislature, and together we funded and redesigned the programs, building on a public leadership lesson I learned from Rahm Emanuel,[3] who said, civically, you never want a serious crisis to go to waste. What he meant is if you have a crisis, take advantage of it to do something that needs to be done—like redesign a program. There is so much inertia in our institutions today, and so many people defending their own economic interests or political interests, with not much thought to public values. You really do have to take advantage of crises to illustrate challenges in terms that draw people toward the cause.

People who have intellectual and physical disabilities have the highest unemployment rates in the United States. We considered that in designing a new program. Because we began to provide the opportunities, we also got more engaged with the family members. Their big challenge was that the government-funded makeshift work programs were not real work. The government was warehousing people and claiming they were working. A whole lot of disabled people actually could work, and they added a vitality to the workforce because of the unique nature of who they were.

What I've learned about all these public values programs is that you must be actively engaged in these issues. As you act, it creates other opportunities to act. It becomes a self-fulfilling prophecy—once you build a new model or have some success in fixing a mess, it creates a new opportunity.

We discovered we had a lot of work to do with managing disabilities in our school systems. We tore down all the silos and changed the relationship we had with a very important group of people. We began to make schools more accountable for people with disabilities.

We developed a community-based care model where families were empowered. And then the same thing applied to our child welfare system. Florida had a disastrous child welfare system. It was underfunded, totally static in its approach, and very cautious, because the only time that the child welfare system creeps into people's life is when it's in a headline of a tragic case of abuse. They were constantly in defense mode.

We were the first state in the country to create a community-based model for our foster care system. Now people consider it a model for other states, and other states are applying it. It's the same principle—who's the most vulnerable in society? A child who's been abandoned, neglected, or abused. I don't know how it was in other places, but in Florida there was an epidemic of families abandoning their beloved children either because they were being abused or because of drug or alcohol abuse. There were many reasons why it happened and we weren't good at solving it.

The old model was a top-down model that didn't respect families, basically. The state had a binary choice: take the child out of the family or leave them in. Nobody asked, "What are the issues that drive this abuse? Is there a way for us to look at this in a broader context, and how do we keep families intact, and make them healthier, and more wholesome, so a child can live there?"

In the child welfare system, there were many 18-year-olds leaving the system. The previous system was, "You're 18. You're out. There's no more support." Well, if you're an 18-year-old kid in America today and you have no family, what do you do? They didn't have many options.

So, we got private-sector support to work on this problem. We matched it with government money to build a bridge for access to college, but also a bridge to provide support, so that these young people who graduated out of the foster care system could at least receive some support by living together between 18 and 21.

Ultimately, the waiting list for services went away. That outcome required being all in on the subject and mobilizing support from many places.

B&C: Most people agree that disabled people need support and opportunity. How did things get so bad for values that most people agree on? What happened for things to reach a point that a federal judge was about to step in?

Bush: I think the legislature didn't agree with how my predecessor was administering the program. If they don't agree about what's being done with a program, they don't fund it. With no funding, things got worse, even though everyone agreed helping the disabled is a public value. The legislature saw what they viewed as mismanagement, that drew their ire, they withheld funding, and things got worse and worse.

B&C: How did you go about putting together a team and bringing people together to solve the disabilities program problem? Who did you bring together and why?

Bush: It began when I was running for office. Running for office is not my idea of fun, to be honest with you. So, I told my team I was happy to do all of the fundraising and campaign work, but I also want to learn something. Learning is what really got me fired up. One of the things I did was visit 250 schools.

During one of my school visits, I met a woman named Berthie and her daughter Lucy, who is now probably 35. Berthie told me in front of about 800 people that her biggest fear was outliving her child. The system she was experiencing had big shortfalls and no access to care. She asked what I was going to do about it. She was so angry that I couldn't smile my way through it or schmooze my way out.

Instead, I said, "In the next few months, I'll give you four full days, and you teach me so I can understand what it is to have a child with an IQ of 20, and who lives in a wheelchair with physical ailments that are awful, and yet is not able to express what is happening." And then I went to group homes, I went to these industrial facilities. I listened and I learned.

By the time I met with Judge Ferguson regarding the court order, I knew a lot about the program because I took the time to meet with families in group home settings and work environments. And I had ideas on what to do about it because I had listened to the people directly impacted.

Community by community, we organized, and I found some leaders for these changes. Publix [supermarket chain] was a big supporter, as was Holland and Knight [international law firm established in Polk County, Florida]. In every community, we would have an organizing event where someone from the private sector would take the lead in providing job opportunities to disabled people who were otherwise getting little help and few services.

There are many things about the chance to be in a leadership position that are gratifying, but that's one I will not forget. It wasn't as big a deal as some of the other fights we had, but it's perhaps the most gratifying. Berthie is probably 72 years old now, and she's not as worried about Lucy. Lucy is now in better care, and even when Berthie is no longer around, Lucy will still get good care.

I use the term stolen from [business writer] Jim Collins, the idea of the Big Hairy Audacious Goal (BHAG). Once you create that and you begin to build toward it, it creates the chance for little mini-BHAGs. People get enthusiastic about engagement, to be able to be a part of it. I know that's what you do at ASU too, lots of Big Hairy Audacious Goals.

B&C: How do you sustain progress?

Bush: You have to improve outcomes, but also measure it, engage people, and be all in. You also have to accept the fact when something is not working. You adjust, and just keep going forward. I'll give you an example. The largest gathering for the developmentally disabled in Florida, and maybe the United States, is an event that takes place in June called Family Café. Literally 10,000 people come to the convention center in Orlando. I went all eight years of my terms to show my respect. I gave them the State of the Union for the developmentally disabled, and we'd have a Q and A. I probably spent an hour and a half taking pictures with people.

There's so much cynicism that people will ascribe bad motives to your actions, but you can't worry about that. You have to just constantly show your heart in a public leadership position, or any leadership position if you believe in these things. You can't be passive. You can't be watching your peripheral vision. You have to be fully engaged, that's the key. Because if you are a leader, you have to know that you can't do 20 things well at the same time. You have to do a few and do them really intensely. I believe success will sustain the programs.

Bozeman and Crow Comments

As we reviewed the Jeb Bush case, it seemed to us to raise many questions that transcended the particular experiences with mental health programs in Florida and provided lessons that add to the ideas provided in mutable leadership. We loved the BHAG acronym, and, more importantly, Governor Bush makes the crucial point that it is often easier to motivate people with an enormously difficult problem than a significant but relatively low stakes problem. The reason we here so much today about "Grand Challenges," a term so common as to have become hackneyed, is that others well understand that grand challenges have more allure than middling challenges. Does the *motivation* of the BHAG or the Grand Challenge contribute much to accomplishment? That is not so easy to determine. It seems likely that focusing on the big prize will at least provide some initial impetus and perhaps attract some parties who would not otherwise have been attracted. But the BHAG is hairy even when people are motivated, and a key is to use the motivation in productive ways.

The quotation about not squandering a good crisis is one that we have heard before, not only from Jeb Bush and Rahm Emanuel but also in several biographies of leaders. It is well understood that times of crisis are also particular times of opportunities. When things are not going well, people are much more receptive to new approaches. By the same token, innovation often falls on deaf ears when there is a general perception that all is well. We do not imply that walking into a crisis is necessarily a key to success.

In the case above, Governor Bush was, at least with respect to mental health, a turnaround artist. He obviously had many of the requirements needed for such crisis events, including, perhaps most importantly, listening to other people. He notes that he spent a good deal of time soliciting ideas and visiting group homes. Doing so has many values, including engendering trust and blunting cynicism.

Finally, the problem of cynicism resonates with us (especially Crow). Nearly every leader who is also an executive in an organization faces suspicions of careerism, looking for the next job, or payoffs to friends and supporters. Perhaps some are exempt. Few people manage a food bank, a group home, or an elementary school because doing so is a strong career move or enhances their power or personal fortune. But most leaders, including public values leaders, are subject to suspicions and doubts, especially among those who do not know them well or personally. Cynicism is perhaps strongest in relation to elected officials. In the first place, few win elections with as much as 60% of the vote, and that means that at least 40% of the people being represented have their doubts even before the winner assumes office. What many skeptics miss is the point we made earlier in the book—being a public values leader is not necessarily a full-time, everyday focus. It is quite possible to be committed to and to achieve public values even while pursuing other objectives, such as job advancement, reelection, professional status, or profit.

Most college presidents continually face some degree of skepticism, especially early in their service. Consider the following example of cynicism facing Crow during his effort to make changes at ASU.

Mini-case. Michael Crow on Cynicism and the New American University

Anyone committed to public values–based leadership and management will almost certainly face skeptics and cynics. If a public values focus is combined with a commitment to innovation, then the old guard will see it as its holy duty to combat the new and the fractious.

Here I am going to give just a few anecdotes about how, as a disruptive president of a disruptive institution, I have learned to expect cynicism about most everything our institution holds dearest. I also have a few ideas about how one can deal with cynics and doubters and sometimes, not often, even win them over.

One of the organizations that seemed to me well aligned with my own public values objectives and those of Arizona State University was the Pew Charitable Trust, a foundation that has supported a great many initiatives one might view as public values projects. Thus, I approached them when we were developing support for a program in responsible innovation for our Consortium for Science, Policy and Outcomes (CSPO). We approached Pew about this, and they invited us to meet. Their basic reaction was, "Well you're not one of the top research universities or one of the top research institutions, it looks like you just want to muck up the science policy system and there is nothing wrong with it." Pew, or at least the people we met with, had completely bought into the "Republic of Science" idea that science policy needed no social or cultural guidance and that all would work out for the best if scientists were just given money to pursue their curiosity. So, they were not at all interested in funding us, and they seemed hopeful that CSPO would not survive. They were not just uninterested; they thought what we were doing was inimical to science.

This was just one of the first of many types and purveyors of cynicism aimed at what we were trying to achieve with a new sort of university, one we refer to as the New American University. Public values–based institutions are not without enemies, and the enemies' views are most often rooted in doubt and cynicism. In our case, the overarching criticism has been this: "If you make your university large and inclusive it can't be any good." The Pew experience was just one of many where institutions doubted the mission in part because of who was performing it.

A potentially more significant example was an experience we had with an ASU accrediting authority. We have all kinds of accrediting, and most of them are quite important. We have topic accrediting, unit accrediting authorities, and university accrediting, among others. In our last full university accreditation we were confronted with the extreme skepticism of one member of the team, a professor who was focusing on our mathematics education. He said, baldly, "I know you are cheating. I just don't know exactly how." His view: we could not possibly be getting the reported math test scores from our students, many of whom were "only" B students in high school and had had little previous exposure to math.

Our measured response: "Yes, the scores are really good, but we changed the entire method of teaching; we changed its structure and design." We had developed a computationally based adaptive learning system, with teachers who went from 20 or 30 students in each math section to 50–150 students. It was this increase in size that drew fire. Our reviewer said, "That's impossible, this data cannot be true. You cannot expand class size in math and get better results. There is something wrong with the way you are reporting this." We walked him though the data and our teaching system in great detail. He was never fully convinced; he still thought that there must be some way we cheated, and that we were just very clever about it. Cynicism in the face of innovation. Fortunately, the entire accreditation committee, when they examined our data, came to the conclusion that not only were the numbers honest but also we had shown the possibility that learning technology can improve math performance even at a larger scale.

This is not much different from a similar problem we encountered when reporting our NSF HERD (Higher Education Research and Development Survey) numbers. We received a complaint from a high-level politician saying that our numbers cannot be correct because they exceed the research performance of some of the nation's top research universities, the often experienced "new kid on the block" sort of skepticism. We provided the data in a greater level of detail, showing that our data sources were the same as all 10 of the universities in the University of California system and, most gallingly to our critics, that these numbers exceeded every campus but one. The response from the official: "You must be fudging; you must be making stuff up."

One last case. The Association of American Universities (AAU) is a sort of club composed of the top research universities in the United States. If you are going to climb up to the top tier, then AAU membership is considered, well, maybe not a prerequisite but the icing on the cake. At one point I petitioned one of the officers of the AAU, a distinguished educator who was former president of Cornell University, former president of the University of Iowa, former president of the AAU. I wrote him and said, essentially, "Hunter [his actual first name], you know we made a lot of progress as a research university and we're performing at a level very similar to a lot of the AAU schools, I hope you and your colleagues will take a look at us for possible membership." He writes back and says, "We're not going to take a look at you, we're not *ever* going to take a look at you. You are so large and have so many faculty, your research funding should be in the billions." I write back and I say, "Well, we have so many faculty because we decided to serve the state and region by admitting all qualified students. We have some faculty that are very much focused on research, some on teaching, and some equally on both. But we not only produce a great deal of research and research funds but also do quite well on a per faculty basis." Hunter wrote back and said, "Well, that's your problem." So I wrote again and said, "We've gone and looked at the output of all your more than 60 AAU member universities, and we have comparable research output while at the same time producing more Native American graduates than all the AAU universities combined, we produce more Hispanic graduates than your entire list of universities, and only three AAU members produce more African American graduates than we do." He gets back to me and says, "Well, so you are playing the race card." I write back and tell him, "No, we are not playing the race card, I'm trying to show you that we are developing an entirely new type of university, one that is inclusive and at the same time high quality." He communicated with me one last time and said, "The process is the process, we will vote and you will not make it." Again, public values and innovation—dual threat.

Cynicism and doubt are inevitable when combining public values and innovation. How does one combat it? Having a thick skin is a good start, but not enough. You have to keep your eye on the prize, focusing on doing quality work on quality goals, and if the accolades come, they come. If others fail to recognize innovation and quality and question service to public values, then the best approach is to develop indisputable evidence and then challenge doubters to dispute it.

Leadership Case. Steve Zabilski and the St. Vincent de Paul's Human Services Campus

This story focuses on a major initiative headed by Steve Zabilski, executive director of the Phoenix St. Vincent de Paul, to develop a "Human Services Campus," located in downtown Phoenix. From the outset, moving the services facility from its long-time location generated controversy, and the project faced particular resistance from the business community. While there are many lessons to be learned from this case, one of the most important is that it is often possible to overcome resistance to change, provided that one is prepared to listen and to accommodate and negotiate among multiple interests. One of several questions to ponder in this case is this: to what extent was Zabilski's leadership effective because, unlike top officials at nonprofit organizations, he has extensive business experience and considerable experience dealing with business executives?

Zabilski: St. Vincent de Paul's downtown office had its genesis in our Human Services Campus. Before we developed the Human Services Campus, we had been operating a dining room for the poor and homeless in a south Phoenix building for about 50 years.[4] When we first moved into our original building, we thought we would be there for about a year, not 50 years. The building was very old and broken down, and it wasn't designed to be a dining room.

About 15 years ago, we were able to convince the state legislature to give us a permit to build a new dining room. There was opposition from the business community; no business really wants a dining room for the poor and homeless next door to them. But we were already there operating our other programs. When we received the permit, people got interested, including some who had been opposed. We tried hard to focus on shared values rather than differences.

At that time, there was almost no dialog between the business and nonprofit communities. Some of the nonprofit community viewed the business leaders as greedy capitalists who only cared about their selfish interest. At the same time, the business community viewed the nonprofit community as naive do-gooders who don't understand anything about building an economy. While there may have been some truth to each of those views, those extreme views were the exception. Most did not have such extreme views. However, the point is there were these stereotypes and there wasn't any dialogue.

I think if there was anything I brought to St. Vincent de Paul, it was the notion that we have that dialogue. We met with three stakeholders—Jerry Colangelo,[5] who had a more positive view about what we were trying to do, but also Marty Shultz[6] and some people from the Phoenix Community Alliance,[7] and they were more skeptical, at least initially. Through our dialog, the business stakeholders began to understand that we, too, want businesses to be successful. We want them to have high return. That said, we also believed there were some things they needed to do to help homeless people.

After many discussions and some shared leadership, the results were very beneficial. What was originally going to be just a single dining room in a new building ended up being this beautiful campus that we have today, one that houses seven nonprofits. Both the county and business community took a leadership role. Today this development is a model for the whole country. People from all around the country come to Phoenix to visit and learn from the Human Services Campus. Some people focus on the buildings. While buildings are nice and impressive, good building design wasn't the secret. The secret was that there was a real dialogue. There was conversation, there was a focus on shared public values about how to help people.

It wasn't easy, and it wasn't just businesspeople who were opposed. Some of the St. Vincent people were very much opposed to moving from our old building. They felt comfortable there because they had been in it for so long. They said, "We're not moving, we're not moving an inch, this is sacred ground." But then there was compromise and a good outcome for all.

It made sense to me that the businesspeople did not want a homeless shelter anchoring the main thoroughfare between the state capitol and downtown. It's not like they were asking us to move to the middle of the desert 100 miles from here. They wanted us to move three or four blocks from the main business district. We did. We compromised. We found shared values, and we built something that none of us could have built by ourselves. The county and the business community and foundations provided more than $25 million. We have a beautiful facility, but, more importantly, we serve more than a thousand people every day. Every day. I watched the Super Bowl with more than 500 homeless people in our dining room downtown.

B&C: The case of the Human Services Campus is a great focal project for showing how public values organizations operate, how public values leadership works. When you were just getting this off the ground, what were some of the processes that you and others employed in order to generate trust and to get buy-in right at the beginning?

Zabilski: We got to know people. We met with David Smith, the county manager, every week for 18 months. The meeting wasn't simply to talk about what kind of table to put in the new room, or what color to paint the wall. It was really about building trust and understanding. That's the hard part. People who visit our Human Services Campus sometimes think, "Oh I'm just going to do the same thing that the Human Services Campus did. I'm going to get a lot of money and build some nice buildings and then good things will happen."

They're missing the point. It's never about the buildings. The mistake is that people want to see quick value. Our response is, "Well, I wish it was that simple, like instant pudding or a magic formula, but unfortunately it's not like that."

We were very fortunate to have people of goodwill on all sides: Jerry Colangelo, Marty Shultz, and Don Keuth,[8] public officials such as Jan Brewer and [County Supervisor] Mary Rose Wilcox. These community and business leaders were all terrific people who came together from different sectors and different political parties.

B&C: Staying in that era, the start-up period, were there any major obstacles that required some creative solutions?

Zabilski: Very much so. There was a real concern on the part of the local community that our programs would make downtown Phoenix a magnet for every homeless person in North America or the western United States. We had to work hard to convince people that helping the homeless was a good idea. Their concerns were legitimate, and we had to convince them that we could accomplish our goals without completely changing the character of downtown Phoenix. Even today, there are still concerns about impacts on property values, and we have to worry about this as we expand. There is still the view "I am all for expansion but do the expansion somewhere else."

We understood the concerns. We didn't want every homeless person in North America to be there either. That's the last thing we want. We can't help everyone. What we wanted to be able to do was effectively help people who were already in Phoenix, and especially to help them transition out of poverty, to give them a chance to have a home. That was the big message we had to convey, that our programs are not about attracting homeless people to come live in Phoenix, but to help those already here to get their life back together.

Bozeman and Crow Comments

There are many lessons in the Human Services Campus case—focusing on shared values rather than divisive issues, meeting face-to-face and regularly to engender trust, fighting against stereotypes based on institutional type—but of particular interest to us is one that does not exactly jump out. Zabilski noted that many of his dedicated and loyal staff were just as opposed to the move as were some of the businesspersons. This special kind of inertia does not receive enough attention. It is easy enough to chalk such reluctance up to obstructionism or lack of commitment, but that is rarely what is going on in staff opposition to massive changes entailed in relocation. Few people find it easy to give up the familiar, especially a comfortable familiar, for the unknown. Moves are personally disruptive. In addition to the obvious problems of just moving offices and physical assets, perhaps habits are disrupted. Commuting patterns change. One suddenly does not know the best places to go to lunch. The longtime office neighbor may no longer be a neighbor.

Leadership Case. Brian and Kelly Swette
and Sweet Earth Natural Foods

Throughout the book, we emphasize the idea of sector agnosticism, the proposition that no sector owns public values (and the less delightful proposition that any sector can thwart public values). However, relatively few private-sector firms are premised on public values, even when the firm includes public values among its motivations. The case of Brian and Kelly Swette's Sweet Earth Natural Foods shows that it is possible and can even be profitable to have public values at the forefront.[9]

We provide a little more background here than for some of the other cases because Brian and Kelly Swette have an especially interesting path to public values work. Brian grew up in Lake Havasu, Arizona, and attended Arizona State University, majoring in economics. He later entered a special training program at Procter & Gamble and then began working for PepsiCo, where two life-changing events occurred: becoming vice president for marketing and, more importantly, meeting his future wife, Kelly, an industrial engineer knowledgeable about production.

Brian went on to become the chief operating officer at eBay, at a time when the company was taking off, and earned a bunch of money, enough to make the family financially independent. One of his interests after leaving eBay was environmental sustainability, and, as an ASU alumnus, he became engaged with ASU's new Sustainability Institute, joining its board of advisors. He and Kelly invested in ASU and helped create what is now known as the Swette Center for Environmental Biotechnology, focusing on fundamental science related to biological engineering and genetic engineering to produce solutions related to sustainability.

After working as CEO of Burger King, he learned a great deal about the realities of how food systems work, a long-standing interest of Kelly's, and when Brian left the position at Burger King, he and Kelly decided to start a new company, one dedicated to improving food and food services and committed to environmental sustainability.

Swette: We established Sweet Earth to advance two of the large challenges in the country, which are sustainability and health. In our view, a good strategy in helping move those goals forward is plant-based eating. Our strategy to make plant-based eating appealing was to find culinary, globally inspired foods that we could provide to the mainstream of America. We like to say it was the democratization of culinary food that is good for you.

B&C: Well, that certainly sounds like clear-cut public values motivation.

Swette: People tend to look at the really big problems, like poverty, world hunger, poor health, greenhouse gases, and global climatic change and assume there's nothing they can do. Our view is there is one behavior everyone engages in that affects all of these problems: the choices all of us make every day when we choose what to eat. By changing what we eat, we can change the groceries supermarkets sell, and the produce grown in the area, and actually, little by little, shape food policy in the United States and in the world.

For us, a first step in the right direction was starting this little plant-based food company. We took all the things that we've learned in our years of business experience and focused our company on a niche of consumers who were environmentally focused but had great expectations for healthier and, at the same time, more interesting culinary food. If we started small, and moved out from there, wouldn't that be a nice little business? It turned out there were a lot of people that felt the way we did. Yet, there weren't products on the market that really addressed what they were looking for, products speaking to them about a broader lifestyle, the concerns they had as individuals, and their ability to make changes.

We've been advocates for what we call the "art of mindful eating." It's an attempt to encourage people to become more knowledgeable and self-aware. You take into account how your actions affect every level. Our feeling is, why would you not do that with food? So even if you're just making a frozen meal, why wouldn't you want to have beautiful color and texture and flavors that make you think of, or connect you to, other cultures and traditions? Why would you not want aroma? Even if you're eating alone, all of these things elevate the meal, the mood, your personal stance, and your view of the world and allow you to appreciate a very humble, simple thing. That was the approach we took to everything. Every dish needed to be special and worthy and include all those elements of connection—taste, texture, aroma, flavor, and a story. Just as important was the desire to contribute to sustainability.

We also wanted to enable people to make a living off of their passions. So we had hundreds of thousands of indigenous people in Mexico selling things they cared about. We were interested in helping establish open, democratized markets that had social good because people could get economic remuneration and freedom from that, but also pursue things they cared passionately about, namely, high-quality agricultural products. Our partners produce everything from tortillas to fungi.

B&C: How do you choose your partners? What were your criteria for good partners and partnerships?

Swette: We have standards as part of our mission to promote more organic and non-GMO foods. Right now, only 1% of the agriculture in the United States is organic, and yet if you asked people whether they want to eat pesticides and want added hormones and preservatives in their food, they would say no. Presented with a choice, many consumers are choosing more organic. They don't want to have their food genetically modified to accept pesticides. We thought if we made the use of organic, non-GMO foods part of our sourcing policy and bundled it into the price, that makes the choice simpler. So, we use the Far West Fungi people, who have a small business right around the corner from us. We also use Monterey Mushroom because they're local and they produce a great product.

We wanted to support some new emerging and Hispanic businesses, so we helped the tortilla supplier you see on our website [https://www .sweetearthfoods.com/] qualify as a business. We helped them bring their standards up to what they needed to supply our excellent food. We worked with them on custom recipes that were superior quality and allowed us to offer our customer a unique product. It's possible to help simplify choices for consumers. We help consumers make smart food choices that also honor and sustain the land.

Bozeman and Crow Comments

The Sweet Earth case is notable for many reasons, but not least for providing evidence that a private-sector company can thrive while being strongly committed to achieving public values. As we have mentioned many times, a great many businesses contribute to public values, but most often as secondary to their primary objectives of profit and growth, and typically the amount of resources put into the public values effort is a relatively small fraction of the resources going to the main lines of business. Such is not the case for Sweet Earth. The company was begun with public values in mind, and the company founders are very much self-conscious about the public values mission and supportive of it.

In addition to providing strong evidence that for-profit businesses can have central public values missions while making a profit, the case is important because it illustrates a strategy that is frequently and often effectively followed by public values leaders: achieving your organization's objectives by helping others achieve theirs. Almost all the cases and anecdotes in our book show the importance of organizational partnership, but the Sweet Earth strategy is a different sort of partnership. Not only do they choose organizational partners on the basis of shared values, but they also seek to achieve public values by helping strengthen and sustain businesses that share their values. If one starts a business having primary public values objectives, then it is natural to seek like-minded partners, and then it is only a short step to helping sustain a network of organizations with shared public values. Sweet Earth is in many ways a template for how people who are strongly committed to public values can succeed and flourish and help others, all within the framework of markets and profit making.

Leadership Case. Ed Zuercher and Light-Rail to Phoenix

In the early 1980s, Phoenix was one of the largest US cities that still sorely lagged behind in its public transportation, a vital concern in a city with sometimes dangerous heat in the summer, as well as one that is spread out and has low density. The face of public transit began to change in 1985 when the Arizona State Legislature passed legislation allowing citizens of Maricopa County (greater Phoenix) to vote on a sales tax that would be earmarked for funding regional improvements in transportation and would also create the Regional Public Transportation Authority (RPTA). The sales tax was approved, and, significantly, other revenue measures were passed in regional cities, including Tempe and Mesa, during the early 1990s. After the RPTA had established an extensive bus service by 2003, Phoenix and surrounding cities looked to develop a light-rail, which began operation in 2008. Unlike the bus service, the light-rail was accompanied by some significant challenges, especially the fact that street construction requirements were extensive and disruptions unavoidable. Further, rail service is inherently limited in its coverage; thus, the politics of rail service proved complex. Ed Zuercher was city manager of Phoenix for much of the time during the development of the light-rail and played a key role in its establishment. This case focuses on the rigors of developing this public values–focused project.

Zuercher: When I was in graduate school [public administration at University of Kansas], I learned that public policy entails balancing competing American values of representation or responsiveness, equity, individual rights, and efficiency.[10] What I often find is that when you decide which of those values predominates, it provides a signpost as to what you should be doing. When I was in school, we were in the middle of the whole Gaebler and Osborne *Reinventing Government* stuff.[11] Efficiency was presumed to be the driving force in government. It often became the predominant value. The problem is that efficiency values don't help much when we are considering public transit systems and accessibility for people with disabilities.

In Phoenix, the Americans with Disabilities Act conversation drove much of public transit development. We had to find better measures than just efficiency if we were going to have accessibility. At that time, I remember having many conversations about money and the costs of accessibility. Of course, 20 years later, there's not even an efficiency argument that gets made when it comes to the Americans with Disability Act—people no longer even question the value of a wheelchair-accessible bus or a light-rail system that's built at levels where disability access is prominent. The value that triumphed in this case was not efficiency, but the rights of individuals.

But public transit is not only about accessibility and rights. That's sort of the framework I come to it from—balancing values, pointing out value traps where people may be too focused on the value that they are exalting, not considering other competing values. Where we get in trouble is when we think there's only one value and that anybody who disagrees with that is wrong.

B&C: Who was responsible for formulating the vision behind Phoenix public transit?

Zuercher: Early on it was the political leadership. Skip Rimsza (former Phoenix mayor) recognized that the differentiation and the viability of central Phoenix was going to depend, in the long term, on improved mobility. We had to expand our concept of mobility from mobility equals freeways to mobility equals people moving in many different ways—how long it takes you to get from one place to another and not how many miles of freeway you have between this point and that point. We felt that if you're depending on freeways to be able to build your way out of congestion and intensity of development, you're going to fail. You can't expand the arterials without destroying the very places that people are trying to get to.

Light-rail was seen as the way for mobility to happen. That was built into a transit tax proposal by a conservative Republican mayor who understood the value of mobility for the survival of the central part of his city. There were objections, but they had to be overcome. Light-rail provides mobility but also spurs development. When a developer looks out their window and sees tracks on the ground, they believe there's going to be transit there for 50 or 80 years. They don't have the same feeling about a bus. All those things played into the ability to get the public to tax themselves to build this system. Once the system was built, the momentum built. They saw the ASU development downtown and the downtown campus, the light-rail link to Tempe and the Tempe ASU campus, the route along north Central Avenue, and they began to think "Where's mine?" as opposed to "Why are you doing this?"

B&C: When this project began, there was opposition. What was the nature of the opposition? To what extent were people like you who were committed to this set of public values able to win them over or at least accommodate the opposition?

Zuercher: I think the nature of the opposition had to do with a very narrow focus on what money means in the "right now." How much is it going to cost us to build this today? And there was a lack of imagination about a world where ever-expanding lanes of road aren't possible. The transportation answers for a long time had been, "Everybody should have their own car and we should have enough freeways so that everyone can get in their car and easily travel to wherever they wish to go." Of course, it's just not possible in a rapidly growing and urbanizing environment. People didn't have the imagination to see something other than a freeway or a street. That took political vision.

Changing minds and changing values was a long process. We first tried in 1997 and lost. The voters weren't ready to embrace a tax increase for a heavy investment in rail. By 2000, the freeways were built and traffic to central Phoenix was intensifying. How were we going to continue this growth? By then the construction interests started understanding that pouring concrete for light-rail is the same as pouring concrete for roads. It's the same kind of business for the contractors; they'll make the money with steel and concrete, just a different way of doing it. People began understanding what urbanization meant here in Phoenix and began to see that more freeways in the urban center was not the answer.

As I said, it took political leadership to bring together a diverse group of people. It was the mayor and the council that understood that diverse leadership was important; in building the plan, we had to have the private sector, the nonprofit sector, and the city all together. We also had the Chamber of Commerce and specific and individual businesses that had an interest in mobility. We had interest groups like the disability community for whom mobility does not necessarily mean a freeway. Then we had government, which ultimately built this thing.

The key was bringing the right people together and then letting them organize the plan themselves and find that common ground. It had to be convened by the government. I think that's an important role that we play now—we're a convener, not the ones with all the ideas. That's part of a change in Phoenix, I think, in the last 20 years.

B&C: Among those people who were not actively engaged or supportive, how did you accommodate them? What about the people who were initially opponents and who remained opponents?

Zuercher: Some of them couldn't be accommodated because they weren't interested in rational dialogue, facts, data, or anything other than their political position. You have to identify that motivation and then just move on from those people. It's important to find the rational spokespeople from the nontraditional sectors. For example, the president of the Chamber of Commerce stands up and says, "This is important because it's going to make it possible for our workers to get to work," or the disability community says, "This is important because it's going to make it possible for our folks to get to jobs." You frame the discussion not about social service, but about economic development, jobs, and education. The school districts stand up and say, "This is about getting our children to school." You begin to change the dialogue. The opponents wanted the dialogue to be about, "You're wasting money on something that other people are going to use."

Our job was to put a face on who the people using the light-rail are and to make everyone understand that maybe they were going to use the light-rail themselves or, if not, their administrative staff would use it or their minimum-wage employees, or people wanting to get to the airport. We had to convince people there would be a competitive advantage for them because their employees would have a better way to get to work than if they just depended on streets and freeways.

B&C: During this process of developing support for the light-rail, was there any sort of racial or economic class problems that had to be confronted?

Zuercher: It's not an absolute no or an absolute yes. There were pockets. There were places we knew the line would never go. There would just be too much opposition. It wasn't particularly feasible. But, in general, there really wasn't much division on the basis of race and income, not nearly to the extent that you see in many other cities.

Those sorts of divides are much less intense in Phoenix than in some other places.

B&C: I would imagine given the nature of this project that you had certain cleavages that were based largely on geography. If so, how do those play out?

Zuercher: Interestingly enough, some of the best voter support for the transit program came from parts of Phoenix that weren't going to be on light-rail for years or maybe ever. North Phoenix, east Phoenix, north-central Phoenix. It was the people who recognized the value of mobility for their city generally, and who also understood the argument about students and low-income workers having mobility, who could see their way to support it.

Bozeman and Crow Comments

"Where we get in trouble is when we think there's only one value and that anybody who disagrees with that is wrong." Ed Zuercher's statement is very much in line with our pragmatism proposition, and we observe, again and again, that people are more likely to accomplish large-scale objectives, including public values–based objectives, if they have some ability to see others' values, acknowledge their legitimacy, and work toward a compromise solution. That does not mean that public values projects thrive only through compromise. Sometimes the power of the zealot rises to the fore, such as with the single-minded public values leader John van Hengel, who began the world's first food bank. But on most occasions, and especially when there are many and diverse conflicting values and needs, an ability to empathize with others and to work with them is an absolute necessity.

Zuercher also noted that sometimes people do not have the imagination to see the finished product and the changes it makes in the status quo. This is entirely understandable, especially in a disruptive technology that has far-reaching social, economic, and public values implications. But part of being a public values leader is to have the vision and make other people see it as well—if not the entirety of the vision at least the part that will most strongly affect them.

Leadership Case. Freeman Hrabowski
and the UMBC Choice Program

In the extensive commentary provided below, Dr. Freeman Hrabowski, long-time president of the University of Maryland–Baltimore County (UMBC), focuses on a university program that many view as a model for university engagement with the surrounding community. The UMBC Choice Program works with "at-risk" children in the Baltimore area, not as a direct effort to enroll them in their university, or necessarily any university, but to give them knowledge and support that increases the likelihood of their becoming productive citizens, improving their socioeconomic prospects and their individual safety and well-being. One of the many notable things about this public values project is the extensive buy-in of many diverse groups, some of which do not typically interact with one another.

Hrabowski: The Choice Program is a signature program at UMBC involving civic engagement, and we have been doing this since 1989. It began when Sargent Shriver[12] called his former deputy Adam Yarmolinsky, who was provost of UMBC at the time, and my boss (I was vice provost). Sargent Shriver asked Adam to help his son, Mark Shriver, who was beginning a program in inner-city Baltimore involving first-time offenders. Keep in mind that UMBC is near the BWI Airport, a suburban area with almost 600 acres that is about five miles from the inner city. We had always been focused on what happens in the suburbs and in Washington, DC, and less so on inner-city Baltimore. But Adam asked me to support Mark.

We came up with the idea for a program working with the families of first-time offenders of nonviolent crimes between the ages of 8 and 17, mainly boys of color. We included a few low-income white kids and a few girls, but mainly black and Hispanic boys. When the boys go to court, the judge gives the parent or grandparent a choice of either having the child go to jail for six months to a year or coming to the UMBC Choice Program.

Mark and I went to a major community meeting to talk about it. The community was all African Americans. The community members at the meeting wanted to know why they would trust what they called "that big white school out there in the Catonsville suburbs" to take their kids in. Fortunately, I had worked at an inner-city college and knew enough people in inner-city Baltimore that I could just be frank. I said I'm not a politician; I'm not here to promise you anything. Think about why we would want to do this. We're not getting any money out of this. I mean why would we want to do this for any reason other than because we care? You either believe that or not, but I hope you will give us a chance. But if you want us to go away, that is up to you.

I wanted them to know we were not afraid to speak the truth. The truth is this was not about money. This was about helping children. It was about building trust, but I had to use the tone that they had used with me. They had to know I was no-nonsense, and I was not a politician trying to sell them something in return for votes. The key is that I was able to use my street cred, as the kids would say, in inner-city Baltimore. I had spent ten years working on issues of poverty at an inner-city college there before coming here, and I could use some of the respect people had for me to say, "Listen, I am there [UMBC] now because this is the place that cares about people of all races. What you need to do is just to watch what we do, and you will see it. You have to give us a chance. The program will grow, and we'll be able to help more and more kids."

The community leaders were willing to do that with the understanding that we would have regular sessions, we would show them what was going on and give them a chance to come to the campus and get a sense of it for themselves. Because the environment on campus is so different from their lives in Cherry Hill, which is one of the most impoverished parts of Baltimore, it helped to have them visit and see what we were doing. I mean they come out here, it's a lovely 600 acres. The contrast with Cherry Hill is between night and day. So, the community gave us a chance, and we brought those children to our campus. And we have served more than 10,000 families over this past almost 30 years.

B&C: How did you go about building trust among such a disparate group?

Hrabowski: The key is that we started out developing trust and familiarity with community leaders, but we also worked hard with the judicial system, the criminal justice system, particularly the juvenile part. We were able to build a partnership with the Department of Juvenile Services that allowed us to get a certain amount of money, I think it was $5,000 per child, to keep them in the program for a year with the understanding that if, at any point, we couldn't make progress and couldn't get the young people to do what we needed, they would then go to jail. That was the leverage we had all along; the alternative to our program was jail. We worked with the families too: grandmothers, mothers, and fathers (when we could get them to participate), getting the families to have conversations about their children with UMBC colleagues, including faculty and students from social work, psychology, and other areas.

Here's what surprises people. We took on the responsibility for making sure the kids got up and got to school. We brought them on campus several days a week. We even set up sites out in their community. We were working with them, literally, 24 hours a day, seven days a week. We still do that. We hire young people, usually in their early twenties, and pay them a little bit, around $20,000. We've actually had returning Peace Corps volunteers involved with the program. There are also lots of people who come here for graduate degrees, and we hire them as youth counselors or supervisors. We have UMBC students who are very involved in the tutoring and the counseling. These children are on campus seven days a week. They get a chance to play a little basketball, but they also have to do math and reading.

B&C: This program was probably a challenge for some of the faculty who were more accustomed to traditional college students. Any trust problems among university faculty and staff?

Hrabowski: The fact is we needed to build trust not only in the community, but trust on this campus. The first question that colleagues raised was what do you mean you're going to bring hundreds of criminals to the campus? From inner-city Baltimore? But I had the support of Adam, our president at the time, and our chancellor, Michael Hooker (wonderful guy, now deceased).

B&C: And what about the children and the UMBC students?

Hrabowski: I'm accustomed to working with inner-city children. I'm a mathematician and I do math problems with them. What always surprises people is I can always tell the children who have become very sophisticated in drug dealing. They have been accustomed to doing math in their work with drugs. They have been trained by the streets. This is very different from the middle-class, higher education world here or anyplace else. These are children who are watching you very carefully. They rarely smile, but when I give them a math problem, often they are the first ones to solve it. The challenge we face is to get them to understand there are better ways to keep them from the two outcomes that I always talk to the kids about: if you don't stop with the drug dealing and all of that, you're going to be either in jail or dead.

The first response that you hear from the boys will be, "Well, you don't get the street cred until you go to jail. We know we're not gonna live to be 30, so what are you talking about?" That's in contrast to my middle-class and upper-middle-class kids on this campus of all races. Remember, we have students from 100 countries, and from the wealthiest parts of our state. One of our values says, "to those whom much is given, much is required."

Many of our students decide to continue in their majors, but to focus on the issues of underprivileged people. Whether it's in medicine, law, social work, or whatever. The program finally got a lot of support from the campus because people saw the results, the impact that it was having on not only the children, but on my students and on people involved in the program and its evaluation. In any of our initiatives, we always ask, "Are these children getting educations? Are they getting jobs?"

People ask if, when they finish the Choice Program, will they come to UMBC and enroll as college students. Usually, no. These are children at the bottom. We have been working to get them to read, we are working to get them through high school. We're working to get them through community college, or their other options, including good jobs. We have started a number of partnerships with people in the region so that they can get jobs, get experience, and begin that education through a community college as we work to build the reading skills and the math skills.

B&C: It looks like you've identified a series of problems, getting buy-in, among other things. Are there other obstacles that proved equally difficult?

Hrabowski: Yeah, we have funding from the state, and state politics change. We go through Republican and Democratic governors, and usually the new governor who comes in doesn't want to keep on with the programs of governors who came before. The idea of keeping a sustained effort going through Democratic and Republican governors is a challenge. Nobody is interested in programs that other people will get credit for, that other people started.

What saved us, and this is another value that we talk about a lot, was rigorous evaluation of whatever we were doing, and we actually publish a lot on evaluations. We've got a number of people who are working on rigorous evaluations of the Choice program. These evaluations prove that a child is much more likely not to go back into the system if they'd come through our program. The evaluations show that program participants finish high school and don't go to jail.

Our evaluations go all the way back, to K through 12. We are always looking at trends. We are looking at what's happening in more recent years with the violence in Baltimore after the Freddie Gray incident.[13] We are looking at the proportion of kids from different zip codes who are getting into difficulty. We are looking at relationships between the police and the children, because we have developed strong relationships working on that through art, of all things, and restorative circles having police and children working together. It helps to have police officers who are of all races, but also who see juvenile offenders as children, not as thugs. As a police officer gets to know a child better, that child becomes more of a child, maybe more like the police officer's son, not a thug. We are working to build those relationships.

Again, what makes this so strikingly visible here is you go from the campus to that Cherry Hill, and you see the significance of the growing inequality gap. We've had three-quarters of a billion dollars of construction on this campus in recent years. The only disruption we've had here is building and cranes. When the Freddie Gray stuff was coming up, people were calling saying, "Are your students okay?" It was hard to explain how different it is within five miles.

We've had many conversations in the academic program about those differences, about inequality, but also about the use of analytics in understanding what we're doing to make a difference in particular zip codes where children are the least advantaged. We do that through the Choice Program, but also through some very rigorous programs in reading and mathematics with Lincoln Elementary, for example. We are piloting efforts to substantially increase the number of children who actually can come up to the state's average in math and verbal, 90% of whom are on the free lunch program. Unfortunately, in Baltimore, when you look at third and fourth graders, not even 20% will come up to proficiency on the Common Core tests right now. We are moving toward 50% in our schools. We are analyzing every step of the way. Not just test scores, but attitudes, involvement of the parents. These are Hispanic, black, and a few white kids, but they are 90% free lunch. This is what I want you to hear, and this is one of those values: I am always saying to my colleagues, it's not enough to write books and do research. If you're in education, we should all be out in the schools, understanding children and teachers and families' outcomes and writing about those things.

It's not enough to be smart. Most of the (Choice Program) kids we work with are smart, they're just not well educated when they come to us. We have learned to stop talking about particular children as smart or not. Because when you say "that's the smart group over here," what are you saying to the other two-thirds? What the hell are you saying about the rest of the people? You tell people they're not smart, and it's like a self-fulfilling prophesy. It's awful. What we do is say high achievement is about grit. It's about perseverance, resilience, never, never, never giving up. We celebrate people who didn't have all the benefits, didn't have all the advantages, didn't have SAT prep, or AP classes. We build on whatever they have when they come to us.

We are a hungry place. We have a saying: success is never final. We are always working to be better. We call UMBC the "House of Grit." When they arrive, we say, "Welcome to the House of Grit." Our mascot is a Chesapeake Bay retriever. The mascot's name? True Grit.

Bozeman and Crow Comments

True grit would be an appropriate motto for those interested in achieving public values; determination is the one characteristic that all public values leaders have in common because it is perhaps the only unchanging prerequisite. But aside from excellent mottos, many elements of the Choice Program case speak to public values leadership. Trust is an important element of this story. True, engendering trust is a requirement of most public values efforts, but the difference here is the vast divides among parties. In the previous case, the Salvation Army's Human Resources Campus, the mistrusting parties were ones often found in public values cases—the public values aspirants and the established business interests. The challenges in such cases are formidable, as the case shows, but pale in comparison to those of the Choice Program case, where trust must be developed among people of different educational backgrounds, different races, different ages, and in many cases within a surrounding atmosphere of well-earned distrust owing to mistreatment, neglect, and even hostility. But the Choice Program case shows that even extreme mistrust can be overcome with frequent interaction, empathy, focus on shared values, a let-us-show-not-just-talk approach, and a little bit of street cred.

Another public values conundrum illustrated in the case is the problem of sustained effort. The Choice Program has survived for a long time and, most importantly, thrived during periods of partisan and political change. As Hrabowski observes, it is second nature for politicians to want to have their own policy victories rather than embrace those of the previous incumbent. But the Choice Program has managed to adapt to political change. To some degree this has been accomplished by "evidence-based public values." Perhaps because of his background as a mathematician, Hrabowski has insisted on careful measurement of the program and its accomplishments, making sure that the resultant evidence is provided, in the most palatable manner possible, to political decision makers. To be sure, evidence is typically not sufficient to carry the day by itself. Politicians are known for being able to turn a blind eye to evidence that contrasts with their own strongly held beliefs or their perceived political self-interest. But evidence, when combined with a strong and consensus-based public values problem and, not least, a master salesman such as Hrabowski, can help counter the tendency to disown other peoples' policy children.

Public Values Leadership—Conclusions

One good reason to develop and analyze case studies is to identify points of commonality among the cases, but historians know that idiosyncrasy and unique elements of cases are often just as edifying as generalizations. Thus, for example, the Choice Program may not have thrived except for particular characteristics of President Hrabowski, many of them unique to him. Likewise, the Bush family history of attending to issues pertaining to mental and physical disabilities was a distinctive resource Governor Bush was able to bring to his work.

Considering these cases together, we see strong elements of both commonality and uniqueness. However, it is easier and, in some ways, more fruitful to conclude with tentative generalizations, in part because the unique elements are manifest in reading of the cases. One point these cases have in common is the idea of mutable leadership or, related, mutable leadership teams. While these are stories of strong leaders, none is the heroic leader of myth and legend. In each case it was vital to interest others in the mission and to encourage them to contribute, to have them buy into the vision.

Related to the team-building aspects of leadership, each of the cases suggests that developing trust is a prerequisite for many public value leadership endeavors. Trust was vital to Freeman Hrabowski's effort to bring together persons unacquainted and in some ways hostile to one another, as well as to Governor Bush's efforts to galvanize support among families and the disabled persons who had been poorly served by the state system. Brian and Kelly Swette had a very different sort of trust challenge—gaining the trust of consumers, consumers bombarded with marketing and advertising from larger food purveyors and consumers who had understandable difficulties working through the maze of claims about "natural," "organic," "healthy," and "sustainable" foods. Developing nontraditional suppliers also required mutual trust.

Both Ed Zuercher and Steve Zabilski faced distrust between skeptical businesspersons and public values advocates. Ed Zuercher had to bring people together to work on light-rail, despite the political and historical complexities and the very different views in different neighborhoods. Likewise, Steve Zabilski's effort to locate a major homeless facility right in the middle of downtown Phoenix required not only negotiation among parties with different interests but also trust and the ability to see and to respect diverse views.

This particular set of cases underscores a lesson that pervades this book: that no single sector owns public values. Here we have cases involving universities, nonprofits, government, and a business firm, each contributing to public values, usually in partnership with other sectors. The requirements for public values attainment may vary somewhat by sector, but the possibilities for achieving public values are there for those willing to pursue them.

Query for Readers

We did not choose the cases on the basis of the sector or background of the leaders, but, as you see, it turns out that they are quite diverse and include an elected politician, two from industry, the head of a nonprofit, a college president, and a city manager. It would not have been possible to develop a much more diverse set even if we had set out to do so. Here is a difficult question for the reader, one that will perhaps draw from your own experience: to what extent do you think that these particular job sectors require distinctive leadership skills, and to what extent do you think that leadership skills are similar from one sector to another? Yes, this is a classic question in the leadership literature (e.g., Hooijberg and Choi 2001; Hamlin 2004; Schimmoeller 2010; Vogel and Masal 2015), but one that remains controversial. You and your speculation and insight, especially if experience based, will be just as relevant as those of the people who have studied this question in systematic research.

7

Public Values Case

St. Mary's Food Bank and the Durability of the Public Values Leadership

The term "public values organization" should not and need not be used recklessly. Organizations can and do make tremendous contributions to public values even if they are not full-time devotees of public values. Businesses sometimes contribute greatly to public values while at the same time aggressively and competitively pursuing profits. Government organizations in many instances pursue public values, but any student of government organizations knows that they also pursue other values, not least of them their own longevity. Political regimes change, and sometimes political leaders and agency heads seek to overturn actions that many would consider public values–based programs. The public value organization equation is not always a simple one.

Consider the give-and-take over the years at the Environmental Protection Agency, where leaders (e.g., Ann Gorsuch during the Reagan administration, Scott Pruitt in the Trump administration) arrived with the avowed intention of dismantling programs advancing conservation, sustainability, or environmental protection, arguably in pursuit of the goals of coalitions of private interests. Another example of lead-to-cutback is Rick Perry, the Trump administration's secretary of energy. Previously the governor of Texas, Rick Perry was appointed secretary of energy notwithstanding (or more likely because of) a campaign pledge to close down the Department of Energy during his unsuccessful run for the Republican presidential nomination.

More recently, consider the initiative to move significant parts of the US Department of Agriculture (USDA) from Washington, DC, to Kansas City and the Department of the Interior to Colorado. As reported in the *Washington Post* (Guarino 2019), Secretary of Agriculture Sonny Perdue announced a plan to move both the National Institute of Food and Agriculture (which funds more than $1.7 billion in research) and the Economic Research Service out of the District of Columbia to Kansas City. According to Purdue, this was for cost savings. Indeed, cost savings would occur, not least because nearly two-thirds of the affected 400 employees, many of them highly trained experts with special skills, refused to be reassigned and would leave their jobs or be fired. When this was announced at a Republican Party fundraiser, Nick Mulvaney claimed that the attrition would help "drain the swamp," bragging about the fact that "half the people quit." He went on to say, "By simply saying to people, 'You know what, we're going to take you outside the bubble, outside the Beltway, outside this liberal haven of Washington, D.C., and move you out in the real part of the country,' and they quit—what a wonderful way to sort of streamline government, and do what we haven't been able to do for a long time." This is not the first time, nor probably the last, that a public official in charge of a federal agency will confuse draining the swamp with a brain drain of professional expertise. But the basic point is quite simple: government agency does not equal public value.

In this chapter, we examine the history of an organization that can, with no caveats, be deemed a public values organization, seeking public values not as a sideline or as one socially responsible program among many private values–based programs, and not on a sometime basis, but throughout its history. St. Mary's Food Bank was the first food bank established in the United States, and perhaps the world. It is also the largest and provides millions of pounds of food to hungry people, at no cost to the recipient. In examining St. Mary's Food Bank, we can learn about the winding path of innovation and innovation diffusion, how to mobilize others in pursuit of public values goals, how to develop trust among public values partners, and the ways in which leadership styles need to be tailored to the context of public values achievement. Before considering St. Mary's and its history, let us first consider the case of one family and their typical struggle to ensure food security.

Mini-case. The Story of Jennifer Williams

Just three years ago, at the age of 19, Jennifer Carpenter (not her real name) was living her dream. True, it was a modest dream, at least compared to some, but experiences condition dreams. Raised by her grandmother, Mary Carpenter, Jennifer had lived most of her life in various Decatur (Georgia) public housing apartments. Jennifer never knew her father. Jennifer's mother, Amanda, an addict and small-time purveyor of drugs, divided her time between jail and the residence of her boyfriend du jour. Jennifer was barely acquainted with her mother, who visited only on Christmas and Thanksgiving and, even then, spent most of the time arguing with Grandma Mary, not only about the "drug life" but also about possible heavenly retribution. Grandma Mary was a devout and lifelong Baptist.

Jennifer was one of five children, only two by the same father. Grandma Mary worked at a downtown Decatur diner, and most of the time she was able to support Jennifer and the one brother with whom she lived. Through her own good character and determination, reinforced by Grandma Mary, Jennifer graduated from Decatur High School, where she was in the marching band. She planned to enroll in DeKalb Community College. Jennifer put that plan on hold the summer after graduation when she met Chad Williams, who had recently become a regular at the Sunday Night Baptist Training Union meetings. Chad had moved to Decatur just a couple of months before from Dothan, Alabama, where for most of his life he worked on his uncle's farm. Chad, seven years older than Jennifer and now an assistant manager at a Stone Mountain tire store, was mature, godly, hardworking, and even handsome—just the sort of man Jennifer always dreamed about.

After only a month of dating, Chad asked Jennifer to move in with him. She declined. Jennifer was crazy in love with Chad but was not willing to disappoint Grandma Mary and "live in sin," as her grandma would think about it. A few weeks later, Chad asked Jennifer to marry him. They didn't wait. They went right to the courthouse. Jennifer Carpenter could not have been more pleased to become Jennifer Williams.

Chad and Jennifer rented a "luxury apartment" near Stone Mountain Park, in an apartment complex with a beautiful view of the huge granite mountain, a swimming pool, and their own reserved parking spot. They chose the two-bedroom model since Chad was anxious to be a dad. The second bedroom was soon put to use; Michael Williams was born after Jennifer had been married only 10 months. Jennifer loved Michael, she loved Chad, and she loved her life. She was looking into taking online courses at the community college, hoping to train to ultimately become a nurse. True, the romance had diminished. Chad was not home that much, preferring to spend time after work "going out with the boys," and he took less interest in Michael than she had hoped. He drank a little too much beer, but the beer just made Chad sleepy, not disagreeable. Generally, they got along fine, fighting only about small things, and she was just happy to have a good man. Both of them still attended church regularly, though now at the Calvary Church in nearby Snellville. On August 4, Jennifer and Chad celebrated their second wedding anniversary, and Jennifer used the occasion to announce a happy, if unplanned, event—a second child was on the way.

On August 7, the good life came to an abrupt end. In the early evening, a pair of uniformed sheriff's deputies knocked on the door and asked for a man named Chad Cotter. Jennifer smiled and said, "I'm sorry officers, but you have the wrong house, there is no Chad Cotter here." Her smile was interrupted by the sound of a commotion, and when she turned, she was astonished to see her husband bolting out the back door. There was a third policeman waiting for him there, and in short order Chad was in handcuffs.

Over the next day, a sad truth emerged. Jennifer was not legally wedded. Chad was, indeed, Chad Cotter, from Jacksonville, Florida. In Jacksonville, he had a wife and two children he had abandoned, all still living in Jacksonville. The authorities had been pursuing Cotter for three years, not only for failure to make child support payments but also because on his way out of Jacksonville he had stolen $4,000 from the auto body shop where he worked. Now, in addition to the robbery and the failure to pay child support, Chad Williams/Cotter was charged with bigamy. After a quick plea deal, he was sentenced to three years, to be served in a north Florida state penitentiary.

With no job and, suddenly, no source of income, Jennifer had to quickly make some decisions. She would have preferred to move back in with Grandma Mary, but that was not feasible. Grandma Mary did not have room in her small apartment and, worse, was very ill, likely to live less than a year. Jennifer soon discovered there was literally no money in the bank, nor, apparently, anywhere else. She suspected that Chad had a hidden bank account, but if so, she could not find it. Her "savings" included the two $20 bills she had in her pocketbook. When she tried to use their joint credit card, she found that Chad's attorney had closed the account. Chad's car had been repossessed, leaving her without transportation.

Jennifer did have some assets she could pawn. A neighbor drove her to the pawn shop, where she pawned the television, the music system, and a microwave oven. She tried to pawn her wedding ring, but the pawnbroker let her know that it was not gold but rather gold-plated over stainless steel, worth $10 or less when new. She left the pawn broker's shop with $157.

Jennifer had been poor most of her life, but not desperately poor. Now, she was. She took her remaining cash and went to the Big Lots to purchase much of her food, including large quantities of beef and chicken broth, closed-out pasta, and canned meat products that had not done well in the market—innovations such as chorizo-in-the-shell and cheese-filled Vienna sausage. She brought her remaining cash and a purse load of coupons to the Walmart, where she bought milk that was on sale, large quantities of grits and butter, several packages of dried beans, and vegetables that had been discounted because they were bruised or had nearly reached their sell-by date. She had not eaten chitterlings since her youth and was surprised to find that even this form of unappetizing (to her at least) protein had become quite a bit more expensive than she expected. Forget about bacon at $5.99 for 11 ounces! Jennifer began to apply the culinary arts of the desperate: watering down her food, making soup from nearly everything, dispensing meat chiefly as seasoning for beans. After a few weeks of stretching food beyond the hunger breaking point, Jennifer had begun to lose weight and to have a constant nagging hunger, not extreme but always there. More importantly, she was not sure that baby Michael was getting enough nutrition, and she was in great anguish about possible damage to the unborn child inside her.

Fortunately, Grandma Mary was, as ever, a rock of dependability. While Grandma Mary's health was failing, she remained loving, wise, and as cheerful as someone could be who had received a death sentence from her doctor. Concerned about Jennifer, whom she still saw regularly in church and with Sunday visits for dinner, Grandma Mary told Jennifer that she would like to help her develop a help network. After so many years living in Decatur public housing, Grandma Mary knew a great many people, all of whom had developed strong survival skills. Not only did Grandma Mary advise Jennifer, but she held a sort of block meeting with friends who could educate Jennifer on the art of making it as a single parent.

In short order, Jennifer learned from Grandma Mary's friends such mysteries as the ins and outs of the WIC program, the foods available from SNAP, and, most importantly, strategies for dealing with both the food and public housing bureaucracies. Just as importantly, she learned about the services of nonprofit helping organizations, including the Atlanta Community Food Bank, the Southwest Emergency Assistance Center, the Hosea Williams food pantry program, and various faith-based programs run by the Salvation Army, St. Vincent de Paul, and even her own church. Jennifer reacquainted herself with the MARTA transportation system and learned about the informal ride sharing among the residents of the city of Decatur's Swanton Heights public housing, where she would soon be living. One of the 98 units had become available, and she was moved up on the list owing to her status as a pregnant, single mother. To her great relief, one of her grandma's friends, who had worked at the Decatur Walmart since it opened in 2015, recommended Jennifer for a cashier's job, and Jennifer was hired, working 60 hours a week with overtime. Day care for little Michael remained a problem, but mothers in Swanton Heights took care of one another, and she was able to get reliable day care from a trusted neighbor.

By this point, Jennifer's dream life seemed a distant memory, but it also seemed that the nightmare life she had experienced for the past six weeks might be fading. Her fears about being homeless and about not having enough food for her children, though not entirely disappearing, were greatly reduced. Life once again seemed to hold some attractive possibilities.

Food Security as a Public Value

One could draw a number of lessons from the story of Jennifer Williams, lessons about resilience and about people in need helping one another. But perhaps the most universal lesson is about life's uncertainty. Life shifts unpredictably. Things seem to be going quite well, and then there is an unexpected second child, a dying grandmother, and a bigamist "husband." The factors implicated in a downward shift are not always the same. Sometimes it is poor or no insurance and a chronic illness, sometimes substance dependence, or sometimes being unexpectedly laid off from a good job at a time in life when one encounters age discrimination. Millions of Americans are just one really bad break away from homelessness and food insecurity. In the United States, with its accelerating income inequality, middle-income status no longer guarantees economic resilience. A 2019 study by the Federal Reserve (Brainard 2019) found that one-third of American families would not be able to meet an unexpected expense of just $400, some saying they would have to sell assets or take out a loan to meet the obligation and others saying they could not meet the expense under any circumstance. In the United States, with its rapidly expanding income inequality, middle-income status no longer ensures the ability to cope with even relatively minor financial setbacks, much less a job loss or major illness.

Even middle-income families are at risk for "food insecurity" (in today's parlance). Hunger is no longer just a "poor people problem" but also a problem for people who have nice houses and nice cars and good jobs but who are also highly leveraged with credit card debt or poor health insurance. Hunger is a problem that occupies every society, and there are few if any societies in which the problem is truly solved, including the United States. Food insecurity is inarguably a corner-stone of public values. No one but an extreme misanthrope would fail to see the humanitarian and social needs of ensuring that citizens have enough food and nutrition for good health.

The USDA provides definitions of food security, with "high food security" as the goal of government programs.[1] Most societies and governments in the world have a goal that citizens have "no reported indications of food access problems or limitations." But many people in the United States and elsewhere do not qualify as having high food security. Instead, they fall in one of three undesirable categories:

- **Marginal food security:** one or two reported indications, typically anxiety over food sufficiency or shortage of food in the house. Little or no indication of changes in diets or food intake.
- **Low food security:** reports of reduced quality, variety, or desirability of diet. Little or no indication of reduced food intake.
- **Very low food security:** reports of multiple indications of disrupted eating patterns and reduced food intake.

As we see in figure 2, according to the USDA's statistics on food security, those with low or very low food security are sometimes hungry, reporting routine anxiety about eating, losing weight, and skipping meals for lack of food.

Among families with very low food security, one-third reported they did not eat food for a whole day because there was not enough money for food, and 68% reported being hungry because they could not afford enough food. As a result of research from Feeding America in its Hunger in America 2014 study, we know about the sacrifices people who do not have enough money for food are required to make (in this case Feeding America clients):

- 69% report having to choose between food and utilities
- 67% have to choose between food and transportation
- 57% must choose between food and housing
- 40% water down food to make it last longer
- 35% pawn goods they own to buy food

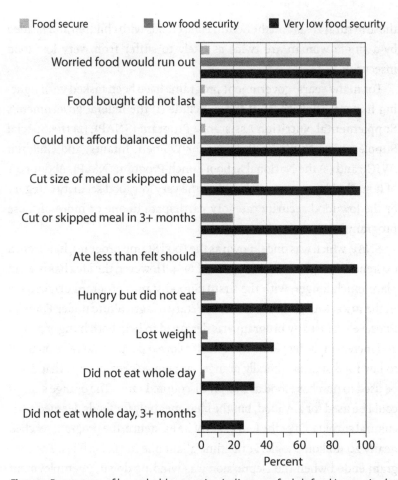

■ Food secure   ■ Low food security   ■ Very low food security

Figure 2. Percentage of households reporting indicators of adult food insecurity, by food security status, 2016. USDA, Economic Research Service, using data from the December 2016 Current Population Survey Food Security Supplement.

How many people in the United States suffer from food insecurity? Millions. According to USDA data, 5% of Americans are in the dire very low food security category—that is more than 15 million. While the problem affects all ages, all races, and every region of the country, food insecurity strikes harder for some groups than others. The very low food insecurity group is overrepresented (in terms of population prevalence) by persons living alone, Black and Hispanic households, and those in rural areas and the South. Households with children and headed by a single woman are twice as likely to suffer from very low food insecurity.

For many years, government programs have been tasked with fighting hunger. The largest of these include (1) the federal government's Supplemental Nutrition Assistance Program (SNAP); (2) the Special Supplemental Nutrition Program for Women, Infants, and Children (WIC); and (3) the National School Lunch Program (NSLP). About 60% of households categorized in either the very low food security category or the low food security category participate in one or more of these programs.

SNAP, which was once known as the Food Stamp program, has been in existence since the Food Stamp Act of 1964. However, the idea has been in place much longer, with the first US food stamp program originating in the 1930s with Henry Wallace, secretary of agriculture under Franklin Roosevelt. The early program was designed to help both hungry people and increasingly desperate farmers. It allowed people who were on relief to buy food stamps, literally orange- or blue-colored stamps that could be used to purchase food at sharply discounted rates. The orange stamps could be used for any food, but the blue ones only for foods deemed agricultural surplus. Over the four years of its existence, the program reached nearly 20 million people, at the time about one in six families. The program ended when the Depression was winding down, unemployment had been reduced, and farmers had greater ability to sell their produce.

The Food Stamp Act of 1964 accompanied President Johnson's War on Poverty. The official mission statement for the program was to strengthen the agricultural economy and provide improved nutrition for low-income households. (Early critics of the program felt that it was aimed more strongly at the first mission than the second; see MacDonald 1977; Levitan 2003.) Provisions of the Food Stamp Act included

- ability to purchase all foods, except alcoholic beverages and imported foods;
- prohibitions against discrimination on bases of race, religious creed, national origin, or political beliefs;

- the division of responsibilities between states (certification and issuance) and the federal government (funding of benefits and authorization of retailers and wholesalers), with shared responsibility for funding costs of administration;
- appropriations for the first year limited to $75 million; for the second year, to $100 million; and for the third year, to $200 million.

Today's SNAP is a good deal different in terms of the number of people served, the budget, and the fact that the program focuses more on poverty and hunger than agricultural surplus. In 1965, the Food Stamp program included only about half a million participants. The program grew, reaching 10 million by 1971, chiefly due to the geographic expansion of participation. By contrast, in April 2016 (the latest available data) SNAP included 43.6 million participants. It is the largest government-sponsored food assistance program in the nation.

Eligibility for SNAP requires that participants be at least 30% below the established federal poverty level. Currently, 44% of participants are children, two-thirds of them living in single-parent households. Other high-use groups include disabled persons and seniors. The majority are white (39.8%), with African Americans composing the second-largest group (25.5%). Undocumented immigrants are not eligible for SNAP, but documented immigrants who have lived in the United States for at least five years are eligible. Exceptions are in place for children, including those in foster care or under state supervision.

The average SNAP benefit changes over time with legislative additions or federal rules, but in 2015 the average SNAP client received a monthly benefit of $129.39, and households an average of $256.11. The use requirements differ relatively little from the original Food Stamp program but are spelled out much more specifically. The USDA, administratively responsible for SNAP, has developed a measure to calculate monthly allotment, its Thrifty Food Plan. The cost is calculated each month and adjusted. The 15 USDA Food Plan "market baskets" include rations of grains, vegetables, fruits, milk products, meat, and beans, all in accordance with the dietary allowances and guidelines issued by the USDA. The goal is to obtain adequate nutrition through a healthy and balanced diet.

The WIC program serves approximately 8 million people, more than half of them children, with nearly 2 million being infants. Unlike SNAP, the states administer WIC, and thus rules, eligibility, and benefits vary. In most states, WIC participants receive checks, vouchers, or debit cards aimed at helping clients supplement their diets. In many cases, participants receive WIC benefits at the grocery store, but in a few states there are WIC warehouses, or delivery is offered to a participant's residence. Food packages depend in part on the category or participants, with infants of course having different packages than the elderly. WIC foods include infant cereal, juice, eggs, milk, vegetables, infant formula, and baby foods, just to give some examples. Since WIC depends on local agencies, there is no equalization of funds, and thus recipients are prioritized. The first priority is pregnant women and women with infants, then children up to age 5.

The third element of the government-based anti-hunger programs is the NSLP, a federal program designed to provide a balanced school lunch for eligible children either for free or at a reduced price. School lunch programs have long been in place in the United States, including many operated by state and city governments. Two federal policies are particularly noteworthy: the National School Lunch Act and the Healthy, Hunger-Free Kids Act of 2010.

In 1946, the US Congress passed the National School Lunch Act. Section 2 of the act gave its purpose as "to safeguard the health and well-being of the Nation's children and to encourage the domestic consumption of nutritious agricultural commodities and other food, by assisting the States, through grants in aid and other means, in providing an adequate supply of food and other facilities for the establishment, maintenance, operation and expansion of nonprofit school lunch programs." Thus, as was the case with the Food Stamp program, the NSLP sought to achieve what was then viewed as two complementary objectives, attacking hunger and at the same time helping farmers and other agricultural interests. The act gave precise details about the apportionment of funds to the states, with the apportionment based on the number of schoolchildren in the respective states and the need for assistance, as determined by states' per capita income. The matching of federal to state funds was on a step basis, with a dollar-for-dollar match until 1950, then a $1.50-to-$1.00 match from 1951 to 1955, and thereafter two federal dollars for every one state dollar. Much of the actual implementation was left to local school boards, which could use the money not only for food but also for equipment (e.g., kitchen implements) and labor. The law also stipulated minimum nutrition requirements for the food the states offered in lunch programs. Lunches provided by programs included milk, cheese, fresh and processed meat, beans, peanut butter, eggs, and fruit and vegetables (usually canned to ensure storage life). The act was amended in 1962, chiefly to address perceived inequities in state funding, with a focus on participation rates and expansion to private and parochial schools. Calculation of apportionment was now according to more specific factors related to specific schools and school districts rather than broader state statistics.

The school lunch program is still in place, but in 2010 programs were to some extent coordinated after passage of the Healthy, Hunger-Free Kids Act of 2010 (updated through 2018). An objective of the act was to provide coordination among the NLSP, the School Breakfast Program, WIC, the Summer Food Service Program, and the Child and Adult Care Food Program, taking into account the total nutrition offered to those who participated in more than one program. The act also revisited and substantially revised nutrition standards, as well as setting new standards for data gathering and evaluation of programs.

With so many federal and state food assistance programs in place, one might easily begin to assume that food insecurity in the United States is or soon will be a thing of the past. But such is not the case. Private charities and organizations provide about the same amount of food as government programs, and there are still unmet needs.

Unequivocal Public Values: St. Mary's Food Bank

St. Mary's is the oldest continuously operating food bank in the world, celebrating its fiftieth anniversary in 2018. During those 50 years it has been focused unerringly on a single public value—feeding hungry people who do not have the financial resources to ensure sufficient nutrition for themselves and their families.

As we shall see, the St. Mary's Food Bank case provides a great many lessons relevant to the design, development, and perseverance of public values–based organizations and institutions. However, in our view, one of the most important lessons is that the leadership requirements for public values organizations may be quite different than one finds in organizations of other sorts.

Many aspects of the St. Mary's Food Bank warrant careful analysis for lessons in achieving public values. However, we focus particularly on the organization's initial leadership because doing so underscores our strongly held view that leadership comes in many different forms at different times—mutable leadership. The St. Mary's Food Bank founder, its creative visionary, was an eccentric gadfly who played the predominant role in launching an organization that evolved into one of the world's leading nonprofit organizations, one providing more than 50 million pounds of food to needy citizens each year and at minimal cost in terms of administration and fundraising. Eccentrics—take heart in this story.

John van Hengel: An Unconventional Public Value Leader

Despite its wealth, there has never been any point in the history of the United States where all its residents possessed sufficient resources to stave off routine hunger. Neither resources nor access to food are randomly distributed, and thus the need to combat hunger is more severe in some places and some time periods than others. The invention of the food bank has been quite an important one.

To clarify, the term "soup kitchen" is used for any organized effort to feed hungry people by preparing food such as soup, a hot meal, or sandwiches and serving it to them at no cost. Soup kitchens have been around for many years, emerging in the United States in 1929, at the onset of the Great Depression. The chief distinction is that the soup kitchen has a regular time for providing food, and it is done on-site. The food bank is quite a bit different in that food is provided, but for people to take home and prepare when they wish. The idea of the "bank" is also important, but it is more easily explained after some background.

John van Hengel began the world's first continuing food bank in 1967. That effort led to a contemporary organization, St. Mary's Food Bank, which distributed more than 73 million pounds of food, including more than 21 million pounds of fresh produce, in 2016 to people in need. The largest food bank in the world, St. Mary's uses 16 trucks and twice that many trailers to deliver food to distribution sites, schools, and a wide variety of venues where people in need live or work.

But St. Mary's started small and chiefly as the vision of one man. His story is to a large extent the story of food banks. Though the origin story of US food banks begins in Phoenix, Arizona, it first wends its way through John van Hengel's time in Wisconsin and California.

Up and Down and Up Again: Van Hengel's Checkered Career

One does not normally associate the implementation of big ideas with ordinary people who are themselves struggling to make ends meet. But in 1966, when van Hengel began formulating the idea of a food bank, he could have easily, with just a modest decline in standard of living, been a customer rather than a creator. As he said in an interview with the *Los Angeles Times* in 1992, "At 44, I was the oldest public pools lifeguard in Phoenix." Before that and, as we shall see, for long after, his life took many twists and turns as he established himself as one of the leading figures in the history of nonprofit, charitable organizations.

It is easy enough to learn about van Hengel's life as a food bank inventor and entrepreneur. There are several interviews with newspapers, and many people knew him well and have anecdotes to share. And in 1967, he thought it would be a good idea to provide some account of the rise of the food bank idea and used an old typewriter to tell the story in an eight-page, single-spaced narrative that St. Mary's Food Bank officials made available to us. The pre-1967 story is sketchy, less often recounted but in some respects quite relevant.

Born in Waupun, Wisconsin, in 1923, John van Hengel was quite well educated for his time, graduating with a bachelor's degree in government from Lawrence University in Appleton, Wisconsin, and then attending graduate school at the University of Wisconsin and then UCLA. After a brief period at UCLA, he dropped out to be "a first-rate beach bum." Later he received a degree in broadcasting. While he did, in fact, put his broadcasting degree to work as a magazine publicist for an advertising firm, he was anything but a careerist. Among other jobs, he in swift succession worked as a plastic rainwear designer, a maître d', and a beer truck driver, all in Los Angeles or Hollywood. He then married Beverlee Thompson, a model with whom he had two children, and briefly settled into a more stable job, becoming a sales manager for an archery equipment manufacturer. But in 1960 his marriage ended in divorce, and he returned to Wisconsin.

There, van Hengel met the fate that as much as anything contributed to his becoming a social services worker and food bank inventor. He began working in yet another of his string of apparently loosely connected jobs, this time in a limestone quarry, for $1.50 an hour. During that time, he got into a bar fight, apparently as a peacemaker, but nonetheless to bad result. The injuries sustained in the fight required spinal surgery, and the surgery left him with a locked, immobile neck, palsy, and partial paralysis in his legs. Correctly figuring that the Wisconsin winters were not salutary for skeletal problems and arthritis, van Hengel moved to Arizona for exactly the same reason as many early immigrants: seeking to improve health by living in a hot, sunny, low-humidity climate. Once in Arizona, he struggled to regain his health, tirelessly swimming laps at the YMCA pool (thus, the offer of a job as lifeguard).

From Soup Kitchen to Food Bank

In 1967, van Hengel was not only a lifeguard but also a volunteer at a local St. Vincent de Paul soup kitchen, a venue that routinely exposed him to the hungry and needy residents of greater Phoenix. It was during this time that the idea for a food bank emerged. As reported in a 1992 interview with the *Los Angeles Times*, van Hengel's inspiration for the food bank idea occurred when visiting a prison as part of a charitable mission. There he happened to meet a mother of 10 who was visiting her inmate husband, who was on death row. In response to van Hengel's question about how she managed to survive with so little money and so many children, she told him that her children always had plenty to eat. She had for some time been going from one grocery store to the next, visiting their garbage bins and taking home food that was sometimes a bit out of date and a little ugly, but that was both plentiful and quite nutritious. After meeting the woman and her apparently healthy children, van Hengel decided to satisfy his curiosity and determine for himself whether her reported experience seemed to work. He visited several grocery store trash bins himself, dipping in and sampling contents. His "research" uncovered still-edible frozen food, surplus loose carrots that were undamaged, and stale but still-edible bread. As he continued inspecting the trash bins, he became more and more convinced that a great amount of entirely healthy and nutritious food was going to waste and thought perhaps it could be repurposed. Most of the food in the bins could not possibly be sold to traditional, more persnickety consumers, not with brown spots on the apples, or wilted tops on carrots. But he figured hungry people would be delighted to have healthy and plentiful food, even if the food was not aesthetically pleasing.

The next step was convincing grocers to take the trouble to donate surplus food rather than simply putting it in the trash. This turned out not to be particularly difficult since the grocers agreed that it would be great to have their refuse put to good use. After a short time, van Hengel and his few early helpers had a problem: how to distribute a large quantity of mostly perishable food.

Eager to pursue his idea of a new means of providing food, van Hengel used some of his own savings to buy an ancient but still serviceable milk truck that he could use to pick up surplus fruits and vegetables. Soon he had more food than he could deal with and no place to store it. As he told the *Chicago Tribune* in a 1988 interview, "It got to the point where we were getting so much that it was killing me because I was having to deliver the produce in the evening after we finished picking it up." With more food than he could use, any daily excess went to missions, traditional soup kitchens, substance abuse centers, and women's shelters.

A lifelong Catholic, van Hengel soon convinced the parish council of St. Mary's Church to allow him to use one of its abandoned buildings to help him store some of his perishable foods. They also contributed $3,000 to help him get his idea off the ground (later repaid to the church). The woman he met when visiting prison, the one with 10 children and a husband on death row, became his first volunteer and also coined the term "food bank." In the first few months of operation, van Hengel, his first volunteer, and two new ones from St. Mary's Church collected and repurposed more than 250,000 pounds of food. Once the concept had been proven, it was not terribly difficult to enlist farmers, growers, grocers, and wholesalers, and the volume moved ever upward, including early on nearly 200 truckloads of surplus grapefruit juice.

An Early Lesson: Take What Is Offered

One of the interesting aspects of St. Mary's Food Bank's early organizational rules was to never turn down anything that was offered. That rule is still in place. As current St. Mary's Food Bank executive Jerry Brown told us, "It has always been a rule that we turn nothing down. That becomes difficult sometimes because we get a lot more food during some periods than others. For example, we have a great many turkey donations at Thanksgiving, sometimes more than we can use. But we have very good connections with other food banks and soup kitchens, and when we can't store food, we give it to others. We don't want to discourage anyone from donating by telling them, 'We don't need that.'"

The origins of this take-what-is-offered view are reported by van Hengel in an instructive but also amusing anecdote:

I remember one occasion of a man calling me with some chickens to pick up. The temperature in Phoenix was about 120 degrees during the summer and this was in the middle of the summer. We sent out a volunteer driver and a truck. Sometime later I received a call from a lady in one of the suburbs saying, "your truck has just gone through our neighborhood and there are chickens flying out the broken back window." About twenty minutes later the driver showed up, drove into the back of our warehouse, jumped out of the truck and took off down the street. I didn't know until later what was going on and when we looked in the truck there were about 45 or 50 of these 60 chickens flying around. They had made a terrible mess. I never did see the volunteer driver again and I can't blame him. It took us a whole day to clean the truck.

That evening I received a call from the chicken man, "Did you get the chickens?" and I said "yes" and he said, "Well could you use some more?" After cleaning the truck and gathering the chickens with chicken wire and then putting them back in cages . . . I was quite unwilling to ask for more, but I told him "I'll call you in the morning." So, in the morning when I called and asked, "how many chickens are you offering." He said, "how about a thousand?" "Wow," we said, "what can we do with a thousand chickens?" Then we realized that we had boys' homes or ranches around the valley. So, I called one of the ranches and I said to John Morgan . . . who at that time was running a home for delinquent boys, "how would you like a thousand chickens?" He said, "We'd jump it and (we will put the boys to work.)" The next day . . . we delivered them to the ranch property.[2]

The food bank was so good at distributing chickens that shortly thereafter van Hengel received another call—"How about 5,000 chickens?" There were four other boy's homes, and all the chickens were placed and put to good use, with chicken dinners, chickens laying eggs, and an opportunity to enhance skills in chicken farming. As observed above, the waste-not-want-not credo continues today. If the food bank is at surplus, there is always need elsewhere.

Institutional Innovation: Diffusing the Food Bank Organization in the United States

In his memoir, van Hengel recounts that, as a result of early work distributing surpluses, St. Mary's Food Bank began, after about five years, to have a regional reputation as a clearing house, and the fact that they maintained a warehouse provided ample space and a central location for a growing and multiorganizational response to feeding the hungry.

The idea of food banks began to spread, and by the mid-1970s there were five more food banks in the Phoenix area, all of them run by groups of Protestant churches. The concept began to attract attention elsewhere. In the 1970s, a group from California interested in starting food banks visited St. Mary's to obtain information, then representatives from groups in Oregon and Washington. Then, the federal government provided a $40,000 grant for St. Mary's to essentially serve as a demonstration project, showing others how to begin and successfully operate food banks. By 1976, with another federal grant, St. Mary's had established the Second Harvest program, designed explicitly to set up food banks around the nation. By 1977, food banks had been established in 18 US cities.

In 2008, the Second Harvest program changed its name to Feeding America. Today, Feeding America is a national network of more than 200 allied food banks, feeding 46 million people each year, including 12 million children and 7 million seniors.[3]

Mutable Leadership: John van Hengel as an Extreme Example

There are many public values lessons one can learn from the St. Mary's Food Bank case, including the possibility of achieving a public value service that no one is providing, the importance of tenacity, the notion of turning away no one who wants to help, and the fact that trust can be developed by abjuring all but the most basic necessities. We conclude by focusing on one signal lesson in public values leadership.

For many years the idea of contingency or situational leadership has had a prominent place in leadership theory, the idea being that there is no one best way to lead; rather, the leadership style should fit the context in which leadership is exercised (Miner 2015). In the case of John van Hengel, the style is in some ways an odd one, but it seems to have been an excellent fit to the context.

When we conjure up a mental image of a "leader," most of us do not visualize someone unkempt and in cast-off clothes. But the cliché that "clothes make the man" (or woman) does little justice to John van Hengel. His story shows that leadership is about so much more than appearance and, indeed, that different appearances can serve leadership in different ways. In interviews, contemporary St. Mary's personnel offered the following: "John wore old clothes, usually from thrift stores. For many years he wore just one pair of white shoes. When they began to get very dirty, his approach to 'new' shoes was to sit them on the floor and spray-paint them with white paint. In the thrift store there is still an outline of the paint from the last time he spray-painted his shoes."

Having a program leader who resembles a homeless person is not exactly an instant advantage. The first time van Hengel visited one of the most affluent grocers in Phoenix, A. J. Bayless, the security guard sent him out the door several times, until Bayless agreed to see this insistent, apparently indigent man. Van Hengel began his discussion with a query as to why Bayless was wasting so much food, implying that it was Bayless's obligation to help the needy. After some acrimonious discussion, van Hengel convinced Bayless that he should be a donor to the food bank, one of the first major donors. From this unusual beginning, the two became friends and remained so for the remainder of their lives.

According to Jerry Brown of St. Mary's, "one advantage of John looking like a homeless person, dressed in thrift store clothes, is that people trusted him. No one really thought he was in it for himself or that he had some other agenda. He looked like the people he was trying to help." Thus, in this manner at least, the unusual leader garb could in some cases help. Given that van Hengel seemed to care nothing for material goods and, relatedly, he was in most cases asking for perishable goods and not monetary donations, why not take him at his word? After all, for nine years he drew no salary at all, and then when he decided to take some salary it was all of $150 per month to "buy the cigarettes, take care of the teeth, and pay the rent." Likewise, the volunteer employees received no money for many years, just an allotment of food for their families.

Even today, St. Mary's works to keep its spare image as well as its lean reality. The vast majority of monetary gifts go directly to food and food transport. The operation is quite large, as is today's warehouse facility, but it is entirely functional. The reception area includes a couple of chairs that could have come from a thrift store, a very bad piece of framed reproduction art, and a vase with artificial flowers. The offices are likewise entirely functional. As Jerry Brown notes, "This is a place with four walls and a roof and a lot of food [and not much else]."

Another advantage of his unusual (for a leader) appearance is not so evident. As van Hengel describes in his informal memoir, "One of the important things that affected the development of the program was when a writer from a local newspaper used my appearance as his source of humor. He would write about how I was the worst dressed man in Phoenix and that the program had these crazy things happening. He consistently wrote this in his column. We came to be kind of a humorous point of interest in the city." He goes on to describe the advantage of asking for perishables rather than monetary donations: "There are advantages accruing from both trust and from lack of competition. As we grew, we chose never to ask for money! The premise was that we would work with what we had and if we didn't have it, we just wouldn't do anything about it. So, we pursued asking for food rather than money. Because of this, the other charities did not feel threatened. They were searching for money. Thus, we became a service agency. We were servants to all the other agencies in the city. They respected us for that."

Another aspect of the van Hengel style of public values–focused leadership was not so unusual, especially for persons working in non-profit organizations. Many adjectives describe van Hengel: "bulldog," "tenacious," "hardheaded." All add up to the fact that it was nearly impossible to deflect him from his goal once he had set upon its path.

Van Hengel and the St. Mary's workers also invented the operational aspects of the food bank. For example, they developed the idea of food boxes, allocations of meals in small boxes, because they knew that many of the people eating their food would be children who were staying at home while parents worked or were looking for work. They also integrated nutritional education into their services. This was inspired by some of the problems witnessed in early US government food supplement problems. As van Hengel noted, "I had seen some problems in the original government surplus commodity program. People would eat a whole can of meat separately instead of making a casserole from it because they didn't know any better. So, a lot of our work was an educational process—teaching people what to eat and improving their nutritional habits."

Another public values leadership lesson pertains not only to the value of long-term involvement but also to the need to change the nature of one's involvement as a leader, the core of mutable leadership. The mutable leadership concept tells us that different times and events often require different leadership skills and, for that reason, also changes in leadership or in the leader. Mutable leadership can occur when the current leader changes roles or approach. Again, the van Hengel case is illustrative.

Van Hengel's leadership roles changed over the years. For example, while his early work focused on developing St. Mary's and its capacity, he then began to give attention to the Second Harvest program. Later, he focused on dissemination of the food bank concept and, in 1986 and later, the Global Food Bank Association, to which he was an advisor. Ultimately, he founded the Feeding America program, today the third-largest charity in the United States. Feeding America remains a vital part of the social safety net, focusing its efforts almost entirely on the core public value of ensuring food security for as many people as possible.

Jerry Brown notes, "John came in to work up until he died in 2005. He would be in two or three days every week, keeping involved helping with the work and also inspiring." Today the food bank headquarters is in some respects a shrine to van Hengel, with pictures of him and associates on the office walls, in conference rooms, and in hallways, along with postings of news stories and events. In that way he remains influential even in death.

Conclusions

If nothing else, this chapter illustrates the hazards of generalizing about public values institutions and, especially, public values leadership.

There is no golden path or magic formula for achieving public values, and as we note in our mutable leadership concept, different challenges require different kinds of leaders.

Another important lesson embedded in this chapter is one that we have not given enough attention to elsewhere in the book: the idea of never turning anyone away. Interestingly, Steve Zabilski, one of the public values leaders and the director of St. Vincent de Paul's, emphasized the same point. But we feel that one need not be in the business of feeding the poor or housing the homeless to benefit from this lesson. An important part of public values management is husbanding the goodwill, energy, resources, and commitment of one's coworkers and public values allies. A public values leader should ensure that no one who can help goes away thinking, "They don't need me." Human resources cannot be squandered.

A reoccurring them in the book is interorganizational partnerships. It is easy to come away with the idea that the St. Mary's case is about a charismatic leader. But the case shows that charismatic leaders need partners. St. Mary's, a secular food bank, takes its name from the church that offered its initial headquarters and office space. Vitally important, public-spirited businesspeople, especially grocers, have been instrumental to the success of the food bank. John van Hengel was neither grocer nor farmer; he was a part-time lifeguard and full-time visionary.

Query for Readers

John van Hengel may be one of the most important public values leaders who remains unknown to almost everyone, a legend in the food bank community but known to few not in that community. He is the sort of person whom many in the organization studies and leadership literature refer to in their typologies as "the zealot." In one of our favorite organization theory classics, Anthony Downs develops a typology of organization leaders, and one of these, the zealot, is described as narrowly focused, prone to upset those he or she is working with, and dogged about their cause. According to Downs (and "received wisdom" in general), the zealot can be useful in an organization, promoting change and advocating new ideas, but is rarely an effective leader. But van Hengel defies organization theory expectations. Why? Is it just a matter of the right need and the right person coming together at the right time? Or do you think that van Hengel might have proved an effective leader in other types of organizations? Is a zealot leader sometimes just what is needed (Moynihan 2010)? How does the zealot leader fit with the notion of mutable leadership?

8

The Starbucks-ASU Alliance

A fundamental assumption of this book is that no one sector "owns" public values. Instances of government, business, and nonprofit public values activities are provided throughout. In many cases, organizations and sectors working together in partnership reach the public values goals. The case discussed here is one of those instances. The chapter discusses a case with which we are intimately familiar, the Starbucks-ASU partnership College Achievement Plan. In the next chapter, the coauthors, especially Crow, reflect extensively on personal experience with the Starbucks-ASU case.

This case is organized a bit differently than the others in the book, in part because it includes so many of the public values leadership elements we discuss as "premises" and "propositions." Thus, in addition to providing the case description, we do so in relation to the various leadership premises and propositions, at least those that seem relevant.

This chapter is coauthored with Kathryn Scheckel, and, indeed, while Crow and Bozeman contributed, Scheckel is the lead author for this chapter. At the time this was written, Ms. Scheckel was ASU's director for the Starbucks Alliance. Crow has his say, in very personal terms, in the next chapter, which is an extended conversation between the authors.

But before getting a little more analytical, let's begin on a personal note, with the case of one particular Starbucks employee and ASU student.

Mini-case. Mary Hamm, Starbucks Employee and ASU Student

Mary Hamm was married and had one child by the age of 19.[1] The demands of a new family quickly overshadowed her dreams of being a nurse. She placed her education on the back burner until decades later when she took out a loan to attend the University of Phoenix. When tuition increased, Mary left, saddled with debt and no degree. Mary had worked in the hospitality industry for 25 years, the most recent 14 years as a Starbucks partner (employee)—with five surgeries on her tired feet and two metal plates in her right foot.

She greeted customers with a warm smile despite her pain, making Frappuccinos, restocking coffee cup sleeves, and ensuring that her store was clean for her customers in Fredericksburg, Virginia. Yet she had been trying to transition from her in-store role to a corporate position at another company, both to relieve her feet and to earn more income to support her family. Met again and again with rejection from job applications, with the most frequently cited reason as her lack of college degree—a pattern similar among almost three-quarters of her peers at Starbucks—Mary struggled to find her next step. And she certainly did not have any spare funds to continue her dream of finishing a college degree.

Mary first learned about a new program Starbucks was launching in 2014 through an email sent to her Starbucks store—an email that went to tens of thousands of partners across the United States. This email said that partners working 20 hours or more per week at any Starbucks company-operated store in the United States were eligible to attend Arizona State University at no tuition cost through one of its online undergraduate degree programs. For the 150,000 or so partners at the company, this could mean finishing a college degree, like Mary wanted to, or starting and completing a degree. Initially reading through the program details of this new initiative called the Starbucks College Achievement Plan (SCAP), Mary excitedly thought of her younger colleagues in the store who would now have access to such opportunities. She did not immediately see herself attending ASU at her age. Quickly, though, she realized that this could be her chance to finish her degree.

Always action focused and driven, Mary talked to an enrollment advisor at the university and signed up the next day (Ripley 2015). Two years later in 2016, Mary graduated from the university with a bachelor's degree in organizational leadership and a special focus in homeland security.

Balancing the demands of 13-hour days in the store, multiple school-age children, and her own college classes was not easy. But, with her degree now in hand, Mary had attained a path toward potential new opportunity. She had the full support of her peers at Starbucks and the support network of the university, which assigned a personal "success coach" to help her navigate questions about her classes and degree as she worked toward completion. Every day, hundreds of these coaches help the more than 30,000 online degree-seeking students at ASU.

Mary is still at Starbucks in Virginia for now, but she leverages the new skills from her degree and applies them on the job. She is an advocate of the program to peers and helps colleagues also pursuing SCAP find balance between partner work and school obligations. Her degree has also empowered her to more broadly give back to her personal community through a nonprofit organization she's founded in Virginia.

Mary's story is similar to those of other employees at Starbucks and to many longing for a college education. Mary struggled to finish college in the face of increasing student loan debt and diminishing personal financial resources. According to the New York Federal Reserve Bank, there are more than 44 million student borrowers in the United States, with a collective $1.3 trillion in student loan debt. The average student graduating in 2016 had $37,000 in student loan debt. The average student loan debt per capita is $4,920. As of 2015, 415,000 of those students with student loan debt have balances greater than $200,000.

Over the past five years, student debt has grown across every age bracket, but those age 60–69 have experienced an almost 90% increase in student loan debt. As a group, the highest increase in student loan debt is among those between 30 and 39 years old, with a collective $408 billion in student loans (Friedman 2017).

Behind this looming statistic of student loan debt is an outcomes-focused view. We know that the greatest predictor of success in higher education in the United States is not measured by a student's grades or

SAT and ACT scores, but rather by their family income and zip code. In this country, students who come from families that are in the top quartile of family income are *eight times* more likely to complete college as compared to those students from the bottom quartile. While certain programs have targeted financially disadvantaged students, the scale of the challenge is far more widespread (Crow and Dabars 2015). More innovative approaches are needed to help shift the balance of student access to a high-quality and affordable education. SCAP represents a program like this.

With the creation of SCAP, Starbucks put concrete meaning behind the idea of former CEO and chairman Howard Schultz to "link long-term value for shareholders with long-term value for employees." The program demonstrates how a partnership between a major for-profit, multinational corporation and the largest public university in the country under a single administration can help provide opportunity to individuals without tying that opportunity to a zip code.

Articulating the Vision

The Starbucks culture and vision are known and present throughout each storefront, counter, and cup. This vision permeates every interaction and connection: "To inspire and nurture the human spirit—one person, one cup, and one neighborhood at a time."[2] That level of shared mission is rare and requires consistent, dedicated efforts to articulate and share. Only more recently are companies realizing the value of the "triple bottom line," an idea that company profit is linked also to community impact. Schultz is no stranger to this concept. His concerted efforts to create a company based not on the products it serves but on the connections fostered exemplifies Starbucks's commitment "to inspire and nurture the human spirit." This vision is what drove Schultz to idealize and create the SCAP, an innovative model through which eligible Starbucks partners can attend ASU tuition-free.

As mentioned earlier in the book, while there is often a key role for a single visionary, there is rarely a case where one individual moves a vision forward. Rather, a collective group together implements a good idea. Moreover, the idea must be more than rhetoric. It must also contain tangible results that people can see and believe to be sustained. Schultz served that role as chief visionary and communicator for Starbucks broadly, and specifically for SCAP.

SCAP provides a clear example for the "articulating the vision" aspect of public values leadership. What is the vision, and how is it articulated? At the core of SCAP is the idea that a college degree leads to greater economic mobility and opportunity. Of course, this idea, along with the reality that access to higher education is uneven across the American populace, did not originate with Schultz. Scholars, reporters, and other commenters have been describing the rising tide in economic inequality among individuals with and without higher education for decades.

Economists and government agencies use wages as one key metric of economic attainment and mobility when looking at degree attainment and corresponding earnings. In 2005, the difference in median income between an individual with a high school degree and one with a college degree was $29,000 (Haskins 2016, 2). This divide has only continued to increase in the most recent decade. According to the US Bureau of Labor Statistics, earnings for full-time workers age 25 and older as of 2016 are as follows by education attainment: (1) without a high school diploma, median weekly earnings of $494; (2) with a high school diploma but no college, $679; (3) with some college or an associate degree, $782; (4) with a bachelor's degree, $1,155; and (5) with an advanced degree (including master's, professional, or doctoral degree), $1,435.[3]

So, how is it that a business leader, a CEO of a multinational and multibillion-dollar corporation, chooses to place education among its top priorities for its US business—in line with health care, stock options, and other benefits for part-time and full-time employees? This kind of commitment to vision and proclamation of the vision is different from leaders of other companies that support education through more traditional education benefit programs. And, in the case of Starbucks, there is a clear connection in both company rhetoric and also practice that this program is largely helping the middle class access a degree that otherwise might be unattainable.

Arguably, no other business leader in the United States or internationally has articulated so clearly the need to invest in its workforce. This vision supports short-term goals of immediate return on investment (ROI) for the workforce, such as a more positive attitude toward the employer and more energy for the work on the job, potentially leading to greater customer satisfaction. In the longer-term the ROI will improve employees' human capital and their ability to contribute back to society.

This program, as well as the vision of Schultz and the Starbucks leadership team, has resulted in other employers in other corporations emulating the idea of helping provide a comprehensive, higher education benefit for employees. Employers in both the for-profit and nonprofit sectors have seen Starbucks, as a visionary company, modeling the behavior. We see some replication through the design of relationships like Adidas and ASU, who together in 2017 launched a small pilot tuition assistance program to provide a scholarship toward specific undergraduate and graduate degrees for a subset of their US employee base. The hope is that this program may expand after the initial pilot phase, based on the needs of Adidas and the value the benefit ultimately could provide to its employees.

The Adidas program is relatively modest in size compared to the ambition of SCAP, which is to graduate 25,000 partners by 2025 through ASU Online. Further, the focus of the Adidas program is slightly different—cultivating more leaders internally through education growth opportunities. Nevertheless, this program is another instance of a multinational corporation providing additional education opportunities to its employees, exemplifying the public values permeating the organizational design of Adidas.

Returning to SCAP, Schultz's intentional vision for education supported by a global, publicly traded company at the scale of Starbucks has generally stirred positive public sentiment from both others in higher education and corporate America. To give a sense of the company's scale, it was reported in December of 2017 (LaVito 2017) that Starbucks is opening one new store in China every 15 hours. Starbucks already operates more than 3,000 stories in China and has plans to add an additional 2,000 by 2021. In 1971, the first Starbucks opened in the historic Pike Place Market in Seattle, Washington. Store count exceeded 100 in 1991, and Starbucks completed its first initial public offering in 1992 with 165 stores. Acquisitions such as Tazo Tea in 1999 and international expansion through the 1990s and 2000s has led Starbucks now to have more than 25,000 stores in over 70 countries.[4]

While Starbucks itself has a rich history, it is still too early to gauge the full impact and transformation behind SCAP. Human capital development programs return benefits over many years. That said, nearly four years into the ambitious project, launched in June 2014, more than 1,200 Starbucks partners have graduated through the SCAP program. An additional nearly 10,000 partners are currently enrolled in coursework to help them advance toward a degree. The pipeline of prospective students refreshes every month, given the natural turnover of employees in the food and beverage industry. As the number of Starbucks partners continues to grow, it is anticipated that the student pipeline will also naturally grow.

The visions in previously discussed case studies, including Mothers Against Drunk Driving and changes in food safety due to Dr. Wiley and his intentional vision that resulted in the Pure Food and Drug Act, have had time to mature. We can look back and evaluate the real impact. To fully absorb the impact of Starbucks's education benefit policy, we need more time. A continuous flow of individuals moving through the program pipeline, along with more graduates, will help to measure the impact of the vision. That said, we can safely predict that the impact will be large and felt broadly among a significant number of individuals whom SCAP may directly or indirectly touch, as well as among other companies emulating the program to implement a similar kind of tuition benefit.

Multilateral Institutional Interaction

Michael Bojorquez is the first in his family to earn a college degree. His story is common among low socioeconomic communities with limited formal education. In Michael's case, his parents worked tirelessly at multiple jobs to provide better opportunities for him and his siblings as he was growing up. He did not have much free time and had to support himself. Only with the assistance of SCAP was Michael able to complete his degree at ASU, debt-free. "This changes everything for us. This changes everything for me."

In Michael's case, SCAP enabled him to achieve an outcome he never thought possible. Without the multilateral alignment between Starbucks and ASU, the program would not exist, and individuals like Michael would never have the opportunity to experience the impact.

The SCAP case pertains clearly to the multilateral institutional interaction proposition. As a reminder, public value attainment, in contrast to the pursuit of private values, almost always includes working with other institutions in processes requiring participation, mutual learning, and accommodation with a shared commitment to change. In the case of SCAP, Starbucks and ASU are joined hand in hand. This deep, values-driven and energy-matched partnership allows for both institutions to continuously optimize, review inputs, recalibrate, adjust, and re-optimize as needed throughout the program implementation of SCAP.

At the beginning of this ambitious project in 2013, Starbucks leaders sat down with the ASU team and shared their ideas for what a transformational education benefit for its partners could look like. Starbucks had a sense already that education was where they wanted to focus their next big emphasis in terms of benefits for partners. Some design parameters were set, including a focus on US partners.

From early meetings to the present, both sides have found common values. For Starbucks, it was ASU's focus and ability to provide high-quality education at scale through ASU Online, along with its willingness to partner in innovating a new model of education access. It also valued ASU's personalized and focused attention on each of its students. This commitment is demonstrated most noticeably by the ASU Student Success Center, which provides individualized and group support for online degree-seeking students. This center is housed within ASU's EdPlus, a central unit of the university responsible for advancing education technology along with ASU's fully online degree programs at the undergraduate and postgraduate levels. As one example of the work of the Student Success Center, every online degree-seeking student is paired with an individual ASU success coach, who is focused on ensuring that a student continues his or her path successfully from first class through graduation. Each coach fields questions ranging from how to sign up for the next term's courses to what to do if a natural disaster hits and studies need to be paused.

Following an organic meeting between ASU president Michael Crow and then CEO Howard Schultz, senior leadership from both Starbucks and ASU came together to devise a strategy around a new type of education benefit with a few key guidelines in mind: minimal to no cost to partners, accessible higher education at scale leading to a full university degree completion leveraging an online environment, and the ability to support Starbucks partners along their education journey.

The operational elements of the program were vitally important. At ASU, major systems had to be overhauled to prepare for thousands of Starbucks partners to become ASU Online students. Given that the initiative was driven from the top down at ASU, strong implementers inside ASU Online alongside senior leaders were essential to help lead progressive efforts through other areas of the university, such as changes in the admissions procedures, student registration, and financial aid provision. The cross-university coordination resulted in reduced time to make decisions on applications for students, increased accessibility to financial aid counselors, faster financial aid processes, and accelerated review of transcripts for transfer students—all key changes that were implemented before the SCAP launch. These eventually impacted all ASU students, both online and on campus. Without the healthy "push" from Starbucks to implement these changes, they may have happened at a much slower pace or perhaps not at all. Thus, there is true benefit to both organizations interacting in a mutual, reciprocal way.

As a second key example of this public values management proposition, we can turn to two major expansions of the SCAP program since its debut. For some context, when the program was first announced in June 2014, students enrolling as a junior or senior received full tuition reimbursement from Starbucks, while students enrolled as freshmen or sophomores received a scholarship to assist with tuition coverage. It was clear almost immediately that a way to remove the financial burden from all partners, regardless of their entering status at the university, needed to be developed. ASU and Starbucks came together and announced in March 2015 that SCAP would provide full tuition reimbursement for all enrolled partners. This expansion again precipitated a major transformation, allowing Starbucks and ASU to provide even greater value to partners.

An additional expansion in February 2017 allowed individuals not yet qualified for admission to the university to enter the SCAP "Pathway to Admission" program. Through input from ASU financial aid advisors and success coaches and feedback from Starbucks store managers, the leadership of the collaboration discovered that a broader set of individuals wanted access to SCAP. Each month, about one-third of applicants to the university were being denied admission, in large part due to poor academic history. Working together, ASU's Office of the Provost, ASU Online, Office of Undergraduate Admissions, and Office of Financial Aid, along with Starbucks's program leaders, launched an inclusive modification to SCAP affording Starbucks's partners a chance to earn admission to the university by taking rigorous coursework delivered through ASU's Global Freshman Academy online program. In under one year, this new pathway for Starbucks's partners to achieve their college degrees generated over 1,000 successful applicants alone, and it continues to grow. In fact, it has been such a success that ASU has opened its earned admission program to any ASU Online prospective student who was previously denied admission.

Changing a program policy that had taken months and months of legal alignment and the design of a joint steering committee governing the program required an agreed-upon process for making changes rapidly so that SCAP Pathway to Admissions could flourish. Fortunately, the constant attention that both Starbucks and ASU gave to program implementation greatly enhanced program delivery.

Many more examples could highlight this principle of multilateral institutional interaction. At the core, however, is the common understanding and alignment Starbucks and ASU both have in the partnership. This leads to the ability to rapidly implement policies with public value.

Inclusiveness and Accommodation of Minority Interests

The SCAP program is an expansive measure with an intentional focus on inclusion of those left at the fray. Many SCAP-enrolled partners' stories begin in the same way: overwhelmed by debt incurred at a traditional college or rapidly changing familial circumstances, students drop out at a rate of 56%. Disheartened and discouraged, students begin a career, often feeling "stuck" at the bottom, lacking mobility and choice.

With respect to public values management, the inclusiveness proposition requires that various stakeholders' views and needs are all considered. The consistent involvement of partners in the experience and implementation of SCAP has contributed to the ongoing success of the program. Partners through social media platforms like Workplace by Facebook can express their views, both positive and negative, and instigate change. One example rose from one of the most popular degrees among SCAP scholars: a bachelor's degree in organizational leadership.

In the first year of the program, Starbucks partners flocked to this degree, which related to their business sense and interest in growing within the company or outside of Starbucks. Starbucks leadership, upon the requests of partners, asked ASU to consider creating a special elective course (not mandatory for the major). This elective in organizational leadership would focus on how Starbucks has implemented organizational design principles to become a global coffee leader. ASU worked closely with Starbucks, creating an expert faculty, curriculum, and videos featuring Starbucks executives to help bring the coffee company's culture to life through an elective designed for students in this degree program.

Additional examples of inclusiveness in the design process for SCAP are apparent as well, including responding to partner feedback regarding delivery of the benefit. While over 10,000 partners are actively participating in SCAP, there are likely many more who would take part in the benefit if the tuition payment design was changed from a reimbursement model to an upfront model where the employer and university covered tuition directly for the student each academic semester. In 2016, program managers at both Starbucks and ASU partnered to design and deploy a survey to partners across the United States to ask what barriers may exist to participating in this program. Among the top three responses was perceived financial barriers.

Given that the program covers full tuition, this may seem somewhat odd. However, the present design of the program requires partners to first pay tuition costs out of pocket and then receive reimbursement from Starbucks at the end of an academic session. The cash flow in this case, while logical to help create skin in the game among participants, is also not logical for those at or barely above minimum wage, such as baristas, shift supervisors, or other positions at Starbucks, and who likely need cash to cover rent, mortgage, or other bills.

While this example is meant to remove barriers of access for participants, inadvertently it is possible that the program put barriers in place. Now, the program teams are working together to remove these out-of-pocket expenses for Starbucks employees, and hopefully the result will be higher enrollment in SCAP and greater retention. This revamped program feature should help increase the program's ability to actively seek diverse participants from different geographic and socioeconomic backgrounds, a characteristic of public values management. The survey deployed represents an example of a framework Starbucks put in place to solicit the inputs of as many voices as possible, including minority interests that may otherwise go unheard if such a survey were not deployed.

The fact that Starbucks and ASU both put full force behind this investigation to understand barriers to participation and to work together to enact a change further exemplifies how organizations from different sectors working together can have even more positive public value impact.

Engendering Trust

In 2009, after graduating from high school, Tammie Lopez, like many of her peers, started college at California State University. Her father, a construction manager, lost his job soon after, and she was forced to make the difficult decision to quit school and pursue a second job to provide for her family. According to Tammie, she had to make an "adult decision." She abandoned her college ambitions so that she could contribute to family finances and help prevent foreclosure on their home mortgage. Tammie helped her dad study for the GED to obtain his high school diploma; without a high school degree, he had been rejected from one job opportunity after another. After years at Starbucks and the launching of SCAP, Tammie has a new chance at dreams she had long left behind. "Starbucks is lifting such a weight off my shoulders," Tammie shared.[5]

To motivate an individual to return to college or start and finish a degree, one must build trust that there is a promise of some brighter path or future ahead. This trust needs to carry the person from the initial coursework through long study nights, tough exams, and compromises that must be made to balance work, school, and normal life. Starbucks and ASU together have been able to build that trust through SCAP—evidenced by the more than 10,000 (and growing) participating partners. One way that Starbucks works to build this trust is through compelling storytelling. The online Starbucks Newsroom offers weekly stories about real partners and their challenges. Starbucks stores promote programs, including SCAP, through the in-store community board, where both customers and partners have a chance to learn more about what is happening in their community, as well as from headquarters. Baristas and other partners in the program proudly wear "ASU" pins on their green aprons, an invitation to customers and colleagues to ask why are they wearing the pin and thus become advocates and champions for the partner.

In some cases, Starbucks has launched full-scale public campaigns focused on highlighting the work the company does to advance its mission to be a company that cares about more than just the bottom line, emphasizing its commitment to public values and social responsibility. In 2017, Starbucks ran a campaign termed "A Year of Good," where the company featured how it is giving back to the community. SCAP was a key part of that storytelling in the second quarter of the year. Authentic, public storytelling has helped Starbucks build credibility and trust among both its employees and its patrons, as well as the general public—and is an essential part of public values management.

Taken together, these public efforts highlighting stories like those of Mary, Allison, Michael, Tammie, and so many other partners help build trust among partners who are intrigued by the program but may not yet have taken the steps to sign up. These efforts also reveal the company's transparency that they celebrate partners who have taken new journeys after their college degree, whether that be moving up in the company or leaving to take on a new challenge and role. Last, by inviting the customer to be a part of the story, assessing employees, helping reward them, and providing ASU pins and cups to those who contribute small amounts to the program, customers feel included in the work of the program. This personalization element is one that other companies seeking to implement public values can learn from. The amplification of an initiative and the added impact that is felt become so much greater when more people can participate in the overall objectives of the public value, including those who may not be the direct intended recipients.

Summary

This case study exemplifies several of the public values management propositions—articulating the vision, multilateral institutional interaction, inclusivity and accommodating minority interests, and engendering trust. Table 7 summarizes the ways in which these principles manifest in the case study of the SCAP.

We can look to Starbucks and the SCAP case study as one benchmark of what public values management looks like. In the years ahead, SCAP promises to be a continuing example of public values management, and its story will grow only richer as more elements of the program evolve, and ultimately as more individuals graduate with college degrees and experience economic mobility in the form of new work and opportunities that otherwise would not have been possible.

TABLE 7

Public Values Propositions Exemplified in the Starbucks College Achievement Plan

Public Value Proposition	Case Study Example
Articulating the vision	Schultz clearly articulated the SCAP vision from the top of the corporation, and the senior leadership team adopted it in order to implement the public value.
Multilateral institutional interaction	Starbucks and ASU worked closely together to design and implement SCAP and pivot quickly together when necessary. This ability to pivot is critical when implementing a new public values program, as one must navigate to new learnings and feedback that happen once a program is launched.
Inclusivity and accommodating minority interests	Through the inherent design of the program itself, SCAP works to include those who may not necessarily be in the majority and support a concrete pathway to college attainment for anyone who is eligible and qualified. It shows initiative to take meaningful steps forward. Also, program design features like changing how reimbursement is processed show a commitment to understanding what will work for all in the program. Designing to support the needs of all and not only the majority, or minority, makes this public values guideline real in the case of SCAP.
Engendering trust	Through action and also careful storytelling, Starbucks has been able to engender long-lasting trust among its partner base and in the SCAP program specifically. Building on a track record of putting its employees' interests first for decades, Starbucks perhaps has a unique advantage over other corporations from which to build on existing trust and amplify it through new actions and activities. Together with ASU, Starbucks has been able to invite not only partners to the table for SCAP but also customers, amplifying the effects of the public values program.

The next chapter, which presents a concluding conversation between the authors, begins with some considerable attention to Michael Crow's experiences with the Starbucks-ASU Alliance. He adds a personal note and an insider's perspective. However, the conversation broadens, including our reflections on the book and what it contributes to the authors' own (and, we hope, the reader's) understanding of public values.

9

Public Values Management and Leadership

A Conversation

We contemplated several options for concluding this book. The conventional options include distilling most important lessons, summarizing, and discussing needed research. However, since we have tried to make this book more personal than most, maybe a little more relaxed than most, we thought we would try an unusual approach to concluding, one that at least is consistent with the tone of the book. Thus, we conclude with a conversation between the authors, in which we reflected on the book, public values management generally, what we learned and what we hoped readers learned, and, well, whatever else popped up during the conversation.

If nothing else, this conversation/conclusion fits the nature of our relationship. Not only have we been friends and colleagues for nearly 40 years, but we have influenced one another on our separate paths, with Bozeman's writing and research influencing Crow's career as a higher education leader and "knowledge enterprise architect," but also with Crow's practitioner work influencing Bozeman's thinking about both public value theory and practice. By this point, we feel comfortable speaking with one another about almost anything, meaning that we felt we could provide a candid conversation rather than a cleaned-up, edited-for-propriety exchange.

Let us note a couple of points before providing the conversation. First, though there is back-and-forth, the conversation is not an "equal-time" conversation, nor is it intended to be. Crow gets more time. Were this a book about public values theory and research, Bozeman would get more time. But this a book about practice, not theory, and so the person who has done more practice gets more time. Second, we apologize in advance if the conversation seems to show like-minded ideas and perspectives, but that is perhaps to be expected given the nature of our four-decade relationship. We do, at least, highlight a few points of disagreement.

When we sat down to converse, we had recently finished the chapter on the Starbucks-ASU Alliance, and this was very much on our mind. Much of this chapter is, then, a more personalized continuation of the previous one. However, as we reviewed the transcripts, it was also clear enough that we used the Starbucks episode as a combination personal and deep case to understand trials, tribulations, and lessons learned about public values leadership and management. Thus, while the Starbucks episode is a base case for much of the conversation, it was also the jumping-off point for discussion of a wide range of public values–related issues.

After the Starbucks-ASU discussion, the conversation ranges much farther afield. So, we divide up the conversation by a clever organizing scheme: (1) the Starbucks Continuation Part; (2) the ASU, Inclusiveness, and Public Value Part; and, appropriately, we end with (3) the Everything Else Part.

Authors' Comment on Scene-Setting Trivia and Other Not So Important Details

The conversation occurred during the halcyon, pre-pandemic days of summer, July 2019. As usual, the authors did not have an easy time catching up to joint work. Crow is usually the one communicating from 30,000 feet, but in 2019 Bozeman was also a fugitive from headquarters. This was the year that Bozeman made the Delta Airlines million-mile club, with travel to 11 countries, including a month in China and a four-month sabbatical in Spain and France. A good life, but not designed for face-to-face collaboration. So, the meeting was set for a week pre-sabbatical, at Tugaloo State Park in Lavonia, Georgia. The 393-acre park on Lake Hartwell is well adapted to the traditional Bozeman-Crow collaboration pattern—hiking trails, cabins, semi-isolation, friendly argument. Hours of conversation were recorded and transcribed. Here we share most of it, omitting only the completely irrelevant, the embarrassing, or the overly self-revelatory. So, relax, join us, and pretend that we are able to share a beer and some freshly caught, pan-fried largemouth bass.

Conversation: The Starbucks Continuation Part

Bozeman: Okay, we just finished a few days ago writing about the Starbucks-ASU partnership, so at least that's fresh on our mind, so maybe a good place to get started. Since we didn't get up close and personal with that in the last chapter, maybe we can do so here. I think it is a great example of issues in designing and implementing public values.

At one point this project was nothing but a glimmer in someone's brain, but I never knew whether it was your glimmer or Howard Schultz, or someone else. What is the creation story?

Crow: In 2017, Howard Schultz, the chairman and CEO of Starbucks, and I were both in the Markle Foundation's national project called Rework America.[1] The objective of the Markle Foundation was to catalyze the coming together of people from all sectors to think about the fourth wave of change in the Industrial Revolution, which is the digitization and automation of nearly everything. Howard was the cochair of the overall meeting, and I was the cochair of one of the two subgroups. There were about 40 people involved. The group I was responsible for cochairing was the group focused on the future education of the individual.

Howard and I started going to these meetings all over the country. We started talking off to the side, and one of the things we talked about was the student debt issue and especially its relation to student degree completion.

Together we decided to see if we could think of a way to help people who had gone to college but didn't finish. From a public policy design perspective, we have this massive expenditure, $25 billion-plus this year for Pell Grants, exceeding half a trillion dollars since 1980. But more than half the people that have received Pell Grants from the US government to go to college have neither a degree nor a certificate. They have no associate's degree, no bachelor's degree, nothing. The program has not been as successful as one would hope.

Bozeman: Do you happen to know what percentage of those people who, one, have Pell Grants and, two, haven't finished are enrolled in for-profit universities?

Crow: I don't recall the exact figures, but Pell students at for-profit universities are a lot less likely to graduate.[2] Many of the recruiters at the for-profits are overpromising, and the institutions are under-achieving. Many for-profits have little or no support services. They spend a huge amount on marketing and recruitment instead.

At one point during our discussions, Howard said, "Well, let me take a look at Starbucks." He comes back later and says that about half of the Starbucks employees have attended college but never finished. Since they had about 150,000 or more employees at the time, just in the United States, that's a really big number that attended but did not complete.

Bozeman: So why do you think so many students, Starbucks employees and others as well, fail to finish?

Crow: Reasons are many and complicated, and I understand some of it from my own experience. Basically, life happens. For example, someone might say "My mom got cancer, and I dropped out, and I couldn't go back," or "I had to work full time and got a .08 grade point and they wouldn't take me back," or "My dad died, and I had no money." It could be anything. I experienced similar things myself, so did you.

Bozeman: Yep, I can relate. As you know, I was able to go to college because I started out in a really inexpensive community college and had a modest athletic scholarship and then a work-study job. My parents, who didn't have much money, did what they could to help, even though my dad was unemployed for part of the time.

Crow: Right, life happens. My family had challenges, yours did, and so did a lot of people working at Starbucks.

Bozeman: So how did ASU become part of the solution?

Crow: The timing was good. At about the same time I was working with Howard and others at Starbucks to see what we could do to help out with the problem of debt and dropout, ASU had made a transformative decision to embrace technology as an egalitarian enabling tool that would allow us to be able to educate across a broader spectrum of students and learners. We had begun launching our online programs, and so I said, "Well, maybe we could build a program where your employees could finish college, allowing them to graduate without cost or debt."

Now, true to form, everybody was really excited about that, but no one had really thought about what it would actually take to do that. The genesis of the idea was to actually do a project that could fundamentally alter the college completion rate, especially among people who had, for whatever reason, not been able to finish college. Then and later, we spent a lot of time just listening to people and the issues or problems they face. Recently, we've gotten together with some of the (to date) more than 3,000 graduates of the ASU-Starbucks partnership and heard these unbelievable stories. No one goes away with a dry eye.

This woman came up to me just last May and she said that she wasn't able to finish her freshman year. She told me her story and what had happened to her and how she always wanted to be a teacher. Then, sure enough, she goes to ASU. She finishes ASU online through the Starbucks Program, no debt, finished the program. Now, she was selected for Teach for America. Where was she going? She was moving to the Mississippi Delta, that delta region in Arkansas and Mississippi along the Mississippi River where the level of educational attainment is low and the poverty index is high. Here we were helping empower this person. Helping her make her contributions to public values.

Bozeman: I guess one of the keys to understanding the ASU-Starbucks partnership is the nexus of timing and technology development. The viability of the technology was just approaching its potential at the same time as the social need was gaining awareness. So, part of the solution was bringing the two together.

Crow: Yes, but it's not just not the technology. If we look back a few years, well before we began thinking about the partnership, we see our own institution, ASU, consistently underperforming. At that time, we had a subpar four-year graduation rate, particularly among minority and low-income students, and a subpar retention rate, again particularly among minority and low-income students.

In tackling that problem, we decided that, just from an affordability perspective, we would have to enhance our faculty's capabilities with technology. We began a process of acquiring technological partners and then synthesizing and integrating those partners. We were willing to think differently, to think about the need for multiple institutional partners. No need to go it alone. Ultimately, ASU acquired more than 200 technology partners. We integrated those partners, not in a "learning platform" that would be too simple and wouldn't solve the problem, but into a learning network. In that learning network, partnering in technology, but also with new organizational and education delivery programs, we drove up our retention and graduation rate. We changed our math outcomes, which had been one of the big bugaboos. We changed our outcomes in other courses that we call gateway courses. We have no remedial courses, just gateway courses that you have to make it through, but at your own pace. Then we could begin to see the power of the technology. For example, with Math 142, which is first-year math, we did an experiment with more than 1,000 students where we tracked their learning pathways using a new adaptive learning technology that we had put in place, which allows a student to be computationally tutored individually, relative to their strengths and their weaknesses in math. We anticipated that, with 1,000 freshmen, we'd get 40 or 50 different pathways.

Bozeman: So, did you actually get 40 or 50 different pathways?

Crow: No, we got 1,000 different pathways. Every student learned in a completely different way. They would go from section 1 to section 2.8 to section 3.5 to section 6 and then, ultimately, make their way through the course. We learned that we had been approaching things wrong. We changed our logic relative to the introduction of technology within the institution. We began expanding that approach and began to think, "Well, if we can do this, then these same technologies can reach people at scale outside of the university."

Bozeman: From a technology standpoint, I guess timing must have been a key issue?

Crow: Sure. This could not have happened much earlier. Technology hadn't been good enough in the past. The bandwidth hadn't been good enough. The scale hadn't been large enough. The learning methodologies, the big data analytics—none of those had been capable enough. But now the technologies had improved, and we brought all these advances together. That allowed us to build a mix of on-campus and online programs, each using enhanced digital technology. These technology-based learning enhancements played a major role in allowing us to double our four-year graduation rate, increase our retention rate to the same level of those universities that only admit A students, whereas we admit A and B students from high school to our first-year class. We had just had the new technology up and running for a couple of years at the time we encountered this Starbucks partnership opportunity. Now the relationship has taken many, many expansive twists and turns, all positive. But that's where we started: need, technology, and partnership, all coming together.

Bozeman: One of the things that we talk a lot about in this book is mutable leadership, the idea that leaders play different roles at different times and different leaders step to the fore as needed. You gave me an excellent overview of events, but not much indication of the particular people and partners. Tell me about some of the people, particularly, at ASU and what they did to advance these public value objectives.

Crow: I know most of them. At ASU, first the faculty, the ones who have to design the courses from their experience and research and build the courses and build the materials. The faculty's willingness to participate and support something like the Starbucks College Achievement Program—this was crucial. It wouldn't happen everywhere, maybe nowhere, at least at this scale and at this time. Our faculty thought this was something we needed to be doing, that it wasn't just some sort of strange sideshow. Nobody said, "Why would we help Starbucks baristas? That's not our job." Most of our faculty, deans, and school chairs said, "Hell yeah, we wanna do that. If we can be of service to them and not blow this place up, then let's do it."

Bozeman: That sounds a lot like the points that Freeman Hrabowski was making with his youth program—that nothing much happens if you don't have a faculty motivated by the idea.

Crow: Yes, that's at UMBC and here at ASU and probably any university that has an interest in public values as a key function.

Bozeman: But there was also a big role for staff and administrators.

Crow: With the faculty buy-in we began to construct teams, especially in the entity we call EdPlus at ASU, our online education experts. EdPlus is led by Phil Regier, Leah Lommel, and Sean Hobson. Those would be the three main people in that part of the organization. Those three people then began working with our chief marketing officer within the university, Dan Dillon, our senior vice president Jim O'Brien for university affairs, our technology team, and Lev Gonick, who now manages our technology platform. These folks and many others were the architects of the program. They designed the program, set up the financial structure of the program, developed the marketing strategy that we used to reach tens of thousands of people spread out across all 50 states.

Bozeman: Given the nature of the student clientele, I guess some of the challenges were a little different than the norm?

Crow: Right. It's not like you just flip a switch and people who haven't been to college for years just conclude all of a sudden, say, "Yeah, I'm goin' back to college. Colleges have always screwed me my entire life and failed to help when I was down, but now I'm going to college again. I'm going back to college despite the fact they threw me out, despite the fact they helped me accumulate a massive debt. Yeah, now I'm ready to get back with those same people who hurt me." It's not an easy sell for people; many have had really bad experiences. We found just how much anger and hurt and, I guess, disenchantment many of these people felt. Most were wary and needed to be convinced.

Bozeman: I know exactly what you mean. I'm sure I've never told you this, but when I go to Starbucks, I often ask the employees, "Do you know about the ASU-Starbucks program? What do you think about it?" I often hear what you just said: "Well, I was in college, it didn't work, I don't want to get screwed again." Bad treatment, lots of debt, that leaves scars.

Crow: Yes, so that was one of our biggest lessons—the level of social alienation shocked us. We had to start by getting their trust. Not just ASU, but the whole higher education sector was something many didn't trust. Three-fourths of the people eligible for the program already had some debt from some previous educational experience. I met one young woman who went to Scottsdale Community College. She was living in California at the time she signed up for this. She had $20,000 of debt from her community college experience, not that the college was that expensive, but she was borrowing money to live on while she went to college.

Bozeman: You've talked about the ASU team contribution. What about Starbucks?

Crow: It's really kind of a complicated thing. We formed a management committee that then would work with the Starbucks people. At Starbucks, Howard Schultz was personally involved all along the way. One of his staff and key leaders, an executive vice president named Vivek Varma, played a major role. He and several senior officers focused on social responsibility. Many people had a role to play at Starbucks, but the CEO investment was vital. As we encountered different decision points along the way, if the CEO hadn't been personally invested and personally involved, it would've gotten killed off along the way. We had to work with them closely on price. It's not like Starbucks can just pay whatever we want to charge. They work on a business model. But we also had to break even. We couldn't keep it going if we were losing massive amounts of money.

Bozeman: Setting up a financial model that works for all parities is very difficult. Who at ASU helped with that?

Crow: Rich Stanley, ASU senior vice president and university planner, designed the financial model, working with Starbucks and then later with our EdPlus people, Phil Regier, as the head of that unit, and Leah Lommel. That was back-and-forth negotiation. Ultimately, we had to decide, as a university, to keep our margins just as low as possible so the program would be affordable.

The Starbucks employees and our students helped us deal with all this. There's a video I can show you where I gave a speech to 35 governors at the National Governor's Association, and then a Starbucks student gets up behind me to talk about her experience.[3] Well, I'm just the wrapper of the package. The package is the student. One student steps up and talks about going to college, dropping out, marrying her husband in the Coast Guard, moving around, starting a family, working in Starbucks to support her family along with her service-oriented husband. She thought there was no way to ever finish college, no way to advance her life. She hoped to support her children in college, but not herself. The end of the story is that she's now graduated from ASU. She's been accepted into the George Mason University School of Public Health.

Bozeman: A great story. Resonates with me. As you know, my parents didn't go to college. Both were really smart, incredibly well-read, and neither finished high school. Like the woman you're talking about, they just spent their time and resources hoping to help me get to college, no thought about themselves having such a chance.

Crow: Right, both of our families were working-class families, and so most of the people we knew didn't go to college. Our parents didn't go to college, and then we found our way somewhere along the way, and we lucked out. Not everybody lucks out. In fact, most people don't luck out. The people at ASU and at Starbucks viewed this, at the time, as a socially important—unbelievably important—project to get started. There was a big article in *Atlantic* magazine on this ASU-Starbucks partnership.[4] The writer asked me, "Well, do you guys think you can save the world?" And we said, "No. One university and one company, no, we're not going to save the world. But we might show how the world might be saved." Meaning, if we had 40 major universities and 40 major companies, that might come closer to saving the world. In this program we're going to graduate 25,000 people. We have 12,000 students involved in it right now, 8,000 in the College Achievement Program alone.

Bozeman: Some people leave college with "bad paper," low grades, dismissal. Some of these people, as you know, have a lot of potential but initially fail because of chance and circumstance. What, if anything, does the program do to help these people?

Crow: When people are not yet eligible for admission, we don't turn them away. Right now we have 3,000 people who are not eligible to be admitted to ASU who are now on what we call our College Pathways Program. We give them four courses through our Global Freshman Academy, where if you take these four courses and you get a B or better, we'll admit you to the university. We call it our 400-hour SAT test. One of them is a math course that we have, this unbelievable math course with adaptive learning technology, intelligent tutors—all these things. What we're finding is those 100 students that we've admitted so far, when they get to the university their GPA is half a standard deviation above the norm. It's 3.65. What we've been doing here—and the people that have been involved in this—is we realize we're reaching out to a group of people that have been abandoned by higher education.

The system that we inherited in higher education is a crushing elitist sorting system that basically sorts for certain kinds of intelligence, certain kinds of ability, and gives little credit for much else. In this old system, if you succeed, you're going to make it; if you don't succeed, too bad for you. This system just casts you off to the side. In a society that can't produce enough college graduates, and where there aren't enough college graduates coming from the lower half of family incomes, we need a new model for empowering success. Most of the Starbucks employees we work with are from this group, not the elite group. Most are baristas, and 95% are from low- and middle-income families and are Pell-eligible based on their family income. Almost all of them have debt, much of it still on the books due to student loans. They all, or nearly all of them, have debt.

Bozeman: It seems as though both sides, both ASU and Starbucks, started with big concepts and a clear public values vision.

Crow: That's right. From the outset we said, "We have no interest in getting together on this if it is just an incremental HR benefit." They already had a tuition benefit of up to $5,800 a year. But not many people took it. We made this an exclusive Starbucks-ASU partnership, partly to ensure quality control and increase the chances for achievement. We told Starbucks, "You need to educate your managers, so they know this is not just another benefit, it's part of your culture." And they did just that.

Bozeman: The partnership received a good deal of attention, right from the get-go. Can you say a little bit about how it was launched?

Crow: When we announced this program, Howard and I sat before the *Wall Street Journal* editorial board, the *New York Times* editorial board, and the *Washington Post* editorial board. We had a three-day campaign. We were traveling all over, but mostly Washington and New York, and we were announcing the program and holding meetings and had both ASU and Starbucks people there. We had about four billion media impressions associated with the announcement, some neutral, some positive, some negative. We expected that the higher education press would be against us, and we were right. Initially, there was not a single positive article or editorial out of anything associated with the higher education press.

Bozeman: Why do you think that is?

Crow: Because the higher education press, at least many of them, buy into the traditional model that higher education is a privilege for the gifted, and so why would you go back and pick up dropouts and people who had for some reason "failed." Our response, basically, was, "Well, that's not the kind of university we are or wish to be."

Conversation: The ASU, Inclusiveness, and Public Values Part

Bozeman: That relates pretty closely to a cornerstone value of ASU, which I'm sure—well, I know—is quite controversial, which is the idea that we measure our success not by whom we exclude . . .

Crow: . . . but who we include and how they succeed, right. That's the first line in the university charter.[5] And the charter also includes a commitment to public value.

Bozeman: Right, okay. That's in the charter of the university. There was initially strong opposition to the ASU-Starbucks partnership and, in general, to the idea of measuring success by inclusion. That does seem radically different to most people, at least most in charge of universities.

Crow: Yes, there's still lots of pushback. But I think we're winning the debate. Not everyone agrees with our mission, but people are being won over. I think people in Arizona see this university as having a unique institutional mission and most people support it or want to be part of it. But that is not necessarily the case outside of ASU and Arizona. Constantly we hear, "You cannot be good and big at the same time. You're as big as you can get, any bigger and your quality will decline and keep declining." Lots of people still think the mission of the big research university is to be more and more selective. That is the standard operating method for the driving of excellence. When you went to Ohio State in the 1970s anyone with a high school diploma in that state could go there.

Bozeman: Yes, I know those days well, I taught there as an instructor during my doctoral studies, and some of the courses I taught were large introductory classes in American government. The downside of completely open admissions is that some people go just to kill time or because they have no idea what to do with themselves—though that is not always a bad thing at 18 or 19. But at OSU during the open admission days the attrition after one year was remarkable. Still, many of those who remained and flourished would have never had a chance to get an inexpensive, high-quality education. The ability to go to school with free tuition was life changing for thousands.

Crow: Right. But nowadays even the big land-grant state universities, like Ohio State and my own undergraduate school Iowa State University, are looking to move up in the rankings by bragging about how many people do not get accepted. When I became ASU president in 2002, the "standard operating manual" for new presidents said two things about how to make your university better, or at least more reputable. First, you cut out the bottom half of your freshman class in terms of academic credentials coming from high school, and, second, you start a medical school, whether needed or not, so that you can immediately ratchet up your research funding. We self-consciously did neither. We maintained egalitarian admissions standards. Not low standards, egalitarian. Our admission standards are very much the same as those in 1950 at another large, quality state university, the University of California at Los Angeles. In 1950, what you needed at UCLA was a B average minimum, and a B in 15 of 16 courses that you needed to take in high school to be ready for college. If you have those two things, come on down. In 1950, UCLA was already a research university, one with free tuition.

Well, why can't that kind of institution or something that's as close to it as possible still exist today? The main barrier is not financial; it is how excellence is measured—by exclusion. The idea that you can't really be good unless you are excluding more and more students, the idea that size doesn't work because if you are big, then you're not selective enough, you just can't be any good. Well, that is just plain false. We have an egalitarian admission at ASU, but we also have more very high performing students than all but about 10 universities in the nation. In our honor's college, we have 8,000 students, all of whom are high performers who would have been admitted to many so-called elite schools. We have more students in our honors college than Stanford has in their entire undergraduate population. The idea that highly qualified students cannot be attracted to a big behemoth university is wrong.

Bozeman: So, you think both the concepts and the numbers that some people use are just not the right ones?

Crow: It is not always because people don't care about equality; in many cases their ideas about quality education work against equality. For example, there's a guy named David Leonhardt who writes for the *New York Times*.[6] He's a smart guy, good guy, cares about education. He wrote an article a couple years ago that said that America's 275 best universities aren't admitting enough poor kids. If they could just admit more poor kids, the country would be a better place. ASU is not on that list. Why? Because the only universities and colleges on that list are ones that have a 75% six-year graduation rate. The only universities that have a 75% six-year graduation rate do not admit B students, only A students. These are universities where "good" is not enough. So, I explained to him that this was a trap, the reasoning that "they have the best graduation rates, so, therefore, they must be the best." I said, "Oh, by the way, compared to the 275 universities on your list, ASU produces more graduates with A-only averages than all but three others. And, by the way, we have more poor kids than any one of them." Those are not just details. Many people believe it is impossible to have scale, diversity, and quality. They are wrong.

Bozeman: Well, I have some notions about just how higher education works at this time in the evolution of American universities, and educating massive numbers of people is viewed as something for lower-tier universities. But if there is contradiction here, it is not between size and quality but, just my opinion, between public values and elitism. I can't think of too many instances where public values, in education realms or in other institutions, thrive in harmony with elitist assumptions. At this point, ASU is distinctive, if not unique, in part because of the faculty. There is not much pushback at ASU on the size-equality-quality assumptions. By this time, I know a lot of people here, and the faculty tend to fall into two categories, those who don't think much or care too much about public value and equality goals and just want to get on with their own work, and those that are enthusiastic about the public value mission. The third category, those who want to slim down the institution, raise admissions to the "don't-apply-unless-you-are-top-5%level," that category is very sparsely populated.

Crow: That's right. We just developed a partnership with Uber that is in some ways like our work with Starbucks. I didn't get hate mail from the faculty. Instead, I got a lot of email and conversations that said, "Well, great, those Uber drivers that didn't finish college ought to be able to go to college, too."

Bozeman: Something I have wondered about, and I would like to get your take on, why do you think it was possible to win over people here at ASU to what is in some ways a radical idea, the idea of size-equality-quality compatibility?

Crow: I think part of the reason for ASU faculty and staff commitment to inclusiveness is that there has never been an elitist culture here. Second, the university was not hard and rigid in a contest where they believed that their identity depended on comparison to other universities. Those two features were present, and that meant that you could suggest a unique or differentiated design with the social mission as a part of it, and you could at least be heard.

There are some other universities with strong inclusivity values. But it is never easy to get a "quality" institution interested in being just as committed to inclusiveness. An example is Purdue University, where, as you know, the former governor of Indiana, Mitch Daniels, became president. After talking to us and visiting ASU, he said, "Well, you know the land-grant model and we want to build on that model." Purdue is probably one of the five most significant emergent land grants in the last 150 years, and its new president was asking, "Why can't we strive to reach every family?" He's not an academic. He's a business guy and a politician. He goes to his faculty and says, "I'd like to scale the university to engage with everyone." The majority of the Purdue faculty said no, that's not the kind of university we want.

Bozeman: Yeah, I followed this conflict closely. It was in the *Chronicle of Higher Education* nearly every issue for a while.

Crow: Right. So, Daniels says, "Okay, then I'm going to go out and buy a for-profit university intact, Kaplan University. I'm going to convert it into a not-for-profit. I'm going to rename it Purdue University Global, PUG. I'm going to drive it forward on a global basis. The faculty then decided to make their last stand at the higher learning commission to try to make sure PUG would not be accredited. Didn't work. PUG was accredited, and now it's underway.

I am not an expert on Purdue faculty, but I expect they are not much different from many faculty—happy with the trajectory they have been on for years. They are a well-established, high-performing research university, so why look at this new model, the one we call the New American University model or the fifth-wave model? But their president led the way and developed support. Are there are other universities that want to take on the fifth-wave model, quality, and scale? The answer is yes, but they are not in most cases among the top 100 research universities; they are places like Central Florida, places like Georgia State, places that have already had an inclusiveness mission.

Bozeman: You referred to some of the universities in the new University Innovation Alliance, which you helped design and you are the chair. Maybe you can tell me a bit more about the alliance, who is involved, and its goals.

Crow: We got 10 other universities to join us in implementing this new model, the one we call fifth wave. The universities in the alliance include Central Florida, Georgia State, Purdue, Michigan State, Ohio State, Kansas, Texas, Iowa State, Oregon State, and UC Riverside. As you know, this is a group of very diverse universities. Intentionally, we wanted to make sure we had only one university in the state; otherwise, the power dynamics and state politics would get in the way. These 11 schools, including ASU, agree on the following goals: producing more graduates, especially more graduates from lower-income families, including Pell-eligible families; we are going to lower the costs of education; and we will innovate together on some projects. We will produce, in the first four years, 75,000 more Pell-eligible graduates from those 11 schools than would have normally been the case. We may be seeing an emergence of social scale universities that can be critical assets in a national transformation in public values–based higher education.

Bozeman: When institutions develop partnerships, they become, for good or ill, linked in the public's mind. Recently ASU has partnered with Uber, but Uber has had a good deal of publicity. Does that pose problems for ASU or other partners? Seems to me when you partner with a Starbucks or an Uber, you also expose your institution to any bad publicity they generate.

Crow: Yep. With Starbucks the issue was the Philadelphia racial incident.[7] So let me back up on Starbucks. We started with the College Achievement Program. We think that's been very successful. It's continuing to accelerate. We're going to produce 25,000 graduates. That's our goal. We're about 10% or 15% toward that goal right now.

The second program we started was a green apron program where we started becoming their teacher relative to sustainability, allowing a sustainability certificate now to permeate its way through the Starbucks Corporation. The third thing that we started was a global learning academy.

They wanted us to work with them. In a sense, buddying up with this company to help them to be successful relative to human capital development. We deployed a learning platform for the families of all the employees in their new stores in India, Canada, UK, and Brazil. The notion is, if you sign up for Starbucks, well, then your family gets access to this learning platform, and the learning platform is not degrees, but courses on this and that and all these other things.

Then, along the way, they have the Philadelphia event where two African Americans get kicked out of the store, largely because they're black. They were drinking water waiting for their next meeting, and, because they hadn't ordered something, they get kicked out. Now no one gets kicked out of a Starbucks store. Apparently, these two guys did. The ASU involvement in the aftermath of this has been to launch a 30-module course that our School for Social Transformation has built on race sensitivity, gender sensitivity, and sexual identity sensitivity.

Then, turning to the Uber case, Uber has a number of historic issues, mostly related to sexism and human resources problems. Now they are trying to clean these up. They changed the CEO. They changed their chair. In our case, we're going into this relationship with eyes wide open. Can we help the individual to be successful as a learner, and then can we help the company to evolve socially, also, through enhanced thinking and instruction and so forth?

Bozeman: Basically, what you seem to be saying is you start out with a focus on public value, and then it broadens to permeate the institution.

Crow: Yes. That's what we hope to do. We view ASU as a major resource for social transformation of all sorts. We have a modern multidisciplinary, transdisciplinary university, including our School of Social Transformation, our School of Sustainability—we have 50 or so faculty members directly involved in, and committed to, social transformation.

Companies don't have anything like that. Companies are profit-seeking, customer-serving, shareholder-driven institutions. When they move to include a public values orientation, they don't always have the resources they need. Public values–focused universities can help them make these changes.

So, maybe that answers part of your question about the risk of working partnerships, but maybe you have some different ideas?

Bozeman: No, not really. I'm just suggesting that the types of activities you are talking about and actually doing are risky and complicated, but also very much needed. As is so often the case in public values design, a big issue is trust. In the case of university-corporate partnerships, we are often talking about institutions with cultures and resources that are, if not at odds with one another, at least different from one another. But the ASU experience, as well as many of the interviews in this book—St. Vincent de Paul, the Competitiveness Council, UMBC—these show that such partnerships are difficult, but often game-changing. I guess a big part of it is connecting with a corporate leader that is concerned with profit and shareholder wealth, but not only those concerns.

Crow: Right, Howard Shultz is one of those types of corporate leaders, and we knew that before ASU got involved with Starbucks. He had already developed health insurance for everybody at Starbucks, even part-time employees. He set up ownership of the company for everyone, even part-time employees. It is a whole different approach to focusing on the worker, not only the bottom line. Because of that, the risk of partnership was not as great as it might have seemed; they already had a track record of thinking about public values.

Bozeman: I've had the chance to work with a good number of CEOs, partly in my consulting, as members of the National Academy of Sciences committees, and such. Most of them are not Howard Schultz. The ones I know, typically, are smart, accomplished, and honorable, but they are driven by profit maximization and don't give much thought to public values. They are not necessarily working counter to public values, but many simply do not view public values as significantly related to their jobs. Here's a tough question for you: do you think there is any way to recruit people into a public values regime if their corporation is not already led by people who have a public values orientation?

Crow: Well, I think the answer is yes, but here's what we think might also occur: You've got multiple outcomes from this Starbucks-ASU deal. One is, will Starbucks be a better company in its normal measures of success? Shareholder value return, wealth generation—all those are considerations. Will it be a better company with these enhanced investments in human capital and the not yet conclusive but, nonetheless, directional indicators? Absolutely unequivocally yes, because, now, they're seeing higher levels of retention and performance changes and all kinds of other things that they didn't really anticipate.

Many socially conscious, highly public value–driven corporations outperform competitors. We recently started a partnership with another corporation known for taking public values into account—Adidas.

Bozeman: Another company recently receiving bad publicity for commercial deals with college coaches and basketball players.

Crow: Yes, they have had their problems, as almost all companies do from time to time. Universities have scandals too. If you only deal with organizations that never have scandals, then you won't have many to choose from. At any rate, we listened when Adidas came to us a few months ago and said, "ASU seems to have these values about sustainability and transnational education and such." After some talks, we started a relationship with them that now includes a College Achievement Program that's just getting started, that has a series of research projects, including work with our new center on global sports.

But back to your point, what we're looking for are companies that self-select. Now, how do you move public values attainment in a corporate model where it's not CEO to CEO? I don't know if I have an answer to that because it turns out that, in every institution, including this one, if we had just left it to a random series of interactions at the unit level within this university, we wouldn't have many of the corporate partnerships we've put in place. There has to be involvement at the top, but if it is only from the top, you have problems. You need to get people involved throughout the organization.

Bozeman: You have to have leadership at the top. An old prescription, but a good one.

Crow: Right, including at universities. But this requires new forms of leadership; universities can't be command and control. It's like what we are saying with the mutable leadership idea. Universities and most institutions nowadays don't run like the army, not some hierarchical command structure, but on ideas and in most cases competing ideas. Not just ideas, but hopefully ideals.

Bozeman: But how do you sustain public values? Howard Schultz stepped down as CEO. At some point you will step down at ASU either through retirement or another job or going to the great beyond. That brings up the question of the relation of public values–focused leadership and executive succession. What do you think you can do to keep ASU moving in a public values direction?

Crow: One thing we did here was to develop and adopt a university charter, one that includes public values as a major element. You might have noticed we recently put a monument up on campus, stone and metal, that shows the charter to everyone as they enter the north part of the Tempe campus.

Bozeman: Not only do I know about it, I've got a picture of it. I use it in my teaching and many of my presentations at professional conferences. I feel good when I walk by it.[8]

Crow: We are trying to make public values service an immutable goal for ASU. If that happens, and I think it is happening, it won't make any difference if I am around anymore.

Thinking beyond ASU, I am working with some key people to develop the idea of the national service universities, ones focusing explicitly on public service and public values. Here at ASU faculty and administrative leaders are being recruited who embrace the idea of a public values university. We're concentrating a fair amount of energy on succession planning. We want to do all we can to make sure that future leaders are committed to the public values mission that is part of our charter.

Bozeman: It seems to me that ASU has a good chance to stay the course with a public values mission. Many people, almost all the people

I know personally, were attracted by the ASU culture. You have all this base—not just old-timers like me but also young people—who think, "Yeah, this is a great place to be" because of the way this place operates. It's not going to be easy to put the brakes on things. Institutional culture is very hard to change, especially when people embrace it and it seems to be working.

Crow: Right. I think we have designed a new type of university. The Starbucks-ASU partnership is not a one-off project. It is a reflection of the type of university we are and want to be. I'm sure the Starbucks people would say much the same thing; it is about the type of business they want to be.

Conversation: The Everything Else Part

Bozeman: In the old days when you had more time to spend on research, a big part of our joint work was based on interviews, often ones we conducted together. We had this practice, which I am sure you recall, of ending every interview with, "Now that you know what we are trying to get out, is there anything you can think of that we should have asked but didn't?" We also used that question with every one of the public values leaders we interviewed for the book. So, let's ask ourselves that question: "What else should we have asked that we didn't?"

Maybe I'll start out answering my own question. How about this—when it comes to public values in management and policy design, what is the role of education? To what extent is it really possible to educate someone to focus on public values, and to what extent does a commitment to public values relate to early socialization that has very little to do with education? This is something I have thought about a good deal, but never come up with much of an answer. The question does relate to this book. While our book is not exactly a managerial handbook, we do hope it will be useful, maybe as background and context at least, to people who already are or aspire to be public values leaders. I guess we would not be doing this if we did not at least think that it is possible for public values managers and leaders to become better and more effective in the enterprise. However, it seems to me that it is the level of commitment to public values that is most crucial, and that has little if anything to do with managerial technique or education. One of the things I think our public values leader interviews show is that there is more than one way to get to the right place.

Crow: I'm sure you remember that the day we met in 1981, you were leaving your office to go coach your son's baseball team. You had forgotten about our appointment, so you asked me if I wanted to go with you and throw batting practice. So, I went with you and took off my coat and tie and threw batting practice. You told me that day, "I can teach a .250 hitter to be a .275 hitter, but I can't teach a .250 hitter to be a .350 hitter."

Bozeman: I sort of remember that, sounds like something I would say. But I think it's true. A great aspiration for this book would be making a public values leader just a little bit better of a leader. That would be a great outcome. Now that we have repelled a large percentage of our readers with a sports metaphor, can you think of anything else that bears some attention?

Crow: I think that one thing. I have this logic in my head, you may not agree with this, that there are just a few core values—liberty, justice, and equality—and that these are reflected in the US Constitution. They are articulated there, even if we haven't achieved them. But these are the only public values. Most of the public values beyond these few relate to particular things that people want to see happen. Most of our institutions can operate quite well without giving any consideration to either these macro public values or the more specific ones about which there is a great deal of agreement by citizens.

Bozeman: Since we agree on so many things, I was going to ask you about something we disagree on. And here it is! Actually, I don't agree with that. I think there are things that most people agree on, but not everyone, and I think things that almost everyone agrees on at one point in history, they do not agree on at another point. I don't really think there are immutable public values, just the public values that exist during a time and in a society. You would say you are more of an idealist. In a way you are—you are more of a Platonist, that sort of ideal form, than me. But the fact that I don't think there are a few core public values doesn't mean that they are less important. Maybe more important because societies are always sorting and changing, even if slowly, their ideas about public values. Today, liberty seems to be ascendant. Maybe someday equality or opportunity will be ascendant.

Crow: Yes, we have had this debate before. I am unyielding.

Bozeman: Since you and I met up many years ago at the Maxwell School of Citizenship and Public Affairs—I love that name, who else has citizenship in the name?—you've spent your time and energy working on a wide variety of public values–focused projects, leading many of them. To what extent do you think the fact that your academic work—your education in ideas related to public interest, public values, public good—shaped your ideas and strategies about how public values–based organizations and institutions should be run?

Crow: Dramatically, even more than you might realize, I'm probably even more of an idealist than you, in some ways—at least, that's my guess—in the sense that, when I went to Maxwell, the main attraction to me, other than working with you, was it seemed to be a place focused not just on what the democracy had been, but what it could be.

The courses I was able to take [at Syracuse University's Maxwell Graduate School of Citizenship and Public Affairs] in normative political theory, public administration, and organizational theory and design—all of those had a dramatic effect on me. The different kinds of analytical tools we learned to help us make decisions and then the philosophy courses and the philosophy of economics, all of these shaped my thinking fundamentally. Again, I'm the idealist, maybe, but the Athenian oath that is carved into the wall about leaving the city more beautiful than it had been left to us, the ideal of public service democracy,[9] is important.

What about you, what were some of the factors that led you to start writing and doing research on public interest and public values? Did it start with your graduate school education?

Bozeman: Not so much. My graduate school education was focused more on quantitative political science, garden-variety empirical research. I don't think I ever had a course on normative political theory. Most of my work has its root in my own discontents. When I began working on "publicness," the discontent was with the stereotypes that dominated most scholarly work in organization theory and management. Why was everything divided into government and business, when in fact there were so many other organizational forms? When I began to work on public values and public failure, it was a reaction against the widespread belief that the market is invariably the best provider of goods and services. Then labeling government as underperforming when it is presumed to have its responsibilities because market organizations have failed, that made little sense. Most of all, the idea there is simply no role for positive government. I viewed this as a stunning misconception, and one not well supported in history, either US history or world history.

My current research is based on my latest discontent—what I call deep corruption, the undermining of public interest and public values to benefit the powerful few, usually through actions that are entirely legal, but powerful interests have undermined democracy. Your idealism, my discontents. I guess maybe we start from somewhat different places, but get to the same destination—public values realized through democratic institutions.

Crow: Yes, in my mind it's vital to keep the link between education and democracy. Ultimately, you can't have a democracy that works and achieves if educational attainment is not equally available to anyone that wants to give it a shot, or if you have an educational system that is so biased that the brightest kids from the lowest-income families have no chance of moving ahead. In the Starbucks partnership, we began to talk about what we refer to as conscience capitalism, which is a phrase—there's a whole group of corporations that view themselves as capitalists with conscience, ones that have multiple bottom lines. We agreed that institutions, if they work together, can achieve egalitarian outcomes with conscience capitalism. What public value is greater than opportunity for human improvement? All entities can see the importance of pursuing business practices that focus energy, time, and resources on helping those individuals succeed.

I did think of something else we should have spent a little more time on. Most of the book deals with public values leadership and management; that's what we set out to do, so no problem. The book includes quite a bit of our own experiences with organizations and policy making, focusing in some detail on public values at ASU. We have talked a lot about education for public values but have not said much of anything about *teaching* public values, and that's something both of us have been doing for years, especially you. How many years is it now that you've been teaching? I'm afraid to guess. So, maybe you can say a little bit about teaching public values in public policy and management?

Bozeman: That would be a pleasure and, you're right, I think that this teaching public values questions is the answer to "what should I have asked that I didn't." If only I had a good answer. I'll give it a try.

In the first place, I've never taught a course focusing explicitly on public values. However, it's been many years since I taught a course that was not framed by a public values perspective and, in most cases, not just indirectly sneaking into the course, but actually part of it. As you know, I am one of those rare faculty who really like to teach different things all the time rather than have the same teaching prep. What this means is that when I teach Higher Education Policy, its higher ed and public values; when I teach Introduction to Public Management, it is with a strong focus on public values. I even managed to get public values into my recent doctoral seminar on Evaluating Impacts of Science and Innovation.[10] However, when I teach public values, it is not a sneak attack approach. It's part of the syllabus, and we include a discussion of the basic concept and some of the theory.

Since most of my courses, even the interdisciplinary ones, have a significant number of public administration students, many of them interested in having careers motivated by public values (even if they would not express their motives in those terms), I usually have a receptive audience. Still, I try hard not to beat them over the head with my concept of public values, or anyone else's, and my chief interest is in getting them to deliberate, discuss, and sometimes debate some of the hard policy and management questions we raise in this book. I'm not trying to lead them to public values conclusions but public values thinking. As you know, I am a great believer in Socrates, a pretty good teaching model. In most of my classes, especially ones with students who are accustomed to just listening to the teach and the parroting, I tell them right away, "Look, I'm going to argue with just about everything you say," and I explain why I think that is a good way to learn, to have to defend their reasoning. I then tell them, this is even harder, "and I want you to argue with me, all the time, out loud or, if you can't do that, at least in your mind." I think this is a pretty good approach for lots of things, but particularly public values. There is nothing more basic, so it's worth not only the deliberation but also the argument.

Crow: Are there any books that you use for the purpose of getting across public values, other than your own book on public values theory?

Bozeman: Not really. In fact, I don't even use my own book since, as I said, I don't teach courses on public values per se and, not only that, it is usually easy and efficient for me just to talk about some of the ideas in that book rather than assign the whole thing. Usually, I assign books that do not necessarily relate directly to public values and then I try to make connections and get the students to do so as well.

Having said that, my own views and writings about public values, and public policy generally, have been greatly affected by a great many books, not all straight academic books but also novels and books on history. What are some books that have influenced your ideas about public values either as a scholar or as a practitioner?

Crow: I guess this is where I am supposed to say Bozeman's *Public Values and Public Interest*? Okay, not bad, but not number one. Maybe Walter Lippmann's *The Public Philosophy*. Anything by John Rawls. How about you?

Bozeman: I think Ayn Rand's *Fountainhead* is a magnificent book for figuring out exactly what not to do with one's life. It is the antithesis of public values and, I understand, the favorite book of some of my least favorite politicians. But on the positive side, maybe Steinbeck's *Grapes of Wrath*. I read that in high school. I was so inspired by Steinbeck that I went on to read all of his novels and many of his other works. Maybe it was because I was at such an impressionable age. I am still stuck on the literary realism genre, despite the fact that it's been dead for maybe 50 years; can't really compete in a cynical world where irony rules. I just reread a couple of Sinclair Lewis novels; lots of people are rereading *It Can't Happen Here*. I'm old enough to remember when we had a poverty policy, and more than a few people were taking very seriously the idea of eradicating poverty. Not a bad public values mission. When I was in graduate school, I read Frances Fox Piven's *Regulating the Poor* and Michael Harrington's *The Other America*. Harry Caudill's *Night Comes to the Cumberlands*, the latter being the intellectual grandfather of today's *Hillbilly Elegy*. Nonfiction social realism, I guess. These books made an impression. Like most of my favorite books, they are likely out of print. What do you think is the most important thing we have said in this book?

Crow: Anyone who wishes to do so can contribute to public values. It isn't necessary to be a CEO with thousands of employees or to have great power. We focus here on public values leaders, but I hope we also make the point that public values leaders don't get very far by themselves and that different people can lead at different times. Mutable public values leadership.

Bozeman: I can't disagree with that. We have to work hard to find much that we disagree on. I know we disagree on ribeye steak vs. sushi or country rock vs. free jazz, and definitely about David Lynch movies vs. David Lean movies. But not so much about public values, management, or public policy, except perhaps for the fact that I have the "who cares what he thinks?" freedom to be a little more out there in public policy dreamland than you or most people leading big organizations. Maybe we tend to agree on most policies because we have known each other since the dawn of time, but also because we had such similar experiences before that. Do you think that socioeconomic background or life experience makes much difference in whether or not one becomes a public values warrior?

Crow: Well, certainly not socioeconomic background. Look at the public values leaders we interviewed for this book. They have very varied backgrounds and mostly different from mine or yours. Life experience? Sure, but in complicated ways. Also, don't forget education. I think people can be educated to be more concerned about public values or at least about how to pursue them. I guess that is in part what we're trying to do here—start with readers who think maybe it is a pretty good idea to think about public values and give them some ideas about possible ways to get to the public values outcomes that interest them.

Bozeman: Yes, I agree. If you look at the best-known public values leaders, people like Martin Luther King Jr., Lincoln, Kennedy, Franklin and Eleanor Roosevelt, Cesar Chavez, Eisenhower, Sandra Day O'Connor, and, as an Alabamian, my personal favorite, federal judge Frank Johnson (well maybe he is not among the best known)—they have very different backgrounds, rich and poor, great formal education or very little, different race or gender. Nor does it make much difference whether one is a Republican or Democrat or a progressive or conservative, except that they might emphasize different public values to different degrees.

Crow: How do you convince leaders that institutions can have deeper and broader socially transformative impacts while not wounding the shareholder value or organizational self-interest? What if every organization could move beyond maximizing the value and power of the organization, whether business, government, or nonprofit, and give serious attention to maximizing the person, the citizen? What if you add commitments to the sustainability of the environment and a commitment to the community, not just the customer or the stakeholder? What if nearly every institution seriously embraced public values? What would the world be like? Would it be less political or more? Would there be more consensus or less? Okay, not every institution is going to transform. But how many public values organizations and institutions would it take to transform society?

Bozeman: It would take exactly 1,437, exactly.

Crow: Good to know.

Bozeman: Or, to put it another way, organizations and institutions are abstractions, they are made up of people. How many *people* would it take to transform society, to have a society that considers public value not just as the province of the few, the responsibility only of people working in "public service" jobs? The "how many" question is perhaps less important than the "who" and "how much" questions.

Crow: Both of us are history buffs, and I think we agree that history shows us that a relatively few people can bring about great changes, often changes that benefit the few, but sometimes changes that benefit everyone, public values changes. It's always a struggle to achieve public values. It takes energy, it can be exasperating. It takes time and patience. Sometimes it takes a thick skin. There's no textbook on how to do it, including this one.

Bozeman: Maybe we should surprise our friends and colleagues and end with that surprising note of humility.

Crow: No, let's end by asking the reader to answer our usual question: "Now that you know what we are trying to get at, what question should we have asked that we didn't ask?"

Bozeman: Right. Let us know.

COVID-19 and Public Values Leadership

The reader has perhaps observed a significant omission in our book, namely, the failure to discuss a set of contemporary events that are among the most important events in world history. Not even alluding to the COVID-19 pandemic? A serious omission indeed. But in all records and writing, timing is everything. In December 2019, when we were finishing this book, we were ignorant of the COVID-19 menace. Now (October 2020), as we write this, it dominates much of our life and almost everyone's. Thus, before going to press, we developed this afterword. Given the volumes written about the pandemic, we have nothing of general interest to add, but we thought the reader might be interested in how one institution we know well, Arizona State University, has thus far coped with the challenges presented by the pandemic. We focus especially on the difficulties of balancing public values in the face of dire and unrelenting change.

The style in this afterword is much the same as in the final chapter of this book, though it veers more toward an interview than a conversation. Bozeman has had no responsibilities as a COVID-19 decision maker, at least not outside his family, but Crow has faced the challenges confronting college presidents and, indeed, most executives of large institutions. We present this interview and his responses not as a paradigm for achieving public values during this crisis but more as a description of the learning and responses that have occurred in our ASU context. As always, we expect that the reader will engage in critical thinking and will have ideas regarding the wisdom and effectiveness of the ASU response and, we hope, can learn from it.[1]

Bozeman: It is not easy for us to briefly discuss what is perhaps the most critical set of events since at least World War II, but if we focus on its impacts on our own institution and the responses that you and others have made during the past few months, then perhaps we can learn something about public values leadership amid crisis.

Since you are the one deciding and implementing and my role is confined to simply teaching a graduate course on public policy and the pandemic, I think you will have a bit more to say. However, there is no interview protocol here, so let's just plunge in. Timing is everything here, so good to start at the beginning by identifying the beginning; when did you and other ASU decision makers first have COVID-19 on your policy response radar screen?

Crow: We set up our emergency response group in December, as soon as we heard there was a viral outbreak. We had experience with H1N1, and we were aware that something like this could happen any time. We had already stockpiled both resources and capabilities, and as soon as our meeting in December we were focused on policies and supply chain options.

Bozeman: One of the things that I'm curious about is how you decided whom to use as advisors. You say you already had expertise in place.

Crow: We have about 50 people in the university that are a part of this emergency response team, a medical group and a public safety technology group. Purchasing turns out to be a really big thing, having ready access to the right supplies.

What we decided to do was to expand our resources by building on our existing relationship with the Mayo Clinic, especially bringing in more infectious disease experts and more public health experts.

Bozeman: One of the things that's really interesting about this from the standpoint of public values is that COVID-19 is perhaps the best case imaginable to show that public values sometimes conflict and require difficult trade-offs. Everyone agrees that it is important to maintain public health and safety, to educate people for success in life and careers, and to sustain people economically with jobs, wages, and the ability to sustain themselves. The pandemic experience often has pitted these concerns against one another in difficult and challenging ways. Did you and other ASU leaders develop any heuristics or guidelines about how to make trade-offs among these crucial and to some extent competing public values?

Crow: And those are the three public values that we focused on initially. Was it possible to build a structure in which each of those values could be maintained at the highest possible level?

And it turns out that when we went through this logic, we studied masking and we studied all of our ventilation systems. We didn't have a testing technology. So, we built one, invented a saliva-based high-speed test. We learned that the virus is highly contagious. It's less lethal than SARS, but lethal. At least we had time to build a structure, one that would limit the transfer of the virus between the students and the workers, basically. And what we calculated was that the best way to limit the virus was intensive testing, random testing, ubiquitous testing for anyone who wanted it. Also, we tested masking and new social distancing technologies.

We have what we called our community of care, which was freedom of choice. You had to act responsibly. So, if you were, you know, 74 years old, the age group that was susceptible, then you don't come to class at all, you Zoom into class. If you are 30 years old and you don't have any preexisting conditions and you are masking, if you are in the low-probability category, then you can come in for a live class. So, you just basically try to structure things in a way that fits people. You try to control risk, while still allowing education to advance and work to advance. So far, everyone is still employed and everyone is getting an education, and we have tried to make it as safe as possible while at the same time achieving employment and education goals. To this point, we have no cases of transfer between students and staff, none. Our highest positive levels were in July, but at this point we have about 100 students positive out of 74,000, so the tools that we've used seem to have worked within the university bubble.

Bozeman: How did you go about contact tracing? I know just generally universities have had a very hard time doing that.

Crow: We contact trace everyone. We have had probably 3,000 people in social isolation, who were not positive but who had been in contact with someone who was positive, and that has worked out. We designed the institution to be able to operate under the assumption of 1%–2% simultaneously positive; it turns out that the population probably has a higher level of positivity than that right now. Many had to socially isolate, so we helped with food and everything else we possibly could.

Bozeman: One of the things we talked about in our books is the importance of multiorganizational linkages. Could you elaborate on the ways in which you might have linked up with other types of organizations, including other universities, and tried to pool information and expertise?

Crow: Well, one thing we did was we sent out all of our officers to their counterparts at the other universities, student affairs, academic affairs, purchasing, everybody, to see what everyone else was doing and learn from them.

We expanded our relationship with the Mayo Clinic and with a company that we and the Mayo Clinic helped to start. The company, called Safe Health, builds a health check app, for a daily health check. We expanded our relationship dramatically with Zoom. We built new relationships in other areas of educational technology. We partnered with everyone that we could possibly partner with, including the state of Arizona. The state then became an important partner for us. They helped us with funding, but we were also helpful to them with knowledge and expertise. We developed research funding for virus-related needs, including a point-of-need test where you spit into a microfluidic device and it tells you whether or not you have the virus, it talks to your cell phone, you get the green light and you are good to go.

We have a much stronger relationship with the CDC than with the state health department, the county health departments. We had weak relationships with those organizations before, and now we have strong relationships with them.

The numbers of partnerships expanded greatly. There's no way we could have solved all these things by ourselves. We don't have the full breadth of expertise and experiences. We have partners and advisers not just here but in Italy and Germany and England and China. The level of scientific collaboration and exchange has been massive. So, our scientific engagement on this is massive.

We have multiple vaccine groups in preclinical trials; we have testing groups. We have genetic assessment groups. We have epidemiological groups, those groups that are all linking in with everyone else. We have $100 million of new funding for COVID-related projects, we've got technology deals that we've been doing. How do we help develop these technologies and get them into use as quickly as possible? We also forged the largest educational technology deal that we've ever conceived of, right in the middle of the pandemic. This is for a full immersion virtual reality avatar-driven learning platform. That's now built and is up and running in a testing and development phase.

We are linking with first responder organizations. The electric utilities are partners; they have to keep all the electricity going and they're a testing partner. We're now spreading out and trying to partner with every school district, not just on educational content but content formatting, teacher training, testing health checks, everything. There's no way a school district can do these things by themselves.

The partnerships are vital. We can't go it alone. We can't just sit this out and hope for the best. The virus is not going anywhere. We have to have teams of institutions working constantly on this. It's a moving target.

We are now at the highest level of partnership engagement and linkage ever, by far, and I feel this in my own stress level. The relationships are vital, but they require attention and care.

Bozeman: If you look at sources such as the *Chronicle of Higher Education*, they gather information on university strategies for COVID-19 and break them down as face-to-face, fully online, and hybrid.

Clearly, ASU is in the hybrid category, a great deal online but also some face-to-face classes.

When you and other college presidents were choosing among these options, and there have been a lot of differences in the choice made, you knew you were going to get pushback no matter what you did. People had different ideas and felt very strongly about them. That's still the case. So how did you handle the pushback from people who were very upset with ASU's choices for dealing with the pandemic?

Crow: Our principal technique was to talk a lot, not to write a lot, but to talk, to meet to go through the data to talk about what we're doing. I probably have had many significant meetings with the Academic Senate leadership and several meetings with the Academic Senate. We have also used our chief science and technology officer, who has a deep understanding of the testing of the epidemiology, to go and meet with any group that wants to meet, faculty subgroups, schools, colleges, but also people outside ASU, especially school districts.

Our attitude was to be sure not to take offense at people who were throwing rocks, not to push back. This situation is different; everybody is anxious and tense and maybe not as reasonable as we would hope. Anxiety is not easy for anyone to deal with, and anxiety speaks for itself. People don't plan to be anxious or speak directly from anxiety, but they can't help it. This is different. People are worried about their families and their future, so discourse is not relaxed.

One thing we had argument about was random testing. We thought it was important to get good data. But we got pushback, and we expected we would get pushback. We had some faculty take shots at us as we were developing and using the data, but we sat down with them and explained in detail and things changed. We began providing more data on positivity rates and that helped. We also published our random testing data. Yes, we changed some of our approaches, we listened and made changes when needed. Sometimes you had to get beyond people's irritation and negativity and just listen, because sometimes they were right and were making good points. When you make an error, you admit your error. For example, we relied on negativity tests for entry into residential halls. This didn't work, so we changed our approach. Right now we have 30 cases in dorms, whereas at one point we had 600. One thing that helped, we were using an antigen test that is only 85% accurate, and now we are using a PCR test that is 99% accurate. Once we figured these things out and made adjustments, then we reported back to everybody and said, hey, this seems to be working now.

Basic point. Talk a lot. And don't take the bait when conflict escalates. Continue to listen to what people are saying, not the way they are saying it. People have lots of different ideas, and they are relevant. People who are normally very civil aren't always so civil when they are anxious and feel threatened. But their ideas are still important. You have to not only be a careful listener but try to be a hyper-rationalist. Emotion is natural, but it can't control decisions of this sort.

Bozeman: Small college towns with big universities pose particular problems, in part because almost all of them are surrounded by bars and restaurants and places for students to congregate and socialize. It can be difficult for universities or even the state governments to exercise a great deal of control of commerce. How have you been able to deal with this?

Crow: As corny as this "community of care" thing sounds, we have had a lot of buy-in. We have students' attention and something like 95% compliance.

Then, we began writing to businesses, you know, targeting all the stores well before students came back for the term, saying we're going to recommend that no one come to your store unless you follow these safety guidelines. We heard back from almost everyone. No problem. They got it. They were happy to help, and most of them have. But not all, especially the bars, chiefly because we have been opposed to the reopening of the bars.

The bars are sometimes not compliant with state standards and can be significant places for spreading the virus. We communicated with them and told them that we had hired safety investigators to go to the bars to see who is in compliance. Any who were not compliant we would report to the state health department and the state liquor board.

All we were asking them to do was to follow the state regulations. But some were none too happy about us doing that. I don't care. I mean, you know, you're going to follow the health and safety regulations or we're going to report you. And so we did.

But in the vast majority of cases the local business community has been very supporting and understanding. They don't want to threaten their customers' health or their own.

Bozeman: ASU has a great many students, including those from just about all political persuasions and, presumably, with very different ideas about the pandemic and approaches to it. Has ASU had much disruption in the classroom, regarding such things as wearing masks and social distancing?

Crow: We have had almost no problems with students in the classroom. We did have one faculty member who announced to his students, "Well, I don't believe in any of this. I don't know why everyone thinks this virus is a big deal." But he did have his mask on when he said it. We got in touch and said, essentially, "You need to alter your behavior or find some other place to work. You can't undermine university policies."

We did have a couple of threats of anti-mask demonstrations, but these didn't come to anything. As you know, it's not because students are apathetic. We had plenty of Black Lives Matter demonstrations, but nothing on anti-masking or social distance requirements.

We have had student issues, important ones, with mental health and anxiety, but we had no problems with students' compliance with safety standards.

Bozeman: Good to hear. Especially since we see so much in the media now blaming students.

Crow: The student blaming is crazy. That's just laziness. Our students have been great and easy to work with. They are exposed and we say go into isolation and they say "okay." We rarely have problems. They understand. I think that's why our rate of positives is actually lower than the rate for their cohort in the general population, despite the fact that many of them are on campus and actively participating in classes and labs.

Bozeman: So getting back to the students, to what extent and how do you and other ASU administrators communicate with them and address their concerns and worries?

Crow: I do hear from students directly and engage directly. We respond to everybody. Then there's student government, the five elected student government leaders. And then we have a highly skilled student services dean on every campus, and they are engaged all the time. They respond to crises, significant problems, but also to craziness and paranoia. No one is ignored. We are trying very hard to listen and, when we can, help.

Bozeman: One of the things that's always true from any sort of disaster this large scale is a chance to learn from it and make things better and develop innovations. For example, if you send a bunch of people off to war in Afghanistan and Iraq, we learn from the experience and develop new technologies and solutions. So, we now have much improved trauma medicine and improved artificial limbs. Likewise, much of operations research, which now is in effect in everything from traffic light programming for traffic smoothing to ambulance scheduling, developed from techniques invented for World War II bombing routes. Good things happen out of the bad. Even terrible circumstances permit learning.

What are lasting and useful lessons you and others at ASU have learned in the wake of the pandemic?

Crow: Yeah, we do have a list of good things coming out of this awful situation. As you know, we now have a third teaching modality. And what we call ASU Sync. We are making great use of Zoom video technology. So now if you're sick and you have to go home or your family needs you, and you have to leave school, you don't have to drop out. Or you can take care of your family at home and still go to class. We think that's a powerful thing. If you are place bound in any way you can still get a good education.

We also think that we can reshape the workplace to allow ASU families to have more flexibility at work. This change will extend beyond the pandemic. We think this new distance technology gives everyone more degrees of freedom.

We have also begun to seriously rethink the idea of a traditional academic calendar, that there is no reason why the calendar should be rigid. How do we make it more flexible, to the benefit of the students and to the benefit of families.

Our full immersion avatar-based virtual reality learning we think can be a game changer in science, in particular. We are now much ahead in telemedicine and telehealth and telecounseling.

Bozeman: Now a personal question. As I've told you many times, only somewhat facetiously, I would not be able to be paid enough to do your job, worrying every day about this gigantic institution. I can now safely reformulate that idea and say that not only is no pay enough but that I would pay to not have this job. I well understand that, for the entire time you have been president, you routinely make decisions that affect thousands of lives. But now? The stakes are even higher.

I would be driven crazy thinking about all the complications and possible unknowns from decisions you have to make. I would never get to sleep. How do you, personally, manage to deal with this, especially the pandemic-related decisions, and not just want to run away screaming for relief?

Crow: The way that I approach things is to try to make the best decision I can with the information that is available. And to always remember that I will have to adjust decisions after making them. I see very little as fixed and almost everything in need of adjustment. That is the mindset that allows me to not become overly anxious about the decisions. I do the best I can but also stay ready to make changes if it is not working out. So, I try to build options upon each new decision. Every time, every decision. I always have plans for what I call a disciplined retreat option. Bad things can happen when you make a decision that has no retreat option.

In my experience, both with people I know and from reading history, successful decision makers are rarely rigid.

Bozeman: Some leaders of large institutions are not doing so well in the environment of constant crisis. Have you observed an increased burnout rate? I know there have been many more retirements than usual.

Crow: I've seen several very different reactions to the pandemic. Some just hunker down waiting for it to go away, which is an error. Some university administrators are jumping contently from one small fire to the next, flailing at everything. They're using up all their work energy and they're not stable and do not give others either stability or confidence. Others are more focused, set priorities, and try to solve problems they can solve.

In my case it is all about having a managerial structure and then being prepared to adjust, learn, adjust. We don't know where Arizona is going to be in a few months with this pandemic. In July things were really elevated. Now they are much better. But look at Paris and London and Madrid. They were optimistic and now things are getting worse. We have to live and respond to change and expect change. That's why we need a structure for management and leadership. We don't know when the second or third wave will hit, or a new virus, or an altogether different sort of challenge. We can't panic and we can't be confident that all is getting better.

It's the old Eisenhower adage, you know, planning is everything and plans are worthless, once the battle starts. But once the battle starts the very idea of having a plan means you are better able to improvise when needed. So, we have done lots and lots of planning. Not every university has our planning commitment. But those that do not have plans, or those who cannot abandon them when circumstances require, are not likely to flourish.

Bozeman: So this last question is difficult in a different way. We worked on the book for a long time, and it was basically finished before COVID-19 broke out. Given what we said in the book about public values leadership and management, what, if anything, have you learned from the pandemic that gives you new or different thoughts about the points we make in the book?

Crow: It has definitely reinforced some of our ideas. The notions of interinstitutional collaboration and the bringing together of sectors, the pandemic has certainly shown the importance of these approaches. We would be so much worse off had we not reached out to a great many other organizations all over the world. If we had distrusted business, or governments or nonprofits, or universities, and maintained old stereotypes, it would have been difficult to forge effective partnerships. Threats that cut across all sectors. So does the pandemic. So does global climate change.

Maybe one thing we could have emphasized a little more or said in different ways was to avoid the destructive effects of tribalism and social and political fragmentation. Even when there is near-universal agreement on public values, that agreement doesn't mean we can achieve them in an atmosphere of distrust and tribalism, walling ourselves off from other people, institutions, or nations. The US response to the pandemic is especially worrisome. We leave the WHO. We avoid entering into vaccine alliances. We spend time scapegoating—"the China virus." We even make mask wearing and other public health measures into foolish ideological markers. This a near-perfect prescription for public values failure.

We look back to World War II, when people in the United States were overall very motivated to band together against a common enemy. What happened? Maybe it is different when the enemy is visible, when we have newsreels of atrocities, when we have propaganda machines. But when the enemy is a virus? Very different. The virus did not even give us a time window to come together. Wars build up over time, we can see it coming, we can see the political conflicts that lead to war, we can see Poland being invaded and then only months later France and the Netherlands. That's not the way the virus works. Not there, then everywhere. Defeating a terrible virus requires as much collective effort and discipline as defeating a human enemy. Public values require a public, not coalitions of interest groups. A viable public and what you call an effective "public sphere" are not easy to achieve. If public values leadership can contribute even a little to developing a more viable public, a little less discord and distrust, then it will be time to celebrate.

Notes

Introduction

1. The technical definition that is perhaps best known is the one provided by Bozeman (2007, 13): "those values providing normative consensus about (a) the rights, benefits, and prerogatives to which citizens should (and should not) be entitled; (b) the obligations of citizens to society, the state and one another; and (c) the principles on which governments and policies should be based."

2. Not everyone agrees that it was a disaster. See Segal (2003).

Chapter 1. Public Values Theory

1. Caveat lector? We don't know Latin either. To save the Google translation, caveat lector means "let the reader beware." It is our way of pedantically introducing the most pedantic chapter in this book.

2. Lippmann was writing at a time when it was customary in the English language to use masculine pronouns to refer to both genders.

3. In stringing together these economics approaches to making public-private allocation decisions, we understand that some readers may not be familiar with at least a few of these approaches. In the interest of space, and because others can make a better and more enthusiastic presentation of these approaches, we decided not to go into any detail, only showing that economics has been a fecund source of public policy approaches. Those interested in more detail may wish to consult the sources cited, or a public finance text such as Buchanan and Musgrave (1999) or Shoup (2017). In an earlier book, Bozeman (2007) discussed in detail many of these same approaches, but from the perspective of a public values theorist and advocate.

4. The account below is from a variety of sources and, especially, the authors' remembrance of their own economics courses. But for those interested in a useful and detailed single source on market failure, we suggest "Types of Market Failure," available on the Economics Online website at https://www.economicsonline.co.uk /Market_failures/Types_of_market_failure.html.

5. According to a recent Gallup poll, only 32% of Americans (and only 14% of those identifying with the Republican Party) say they have "a great deal" or "a fair amount" of trust in mass media (http://www.gallup.com/poll/195542/americans -trust-mass-media-sinks-new-low.aspx).

6. A 2014 poll by the Pew Research Center found that members of parties have increased distrust of those in the other party, with 38% of Democrats saying they have "very unfavorable" opinions about Republicans and 43% of Republicans saying they have "very unfavorable" opinions about Democrats. Some 27% of Democrats and 36% of Republicans described the other party as "a threat to the nation's well being." These numbers are more than doubled from a similar poll in 1994 and are

significant increases from a similar 2004 poll. See http://www.people-press.org /2014/06/12/political-polarization-in-the-american-public/.

7. Here is an illustration of the Motivation Problem. Bozeman has on many occasions been asked, often with the interrogator answering his or her own question, whether Crow is in any way sincere about the alleged ASU goal of widening participation, or whether this is just a scheme to develop more money, perhaps by currying favor with the Arizona Board of Regents or funding agents. Usually, before Bozeman can even respond, the questioner says something like, "You know, I can tell he is not sincere about this, but he is good at pretending to be." Is Crow sincere? I think so. Does it make any difference? Probably it does not. Maybe there is a small advantage to people at least thinking he *might* be sincere, but in the long run the test of inclusiveness is including people. It is not easy to game that outcome.

8. Here are the procedures: Bozeman used the Amazon Turk crowdsourcing resource, paying individuals to complete the survey. He received responses from 2,509 individuals, all American citizens (as stipulated by our posting). The sample is purposeful but not random. However, the participants were not substantially different from the US population and closely exhibit the attributes of that segment of the population that responds to questionnaire requests. Thus, 80% are white, half are college graduates, and half are men and half women. About one-quarter describe themselves as political independents, about the same number as Republicans, and 43% as Democrats. As one might expect, this is a relatively youthful set of respondents (reflective of the relative youth of the Amazon Turk roster), with nearly half in the 25–34 age group. However, this is a relatively large set of respondents, so, for example, there are responses from about 200 people 55 or older. More details can be found in Bozeman (2019).

Chapter 2. Three Premises of Public Values–Based Management

1. This summary draws from Madrigal (2013).

2. A small number of laboratory researchers have died from exposure to laboratory samples of smallpox.

3. "Smallpox," available on the WHO website at https://www.who.int/health -topics/smallpox#tab=tab_1.

4. Unfortunately, the smallpox case shows the need to remain ever vigilant about preserving public values. Evidence shows that whereas at present natural smallpox presents little or no threat, Russia has been engaged in research seeking to develop a biological weapon based on the smallpox virus and its kin. See http://www.bbc.co.uk/history/british/empire_seapower/smallpox_01.shtml.

5. Especially relevant are Moore (2013) and Bryson (2018).

6. Memory is not perfect, but this paraphrase captures the gist of a much longer conversation.

7. Rightly, the Contract with America is little remembered since it had only modest impacts, serving chiefly as a rallying cry uniting Republican congressional candidates in 1994. Its provisions, almost none of which were enacted, included cutting the number of House committees by one-third, implementing zero-based federal budgeting, limiting the terms of all committee chairs, and, perhaps most

unlikely, requiring all laws pertaining to US citizens to apply equally to members of Congress. The Republicans also promised to slash great swaths of the federal bureaucracy, including cabinet departments and agencies, but in the end managed only one bureaucratic scalp on their belt: the Office of Technology Assessment, which was part of the congressional staff apparatus. Despite its ultimate feckless-ness, the large GOP majority, coupled with the pledges under the contract, caused a short-term panic in Washington, DC.

8. The authors are great believers in multimedia learning. Okay, when pressed we admit that our commitment may be just an excuse for our tendency to watch too many movies. But readers who want to have insights into the founding of a huge and successful American corporation could do worse than spend a couple of hours watching Michael Keaton portraying McDonald's czar Ray Croc in the 2016 movie *The Founder*.

9. Example: both Crow and Bozeman have daughters (Alana Francis-Crow and Brandyn Bozeman) who work tirelessly to achieve public values, though not usually as part of a formal organization.

10. Another multimedia learning opportunity.

11. For some evidence, see North (1989), Weingast (1995), and Nistotskaya and Cingolani (2015).

12. *Cambridge Dictionary*, 2019.

Chapter 3. Public Values Management Propositions I

1. During the past decade or so, the use of prizes to stimulate socially relevant innovation has once again come into prominence. Some examples are the APEC "ASPIRE" awards (see https://www.science.org.au/opportunities/travel/grants -and-exchange/apec-science-prize-innovation-research-and-education-aspire) and the innovation inducement prizes of the US National Science Foundation (https://www.nap.edu/catalog/11816/innovation-inducement-prizes-at-the -national-science-foundation).

2. Personal historical aside: one of coauthor Bozeman's proudest moments was when his work received attention from President Ronald Reagan's White House. His book *All Organizations Are Public* (Bozeman 1987) was listed in the *Washington Monthly*, as "a book being read at the White House," in this case for the purpose of seeing what mischief the liberal political opposition was up to.

3. There it is again: multimedia learning! Bruce Springsteen, "Dancing in the Dark," http://www.azlyrics.com/lyrics/brucespringsteen/dancinginthedark.html.

4. See https://www.merriam-webster.com/dictionary/multilateral.

5. ICANN is the widely used and familiar abbreviation for the Internet Corporation for Assigned Names and Numbers. ICANN is a worldwide nonprofit organization responsible for coordinating the maintenance and procedures of several databases related to the name and naming protocols for the web (e.g., coming up with the country codes and the .com, .org, and .edu distinctions).

6. See https://www.webmd.com/fitness-exercise/ss/slideshow-sitting-health.

Chapter 4. Public Values Management Propositions II

1. According to research reported by the *Washington Post* (Hajnal, Lajevardi, and Nielson 2017), additional requirements from voter fraud legislation have little or no effect on white voters' turnout but reduce turnout of African Americans, Asian Americans, and Hispanics (with Hispanic turnout being affected the most, reduced by 7%).

2. We confess: we just invented this version of the "know thyself" idea. But we like our version, even if not so original. By the way, it's okay with us if you wish to pass it off as the wisdom of the *Tao Te Ching* or, perhaps even better, as an obscure lost passage from Ben Franklin's *Poor Richard's Almanac*.

Chapter 5. Mutable Leadership

1. But this does not apply to all academic leadership books or research articles. Those who study leadership systematically have for many years stressed the importance of contingencies, leadership fit, and context (e.g., Fiedler and Chemers 1967; Graen et al. 1970; Fiedler 1972; Kerr et al. 1974). Somehow, this excellent and well-verified work does not often get much attention from authors of popular leadership books.

2. Doing so would make it very difficult to continue writing this book!

3. In Crow parlance this sort of visionary leader is the "chief design architect."

4. Some evidence that others do not agree with us about the need to lessen boundaries: according to the *Washington Post*, the average US CEO makes 271 times more than the average worker (McGregor 2017). A formidable boundary, indeed!

Chapter 6. Case Studies in Public Values Leadership

1. Not all of the public values leaders we interviewed have cases included here. While all the interviews were useful and informative, we chose those that go into some depth about one particular case. Some of the interviews were wide-ranging and not sufficiently focused on one particular episode to work as a case study.

2. Wilkie D. Ferguson Jr., now deceased, former judge of the Federal District Court, Third District.

3. Former mayor of Chicago.

4. For those not familiar with Phoenix geography, the south Phoenix area is not part of the prime business district, but rather a predominantly residential area composed chiefly of working-class Latino families.

5. Phoenix-based businessman, real estate investor, and sports executive, best known as former owner of the Arizona Diamondbacks major league baseball team and the Phoenix Suns and Phoenix Mercury professional basketball teams.

6. Martin L. Shultz, also known as Marty, served as vice president of government affairs for Pinnacle West Capital Corp. and its principal subsidiary, Arizona Public Service Company (APS), until 2011. Prior to joining APS, he served as chief of staff to three Phoenix mayors.

7. The Phoenix Community Alliance is a community development organization focused on the development of downtown Phoenix.

8. President of the Discovery Triangle Development Corporation and a member of the Phoenix Community Alliance.

9. Unlike all the other interviews, this one was with two people. Since the conversation was comingled to a considerable extent between Brian and Kelly Swette, for convenience we do not (for the most part) provide a separate attribution, but just designate the speaker as "Swette."

10. Zuercher wanted us to be sure to credit his graduate school mentor, who had a great impact on his thinking about public policy and administration issues. That mentor is John Nalbandian (whose fine work is also well known to us), professor emeritus at the University of Kansas.

11. See Osborne and Gaebler (1992).

12. Best known as President John F. Kennedy's and President Lyndon Johnson's head of the Office of Economic Opportunity and one of the leaders in the Poverty Program established under the Economic Opportunity Act. He was also the first director of the Peace Corps and the Democratic Party candidate for vice president in 1972.

13. The Freddie Gray incident refers to a nationally publicized case of a young man who died in police custody while being transported in a police van, resulting in civil unrest, protests, and a trial that ultimately ended in September 2015 with a $6.4 million settlement provided to the Gray family by the city of Baltimore. The episode has been one of the elements spurring the Black Lives Matter movement. For more information see Gordon (2015).

Chapter 7. Public Values Case

1. See https://www.ers.usda.gov/topics/food-nutrition-assistance/food-security-in-the-us/definitions-of-food-security.aspx#.U760j_ldW-g, https://www.ers.usda.gov/topics/food-nutrition-assistance/food-security-in-the-us/key-statistics-graphics.aspx#insecure, and https://www.fns.usda.gov/wic/frequently-asked-questions-about-wic.

2. Private correspondence from organizational officials.

3. See http://www.feedingamerica.org/about-us/our-history/.

Chapter 8. The Starbucks-ASU Alliance

1. A fuller picture of Mary's experiences can be found in Ripley (2015), where she was first profiled.

2. See https://www.starbucks.com/about-us/company-information.

3. See https://www.bls.gov/opub/ted/2016/weekly-earnings-by-educational-attainment-in-first-quarter-2016.htm.

4. See https://www.starbucks.com/about-us/company-information/starbucks-company-timeline.

5. See https://news.starbucks.com/collegeplan/dream-of-a-college-degree.

Chapter 9. Public Values Management and Leadership

1. See https://www.markle.org/rework-america-task-force/#rework-america.

2. According to a recent study (Rossman 2017), 55% of students enrolled in private nonprofit institutions earn a degree within six years, but only 20% of those enrolled in private for-profit institutions do so.

3. See https://www.statepress.com/article/2018/02/sppolitics-crow-speaks-to-nga.

4. See Ripley (2015).

5. The charter, adopted in 2014: "Arizona State University is a comprehensive public research university, measured not by whom it excludes, but by whom it includes and how they succeed; advancing research and discovery of public value; and assuming fundamental responsibility for the economic, social, cultural and overall health of the communities it serves."

6. See Leonhardt (2014).

7. For background see Dias, Eligon, and Oppel (2018).

8. Multimedia learning: for a picture of the ASU charter rock see https://aecoverseas.com/wp-content/uploads/2020/07/CharterMonument2.jpg.

9. The inscription: "We will ever strive for the ideals and sacred things of the city, both alone and with many, we will unceasingly seek to quicken the sense of public duty, we will revere and obey the city's laws, we will transmit this city not only not less, but greater, better, and more beautiful than it was transmitted to us."

10. And managed to publish something on this topic as well; see Bozeman (2020).

Afterword. COVID-19 and Public Values Leadership

1. Interview conducted safely by Zoom on October 14, 2020.

References

Alchian, A. A., and H. Demsetz. 1973. "The Property Right Paradigm." *Journal of Economic History* 33 (1): 16–27.

Amabile, T. M. 1998. *How to Kill Creativity*. Vol. 87. Boston: Harvard Business School Publishing.

Anderson, D. M., and J. M. Stritch. 2015. "Goal Clarity, Task Significance, and Performance: Evidence from a Laboratory Experiment." *Journal of Public Administration Research and Theory* 26 (2): 211–25.

Anderson, D. M., and G. Taggart. 2016. "Organizations, Policies, and the Roots of Public Value Failure: The Case of For-Profit Higher Education." *Public Administration Review* 76 (5): 779–89.

Angulo, A. J. 2016. *Diploma Mills: How For-Profit Colleges Stiffed Students, Taxpayers, and the American Dream*. Baltimore: Johns Hopkins University Press.

Anttiroiko, A. V., S. J. Bailey, and P. Valkama. 2013. "Outsourcing in Sandy Springs and Other US Cities: Insights for Other Countries." *International Public Administration Review* 11 (3–4).

Armbrüster, T. 2004. "Rationality and Its Symbols: Signalling Effects and Subjectification in Management Consulting." *Journal of Management Studies* 41 (8): 1247–69.

Baghdady, G., and J. M. Maddock. 2008. "Marching to a Different Mission." *Stanford Social Innovation Review* 6 (2): 61–65.

Barnett, W., W. E. Block, and M. Saliba. 2005. "Perfect Competition: A Case of Market-Failure." *Corporate Ownership and Control* 2 (4).

Barrick, M. R., G. L. Stewart, M. J. Neubert, and M. K. Mount. 1998. "Relating Member Ability and Personality to Work-Team Processes and Team Effectiveness." *Journal of Applied Psychology* 83 (3): 377.

Bartels, L. M. 2018. *Unequal Democracy: The Political Economy of the New Gilded Age*. Princeton, NJ: Princeton University Press.

Bator, F. M. 1958. "The Anatomy of Market Failure." *Quarterly Journal of Economics* 72 (3): 351–79.

Bazzi, S., M. Fiszbein, and M. Gebresilasse. 2020. "Frontier Culture: The Roots and Persistence of Rugged Individualism in the United States." *Econometrica* 88 (6): 2329–68.

Beehr, T. A., L. Ivanitskaya, C. P. Hansen, D. Erofeev, and D. M. Gudanowski. 2001. "Evaluation of 360 Degree Feedback Ratings: Relationships with Each Other and with Performance and Selection Predictors." *Journal of Organizational Behavior* 22 (7): 775–88.

Beetham, D. 2013. *The Legitimation of Power*. London: Palgrave Macmillan.

Bennet, A., and D. Bennet. 2004. *Organizational Survival in the New World*. London: Routledge.

Berkowitz, E. 2017. "George Bush and the Americans with Disabilities Act." *Social Welfare History Project.* http://socialwelfare.library.vcu.edu/recollections/george -bush-and-the-americans-with-disabilities-act/.

Bhattacherjee, A. 2012. "Social Science Research: Principles, Methods and Practices." Scholar Commons, University of South Florida.

Block, F., and M. R. Somers. 2014. *The Power of Market Fundamentalism.* Cambridge, MA: Harvard University Press.

Bloom, N., R. Griffith, and J. Van Reenen. 2002. "Do R&D Tax Credits Work? Evidence from a Panel of Countries 1979–1997." *Journal of Public Economics* 85 (1): 1–31.

Borzaga, C., and E. Tortia. 2006. "Worker Motivations, Job Satisfaction, and Loyalty in Public and Nonprofit Social Services." *Nonprofit and Voluntary Sector Quarterly* 35 (2): 225–48.

Bozeman, B. 1987. *All Organizations Are Public: Bridging Public and Private Organization Theory.* San Francisco: Jossey-Bass.

———. 2000. *Bureaucracy and Red Tape.* Upper Saddle River, NJ: Prentice Hall.

———. 2002. "Public-Value Failure: When Efficient Markets May Not Do." *Public Administration Review* 62 (2): 145–61.

———. 2007. *Public Values and Public Interest: Counterbalancing Economic Individualism.* Washington, DC: Georgetown University Press.

———. 2019. "Public Values: Citizens' Perspective." *Public Management Review* 21 (6): 817–38.

———. 2020. "Public Value Science." *Issues in Science and Technology* 36 (4): 34–41.

Bozeman, B., and D. Anderson. 2014. "For-Profit Universities Are Not Inherently Bad." *Boston Globe*, November 16, 2014.

Bozeman, B., and M. K. Feeney. 2011. *Rules and Red Tape: A Prism for Public Administration Theory and Research.* Armonk, NY: M. E. Sharpe.

Bozeman, B., and J. Johnson. 2015. "The Political Economy of Public Values: A Case for the Public Sphere and Progressive Opportunity." *American Review of Public Administration* 45 (1): 61–85.

Bozeman, B., and D. Sarewitz. 2011. "Public Value Mapping and Science Policy Evaluation." *Minerva* 49 (1): 1–23.

Bozeman, B., and X. Su. 2015. "Public Service Motivation Concepts and Theory: A Critique." *Public Administration Review* 75 (5): 700–710.

Bozeman, B., and L. Wilson. 2004. "Market-Based Management of Government Laboratories: The Evolution of the US National Laboratories' Government-Owned, Contractor-Operated Management System." *Public Performance and Management Review* 28 (2): 167–85.

Brainard, L. 2019. "Is the Middle Class within Reach for Middle-Income Families?" *Federal Research System*, May 10, 2019. https://www.federalreserve.gov/newsevents /speech/brainard20190510a.htm.

Brennan, J. F., and L. F. Keller. 2017. "Pragmatism, the New Republic, and American Public Administration at Its Founding." *Administration and Society* 49 (4): 491–529.

Brewer, G. A., R. M. Walker, B. Bozeman, C. N. Avellaneda, and G. A. Brewer Jr. 2012. "External Control and Red Tape: The Mediating Effects of Client and

Organizational Feedback." *International Public Management Journal* 15 (3): 288–314.

Bright, L. 2008. "Does Public Service Motivation Really Make a Difference on the Job Satisfaction and Turnover Intentions of Public Employees?" *American Review of Public Administration* 38 (2): 149–66.

Brody, A. L., B. Bugusu, J. H. Han, C. K. Sand, and T. H. McHugh. 2008. "Innovative Food Packaging Solutions." *Journal of Food Science* 73 (8): R107-16.

Bromley, P., and J. W. Meyer. 2017. "'They Are All Organizations': The Cultural Roots of Blurring between the Nonprofit, Business, and Government Sectors." *Administration and Society* 49 (7): 939–66.

Brooks, R. C. 2004. "Privatization of Government Services: An Overview and Review of the Literature." *Journal of Public Budgeting, Accounting and Financial Management* 16 (4): 467.

Brunges, M., and C. Foley-Brinza. 2014. "Projects for Increasing Job Satisfaction and Creating a Healthy Work Environment." *AORN Journal* 100 (6): 670–81.

Bryson, J. M. 2018. *Strategic Planning for Public and Nonprofit Organizations: A Guide to Strengthening and Sustaining Organizational Achievement*. Hoboken, NJ: John Wiley & Sons.

Bryson, J. M., M. J. Gibbons, and G. Shaye. 2001. "Enterprise Schemes for Nonprofit Survival, Growth, and Effectiveness." *Nonprofit Management and Leadership* 11 (3): 271–88.

Buchanan, J. M. 1973. "The Coase Theorem and the Theory of the State." *Natural Resource Journal* 13:579.

Buchanan, J. M., and R. A. Musgrave. 1999. *Public Finance and Public Choice: Two Contrasting Visions of the State*. Cambridge, MA: MIT Press.

Burns, J. M. 1956. *Roosevelt: The Lion and the Fox*. San Diego: Harcourt, Brace & World.

Cafaro, A., H. Vilhjálmsson, T. Bickmore, D. Heylen, K. Jóhannsdóttir, and G. Valgarðsson. 2012. "First Impressions: Users' Judgments of Virtual Agents' Personality and Interpersonal Attitude in First Encounters." In *Intelligent Virtual Agents*, ed. J. Beskow, C. Peters, G. Castellano, C. O'Sullivan, I. Leite, and S. Kopp, 67–80. Berlin: Springer.

Cartwright, S., and C. L. Cooper. 2014. *Mergers and Acquisitions: The Human Factor*. Oxford: Butterworth-Heinemann.

Chandler, J. 2017. *Questioning the New Public Management*. London: Routledge.

Chun, Y. H., and H. G. Rainey. 2005. "Goal Ambiguity and Organizational Performance in US Federal Agencies." *Journal of Public Administration Research and Theory* 15 (4): 529–57.

Cochran, C. E. 1974. "Political Science and the Public Interest." *Journal of Politics* 36 (2): 327–55.

Coppin, C. A., and J. High. 1999. *The Politics of Purity: Harvey Washington Wiley and the Origins of Federal Food Policy*. Ann Arbor: University of Michigan Press.

Corbett, J., and C. Howard. 2017. "Why Perceived Size Matters for Agency Termination." *Public Administration* 95 (1): 196–213.

Coukell, A. 2017. "Proposed Budget Cuts' Potential Effect on Public Health." Pew Charitable Trust, June 7, 2017. http://www.pewtrusts.org/en/research-and

-analysis/analysis/2017/06/07/proposed-budget-cuts-potential-effect-on
-public-health.

Coyne, C. J., and D. Lucas. 2016. "Economists Have No Defense: A Critical Review of National Defense in Economics Textbooks." Available at SSRN 2742391.

Crow, M. M., and W. B. Dabars. 2015. *Designing the New American University*. Baltimore: Johns Hopkins University Press.

Cuervo-Cazurra, A. 2014. "Transparency and Corruption." In *The Oxford Handbook of Economic and Institutional Transparency*, ed. J. Forssbæck and Lars Oxelheim, 323 Oxford: Oxford University Press.

Dasgupta, A. K., and D. W. Pearce. 1972. *Cost-Benefit Analysis: Theory and Practice*. London: Macmillan International Higher Education.

Davies, J. S. 2000. "The Hollowing-Out of Local Democracy and the 'Fatal Conceit' of Governing without Government." *British Journal of Politics and International Relations* 2 (3): 414–28.

Davis, P., and K. West. 2009. "What Do Public Values Mean for Public Action? Putting Public Values in Their Plural Place." *American Review of Public Administration* 39 (6): 602–18.

Dechenaux, E., D. Kovenock, and R. M. Sheremeta. 2015. "A Survey of Experimental Research on Contests, All-Pay Auctions and Tournaments." *Experimental Economics* 18 (4): 609–69.

Dejong, D. N., and C. H. Whiteman. 1992. "More Unsettling Evidence on the Perfect Markets Hypothesis." *Economic Review—Federal Reserve Bank of Atlanta* 77 (6): 1.

Dewey, J. 1927. *The Public and Its Problems*. New York: Henry Holt.

———. 1935. "Peirce's Theory of Quality." *Journal of Philosophy* 26 (2): 701–8.

Dias, E., J. Eligon, and R. Oppel Jr. 2018. "Philadelphia Starbucks Arrests, Outrageous to Some, Are Everyday Life for Others." *New York Times*, April 17, 2018. https://www.nytimes.com/2018/04/17/us/starbucks-arrest-philadelphia.html.

Disch, L. J. 2002. *The Tyranny of the Two-Party System*. New York: Columbia University Press.

Donahue, J. 1991. *The Privatization Decision*. New York: Basic Books.

Dyck, B., M. Mauws, F. A. Starke, and G. A. Mischke. 2002. "Passing the Baton: The Importance of Sequence, Timing, Technique and Communication in Executive Succession." *Journal of Business Venturing* 17 (2): 143–62.

Economist. 2015. "A Crash Course in Probability." *Economist*, January 29, 2015. https://www.economist.com/blogs/gulliver/2015/01/air-safety.

Egnal, M. 1975. "The Economic Development of the Thirteen Continental Colonies, 1720 to 1775." *William and Mary Quarterly* 32 (2): 192–222.

Eldor, L. 2018. "Public Service Sector: The Compassionate Workplace—the Effect of Compassion and Stress on Employee Engagement, Burnout, and Performance." *Journal of Public Administration Research and Theory* 28 (1): 86–103.

Emmert, M. A., and M. M. Crow. 1988. "Public, Private and Hybrid Organizations: An Empirical Examination of the Role of Publicness." *Administration and Society* 20 (2): 216–44.

Feldman, S. 1982. "Economic Self-Interest and Political Behavior." *American Journal of Political Science* 26 (3): 446–66.

Fell, J. C., and R. B. Voas. 2006. "Mothers Against Drunk Driving (MADD): The First 25 Years." *Traffic Injury Prevention* 7 (3): 195–212.

Festenstein, M. 1997. *Pragmatism and Political Theory: From Dewey to Rorty*. Chicago: University of Chicago Press.

Fiedler, F. E. 1972. "The Effects of Leadership Training and Experience: A Contingency Model Interpretation." *Administrative Science Quarterly* 17 (4): 453–70.

Fiedler, F. E., and M. M. Chemers. 1967. *A Theory of Leadership Effectiveness*. New York: McGraw Hill.

Friedman, Zack. 2017. "Student Loan Debt in 2017: A $1.3 Trillion Crisis." *Forbes*, February 21, 2017. https://www.forbes.com/sites/zackfriedman/2017/02/21 /student-loan-debt-statistics-2017/2/.

Fukumoto, E., and B. Bozeman. 2019. "Public Values Theory: What Is Missing?" *American Review of Public Administration* 49 (6): 635–48.

Gares, D. V., and E. A. Delco. 1991. "Ten Steps to Successful Minority Hiring and Retention." *New Directions for Community Colleges* 1991 (74): 103–8.

Gilroy, L., H. Kenny, A. Summers, and S. Staley. 2011. *Annual Privatization Report 2010: Local Government Privatization*. Los Angeles: Reason Foundation.

Glaeser, E. L., A. Hillis, S. D. Kominers, and M. Luca. 2016. "Crowdsourcing City Government: Using Tournaments to Improve Inspection Accuracy." *American Economic Review* 106 (5): 114–18.

Golan, E., T. Roberts, E. Salay, J. Caswell, M. Ollinger, and D. Moore. 2004. "Food Safety Innovation in the United States: Evidence from the Meat Industry." *UDSA Agricultural Economics Reports*, no. 831.

Golembiewski, R. T., R. A. Boudreau, B. C. Sun, and H. Luo. 1998. "Estimates of Burnout in Public Agencies: Worldwide, How Many Employees Have Which Degrees of Burnout, and with What Consequences?" *Public Administration Review* 58 (1): 59–65.

Golub, B., and M. O. Jackson. 2010. "Naive Learning in Social Networks and the Wisdom of Crowds." *American Economic Journal: Microeconomics* 2 (1): 112–49.

Goodwin, Doris Kearns. 2005. *Team of Rivals: The Political Genius of Abraham Lincoln*. New York: Simon & Schuster.

Gordon, Kalani. 2015. "Latest Updates on Baltimore Unrest and Freddie Gray Case—the Charges." *Baltimore Sun*, May 1, 2015.

Gothard, S., and M. J. Austin. 2013. "Leadership Succession Planning: Implications for Nonprofit Human Service Organizations." *Administration in Social Work* 37 (3): 272–85.

Graber, D. A., and J. Dunaway. 2017. *Mass Media and American Politics*. Thousand Oaks, CA: CQ Press.

Graen, G., K. Alvares, J. B. Orris, and J. A. Martella. 1970. "Contingency Model of Leadership Effectiveness: Antecedent and Evidential Results." *Psychological Bulletin* 74 (4): 285–95.

Greer, C. R., and M. Virick. 2008. "Diverse Succession Planning: Lessons from the Industry Leaders." *Human Resource Management* 47 (2): 351–67.

Guarino, B. 2019. "USDA Science Agencies' Relocation May Have Violated Law, Inspector General Report Says." *Washington Post*, August 6, 2019. https://www

.washingtonpost.com/science/2019/08/05/usda-science-agencies-relocation
-may-have-violated-law-inspector-general-report-says/.

Hairston, J. B. 1998. "Water Privatization: Winning Bidder Will Face Debt,
Backlog, Major Upgrade." *Atlanta Journal-Constitution*, 23, D1.

Hajnal, Z., N. Lajevardi, and L. Nielson. 2017. "Do Voter Identification Laws
Suppress Minority Voting? Yes. We Did the Research." *Washington Post*,
February 15, 2017. https://www.washingtonpost.com/news/monkey-cage/wp
/2017/02/15/do-voter-identification-laws-suppress-minority-voting-yes-we
-did-the-research/?utm_term=.e7eff16c8fcc.

Hamlin, R. G. 2004. "In Support of Universalistic Models of Managerial and
Leadership Effectiveness: Implications for HRD Research and Practice."
Human Resource Development Quarterly 15 (2): 189–215.

Haskins, R. 2016. "Education and Economic Mobility." In *Economic Mobility Project:
An Initiative of the Pew Charitable Trusts*. Washington, DC: Brookings Institution
Press. https://www.brookings.edu/wp-content/uploads/2016/07/02_economic
_mobility_sawhill_ch8.pdf.

Haythornthwaite, P. 1991. *Gallipoli 1915: Frontal Assault on Turkey*. Oxford: Osprey.

Helfand, W. H., J. Lazarus, and P. Theerman. 2001. "'. . . So That Others May
Walk': The March of Dimes." *American Journal of Public Health* 91 (8): 1190.

Henig, J. R. 1989. "Privatization in The United States: Theory and Practice."
Political Science Quarterly 104 (4): 649–70.

Herring, E. P. 1936. *Public Administration and the Public Interest*. New York: McGraw
Hill.

Hersey, P., K. H. Blanchard, and W. E. Natemeyer. 1979. "Situational Leadership,
Perception, and the Impact of Power." *Group and Organization Studies* 4 (4):
418–28.

Hilts, P. J. 2003. *Protecting America's Health: The FDA, Business, and One Hundred Years
of Regulation*. Chapel Hill: University of North Carolina Press.

Ho, W. H., C. S. Chang, Y. L. Shih, and R. D. Liang. 2009. "Effects of Job Rotation
and Role Stress among Nurses on Job Satisfaction and Organizational Commitment." *BMC Health Services Research* 9 (1): 8.

Hooijberg, R., and J. Choi. 2001. "The Impact of Organizational Characteristics on
Leadership Effectiveness Models: An Examination of Leadership in a Private
and a Public Sector Organization." *Administration and Society* 33 (4): 403–31.

Hughes, T. P. 1979. "The Electrification of America: The System Builders." *Technology and Culture* 20 (1): 124–61.

Hurley, C. 2014. "A Better Path to Progress on Drunk Driving." *Addiction* 109 (6):
877–78.

Huss, S., and L. Dwight. 2018. "Planned Parenthood: 100 Years of Leadership and
Controversy." In *Leadership and Sexuality*. Cheltenham: Edward Elgar.

Ingersoll, R. 1940. *Report on England, November 1940*. New York: Simon & Schuster.

Innes, S. 1995. *Creating the Commonwealth: The Economic Culture of Puritan New
England*. Vol. 2. New York: W. W. Norton.

James, O., and M. Lodge. 2003. "The Limitations of 'Policy Transfer' and 'Lesson
Drawing' for Public Policy Research." *Political Studies Review* 1 (2): 179–93.

James, O., N. Petrovsky, A. Moseley, and G. A. Boyne. 2016. "The Politics of Agency Death: Ministers and the Survival of Government Agencies in a Parliamentary System." *British Journal of Political Science* 46 (4): 763–84.

James, W. 1907. *Pragmatism: A New Name for Some Old Philosophy, Old Ways of Thinking: Popular Lectures on Philosophy*. London: Longmans, Green.

———. 2015. *Pragmatism: A New Name for Some Old Ways*. Media Galaxy.

Jones, G. R., and J. M. George. 1998. "The Experience and Evolution of Trust: Implications for Cooperation and Teamwork." *Academy of Management Review* 23 (3): 531–46.

Jørgensen, T. B., and B. Bozeman. 2002. "Public Values Lost? Comparing Cases on Contracting Out from Denmark and the United States." *Public Management Review* 4 (1): 63–81.

———. 2007. "Public Values: An Inventory." *Administration and Society* 39 (3): 354–81.

Kaufman, H. 1976. *Are Government Organizations Immortal?* Washington, DC: Brookings Institution Press.

Kenyon, D. A. 1991. *Competition among States and Local Governments: Efficiency and Equity in American Federalism*. Washington, DC: Urban Institute.

Kerr, S., C. A. Schriesheim, C. J. Murphy, and R. M. Stogdill. 1974. "Toward a Contingency Theory of Leadership Based upon the Consideration and Initiating Structure Literature." *Organizational Behavior and Human Performance* 12 (1): 62–82.

Kesner, I. F., and T. C. Sebora. 1994. "Executive Succession: Past, Present and Future." *Journal of Management* 20 (2): 327–72.

Kimball, W. F. 1997. *Forged in War: Roosevelt, Churchill, and the Second World War*. New York: Morrow.

Kimberly, J. R., and R. H. Miles. 1980. *The Organizational Life Cycle: Issues in the Creation, Transformation, and Decline of Organizations*. San Francisco: Jossey-Bass.

King, M. L., Jr. 1964. *Why We Can't Wait*. Boston: Beacon.

Konrad, A. M., and J. Pfeffer. 1991. "Understanding the Hiring of Women and Minorities in Educational Institutions." *Sociology of Education* 64 (3): 141–57.

Koopman, Colin. 2014. "Conduct Pragmatism: Pressing beyond Experientialism and Lingualism." *European Journal of Pragmatism and American Philosophy* 6 (2): 145–74.

Krupnick, A. J., W. E. Oates, and E. Van De Verg. 1983. "On Marketable Air-Pollution Permits: The Case for a System of Pollution Offsets." *Journal of Environmental Economics and Management* 10 (3): 233–47.

Kuttner, R. 1999. *Everything for Sale: The Virtues and Limits of Markets*. Chicago: University of Chicago Press.

Lamberg, J. A., H. Tikkanen, T. Nokelainen, and H. Suur-Inkeroinen. 2009. "Competitive Dynamics, Strategic Consistency, and Organizational Survival." *Strategic Management Journal* 30 (1): 45–60.

Lane, J. E. 2000. *New Public Management*. London: Taylor & Francis.

Larsen, D. 2012. "The March of Dimes and Polio: Lessons in Vaccine Advocacy for Health Educators." *American Journal of Health Education* 43 (1): 47–54.

Lavito, A. 2017. "Starbucks Opening a Store in China Every 15 Hours." CNBC, December 5, 2017. https://www.cnbc.com/2017/12/05/starbucks-is-opening-a-store-in-china-every-15-hours.html.

Lawton, A., and M. Macaulay. 2017. "From Birth to Death: The Life of the Standards Board for England." *Public Administration Review* 77 (5).

Lee, Y. J., and V. M. Wilkins. 2011. "More Similarities or More Differences? Comparing Public and Nonprofit Managers' Job Motivations." *Public Administration Review* 71 (1): 45–56.

Leiner, B. M., V. G. Cerf, D. D. Clark, R. E. Kahn, L. Kleinrock, D. C. Lynch, J. Postel, L. G. Roberts, and S. Wolff. 2009. "A Brief History of the Internet." *ACM SIGCOMM Computer Communication Review* 39 (5): 22–31.

Leonard, D., and S. Straus. 1997. "Putting Your Company's Whole Brain to Work." *Harvard Business Review* 75:110–22.

Leonhardt, D. 2014. "*Is College Worth It? Clearly, New Data Say.*" *New York Times*, May 27, 2014. https://www.nytimes.com/2014/05/27/upshot/is-college-worth-it-clearly-new-data-say.html.

Levitan, S. A. 2003. *Programs in Aid of the Poor*. Baltimore: Johns Hopkins University Press.

Levitt, J. 2014. "A Comprehensive Investigation of Voter Impersonation Finds 31 Credible Incidents out of One Billion Ballots Cast." *Washington Post*, August 6, 2014. https://www.washingtonpost.com/news/wonk/wp/2014/08/06/a-comprehensive-investigation-of-voter-impersonation-finds-31-credible-incidents-out-of-one-billion-ballots-cast/?utm_term=.9c0e3e0640d9.

Lippmann, W. 1955. *Essays in the Public Philosophy*. New Brunswick, NJ: Transaction.

Longwell, S. 2012. "Today's MADD Drives Dangerous New Policies." *Hill*, March 22, 2012. https://thehill.com/blogs/congress-blog/civil-rights/217573-sarah-longwell-managing-director-american-beverage-institute.

Lutz, D. S. 1984. "The Relative Influence of European Writers on Late Eighteenth-Century American Political Thought." *American Political Science Review* 78 (1): 189–97.

Maass, A. 1966. "Benefit-Cost Analysis: Its Relevance to Public Investment Decisions." *Quarterly Journal of Economics* 80 (2): 208–26.

MacDonald, M. 1977. "Food Stamps: An Analytical History." *Social Service Review* 51 (4): 642–58.

Machado, T., V. Sathyanarayanan, P. Bhola, and K. Kamath. 2013. "Psychological Vulnerability, Burnout, and Coping among Employees of a Business Process Outsourcing Organization." *Industrial Psychiatry Journal* 22 (1): 26.

MacIntyre, A. C. 1969. *Hume on 'Is' and 'Ought'*. London: Palgrave Macmillan.

Madrigal, A. C. 2013. "The Last Smallpox Patient on Earth." *Atlantic*, December 9, 2013. https://www.theatlantic.com/health/archive/2013/12/the-last-smallpox-patient-on-earth/282169/.

Magjuka, R. J., and T. T. Baldwin. 1991. "Team-Based Employee Involvement Programs: Effects of Design and Administration." *Personnel Psychology* 44 (4): 793–812.

Marie, T. T. 2016. "Public Values as Essential Criteria for Public Entrepreneurship: Water Management in France." *Utilities Policy* 40:162–69.

Matten, D., and J. Moon. 2005. "Corporate Social Responsibility." *Journal of Business Ethics* 54 (4): 323–37.

McCarthy, J. D., and M. Wolfson. 1996. "Resource Mobilization by Local Social Movement Organizations." *American Sociological Review* 61 (6): 1070–88.

McCoy, T. 2015. "The Surprisingly Simple Way Utah Solved Chronic Homelessness and Saved Millions." *Washington Post*, April 17, 2015. https://www.washingtonpost.com/news/inspired-life/wp/2015/04/17/the-surprisingly-simple-way-utah-solved-chronic-homelessness-and-saved-millions/.

McGregor, Jena. 2017. "Major Company CEOs Make 271 Times More Than the Typical U.S. Worker." *Washington Post*, July 20, 2017.

McNamara, P. 1998. *Political Economy and Statesmanship: Smith, Hamilton, and the Foundation of the Commercial Republic*. DeKalb: Northern Illinois University Press.

McPherson, G., L. Misener, D. McGillivray, and D. Legg. 2017. "Creating Public Value through Parasport Events." *Event Management* 21 (2): 185–99.

Meyer, R. 2011. "The Public Values Failures of Climate Science in the US." *Minerva* 49 (1): 47–70.

Midgley, C., ed. 2014. *Goals, Goal Structures, and Patterns of Adaptive Learning*. London: Routledge.

Milward, H. B., and K. G. Provan. 2000. "Governing the Hollow State." *Journal of Public Administration Research and Theory* 10 (2): 359–80.

Miner, J. B. 2015. *Organizational Behavior 1: Essential Theories of Motivation and Leadership*. London: Routledge.

Monroe-White, T., and T. S. Woodson. 2016. "Inequalities in Scholarly Knowledge: Public Value Failures and Their Impact on Global Science." *African Journal of Science, Technology, Innovation and Development* 8 (2): 178–86.

Moore, M. H. 2013. *Recognizing Public Value*. Cambridge, MA: Harvard University Press.

Morduch, J., and B. Armendariz. 2005. *The Economics of Microfinance*. Cambridge, MA: MIT Press.

Moulton, S. 2009. "Putting Together the Publicness Puzzle: A Framework for Realized Publicness." *Public Administration Review* 69 (5): 889–900.

Moulton, S., and B. Bozeman. 2011. "The Publicness of Policy Environments: An Evaluation of Subprime Mortgage Lending." *Journal of Public Administration Research and Theory* 21 (1): 87–115.

Moynihan, D. P. 2010. "A Workforce of Cynics? The Effects of Contemporary Reforms on Public Service Motivation." *International Public Management Journal* 13 (1): 24–34.

———. 2012. "A Theory of Culture-Switching: Leadership and Red-Tape during Hurricane Katrina." *Public Administration* 90 (4): 851–68.

Moynihan, D. P., and S. K. Pandey. 2007. "The Role of Organizations in Fostering Public Service Motivation." *Public Administration Review* 67 (1): 40–53.

Murphy, J. D. 2013. *Mission Forsaken: The University of Phoenix Affair with Wall Street*. Proving Ground Education.

Nabatchi, T. 2012. "Putting the 'Public' Back in Public Values Research: Designing Participation to Identify and Respond to Values." *Public Administration Review* 72 (5): 699–708.

Needham, K., F. P. De Vries, P. R. Armsworth, and N. Hanley. 2019. "Designing Markets for Biodiversity Offsets: Lessons from Tradable Pollution Permits." *Journal of Applied Ecology* 56 (6): 1429–35.

Nicholson-Crotty, S. 2005. "Bureaucratic Competition in the Policy Process." *Policy Studies Journal* 33 (3): 341–61.

Nistotskaya, M., and L. Cingolani. 2015. "Bureaucratic Structure, Regulatory Quality, and Entrepreneurship in a Comparative Perspective." *Journal of Public Administration Research and Theory* 26 (3): 519–34.

North, D. C. 1989. "Institutions and Economic Growth: An Historical Introduction." *World Development* 17 (9): 1319–32.

O'Neill, John J. 2006. *Prodigal Genius: The Life of Nikola Tesla.* New York: Cosimo Classics.

Osborne, D., and T. Gaebler. 1992. *Reinventing Government: How the Entrepreneurial Spirit Is Transforming Government.* Reading, MA: Addison Wesley.

Oshinsky, D. M. 2005. *Polio: An American Story.* Oxford: Oxford University Press.

Pandey, S. K., and G. A. Kingsley. 2000. "Examining Red Tape in Public and Private Organizations: Alternative Explanations from a Social Psychological Model." *Journal of Public Administration Research and Theory* 10 (4): 779–800.

Patil, S. V., and R. D. Lebel. 2019. "'I Want to Serve but the Public Does Not Understand': Prosocial Motivation, Image Discrepancies, and Proactivity in Public Safety." *Organizational Behavior and Human Decision Processes* 154:34–48.

Payne, B. K. 2006. "Weapon Bias: Split-Second Decisions and Unintended Stereotyping." *Current Directions in Psychological Science* 15 (6): 287–91.

Peirce, C. S. 1905. "What Pragmatism Is." *Monist* 15 (2): 161–81.

Perkins, E. J. 1988. *The Economy of Colonial America.* New York: Columbia University Press.

Perry, J. L. 1997. "Antecedents of Public Service Motivation." *Journal of Public Administration Research and Theory* 7 (2): 181–97.

Perry, J. L., and A. Hondeghem, eds. 2008. *Motivation in Public Management: The Call of Public Service.* Oxford: Oxford University Press.

Perry, J. L., and H. G. Rainey. 1988. "The Public-Private Distinction in Organization Theory: A Critique and Research Strategy." *Academy of Management Review* 13 (2): 182–201.

Pettinger, R. 2012. *Management: A Concise Introduction.* London: Macmillan International Higher Education.

Pfeffer, Jeffrey. 2015. *Leadership BS: Fixing Workplaces and Careers One Truth at a Time.* New York: Harper Business.

Pollitt, C., and S. Dan. 2013. "Searching for Impacts in Performance-Oriented Management Reform: A Review of the European Literature." *Public Performance and Management Review* 37 (1): 7–32.

Pollitt, C., S. Van Thiel, and V. Homburg, eds. 2007. *New Public Management in Europe.* Basingstoke: Palgrave Macmillan.

Posner, R. A. 1979. "Utilitarianism, Economics, and Legal Theory." *Journal of Legal Studies* 8 (1): 103–40.

Pring, R. 2014. *John Dewey.* London: Bloomsbury.

Radaelli, C. M. 2004. "The Puzzle of Regulatory Competition." *Journal of Public Policy* 24 (1): 1–23.

Rainey, H. G. 1993. "Toward a Theory of Goal Ambiguity in Public Organizations." *Research in Public Administration* 2 (1): 121–66.

Rainey, H. G., and B. Bozeman. 2000. "Comparing Public and Private Organizations: Empirical Research and the Power of the A Priori." *Journal of Public Administration Research and Theory* 10 (2): 447–70.

Rempel, M. 2018. "Contemporary Ideological Cleavages in the United States." In *Citizen Politics in Post-industrial Societies,* ed. T. N. Clark and M. Rempel, 195–208. London: Routledge.

Reynolds, D. 2007. *In Command of History: Churchill Fighting and Writing the Second World War.* New York: Basic Books.

Rhodes, R. A. W. 1996. "The New Governance: Governing without Government." *Political Studies* 44 (4): 652–67.

Ripley, A. "The Upwardly Mobile Barista." *Atlantic,* May 2015. https://www.theatlantic.com/magazine/archive/2015/05/the-upwardly-mobile-barista/389513/.

Ritch, W. A., and M. E. Begay. 2001. "Strange Bedfellows: The History of Collaboration between the Massachusetts Restaurant Association and the Tobacco Industry." *American Journal of Public Health* 91 (4): 598.

Ritz, A., G. A. Brewer, and O. Neumann. 2016. "Public Service Motivation: A Systematic Literature Review and Outlook." *Public Administration Review* 76 (3): 414–26.

Robbins, S. P. 1974. *Managing Organizational Conflict: A Nontraditional Approach.* Upper Saddle River, NJ: Prentice Hall.

Roberts, D. 2014. "US Jury Convicts Blackwater Guards in 2007 Killing of Iraqi Civilians." *Guardian,* October 31, 2014. https://www.theguardian.com/us-news/2014/oct/22/us-jury-convicts-blackwater-security-guards-iraq.

Robinson, J. 1953. "Imperfect Competition Revisited." *Economic Journal* 63 (251): 579–93.

Rogers, J. D., and G. Kingsley. 2004. "Denying Public Value: The Role of the Public Sector in Accounts of the Development of the Internet." *Journal of Public Administration Research and Theory* 14 (3): 371–93.

Rosenthal, S. B., C. R. Hausman, and D. R. Anderson, eds. 1999. *Classical American Pragmatism: Its Contemporary Vitality.* Champaign: University of Illinois Press.

Rossman, D. 2017. "New Graduation Data on Pell Recipients Reveals a Gap in Outcomes." *Ithaka S+R,* October 24, 2017. https://sr.ithaka.org/blog/new-graduation-data-on-pell-recipients-reveals-a-gap-in-outcomes/.

Rutgers, M. R. 2015. "As Good as It Gets? On the Meaning of Public Value in the Study of Policy and Management." *American Review of Public Administration* 45 (1): 29–45.

Rynes, S. L., B. Gerhart, and K. A. Minette. 2004. "The Importance of Pay in Employee Motivation: Discrepancies between What People Say and What They Do." *Human Resource Management* 43 (4): 381–94.

Salipante, P. F., and K. Golden-Biddle. 1995. "Managing Traditionality and Strategic Change in Nonprofit Organizations." *Nonprofit Management and Leadership* 6 (1): 3–20.

Samuelson, P. A. 1948. *Economics: An Introductory Analysis*. New York: McGraw-Hill.

———. 1954. "The Pure Theory of Public Expenditure." *Review of Economics and Statistics* 36 (4): 387–89.

Samuelson, P. A., and W. Nordhaus. 2009. *Economics*. 19th Ed. New York: McGraw-Hill.

Satin, M. 2007. *Death in the Pot: The Impact of Food Poisoning on History*. Buffalo, NY: Prometheus Books.

Schedler, K., and I. Proeller. 2000. *New Public Management*. Stuttgart: Wie.

Schimmoeller, L. J. 2010. "Leadership Styles in Competing Organizational Cultures." *Leadership Review* 10 (2): 125–41.

Schlaerth, A., N. Ensari, and J. Christian. 2013. "A Meta-analytical Review of the Relationship between Emotional Intelligence and Leaders' Constructive Conflict Management." *Group Processes and Intergroup Relations* 16 (1): 126–36.

Schlosser, Eric. 2006. "*The Jungle* Was a Socialist's Cry for Labor Justice. It Launched a Consumer Movement Instead." *Chicago Tribune*, May 21, 2006. http://articles.chicagotribune.com/2006-05-21/features/0605210414_1_upton -sinclair-trust-free.

Scott, R. 2015. "Fifty Companies That Crush Giving Back." *Forbes*, February 19, 2015. https://www.forbes.com/sites/causeintegration/2015/02/19/the-50 -companies-that-crush-giving-back/#6af57166502d.

Segal, Geoffrey. 2003. "What Can We Learn from Atlanta's Water Privatization." *Reason Foundation*, January 21, 2003. https://reason.org/commentary/what-can -we-learn-from-atlanta/.

Seifer, M. J. 1996. *Wizard: The Life and Times of Nikola Tesla: Biography of a Genius*. New York: Citadel Press.

Shareef, R. 2008. "Teaching Public Sector Ethics to Graduate Students: The Public Values / Public Failure Decision-Making Model." *Journal of Public Affairs Education* 14 (3): 285–95.

Sharkey, C. M. 2009. "Federalism Accountability: 'Agency-Forcing' Measures." *Duke Law Journal* 58:2125–92.

Sharp, Z., and D. M. Brock. 2012. "Implementation through Risk Mitigation: Strategic Processes in the Nonprofit Organization." *Administration and Society* 44 (5): 571–94.

Shen, F., and H. H. Edwards. 2005. "Economic Individualism, Humanitarianism, and Welfare Reform: A Value-Based Account of Framing Effects." *Journal of Communication* 55 (4): 795–809.

Shen, W. 2003. "The Dynamics of the CEO-Board Relationship: An Evolutionary Perspective." *Academy of Management Review* 28 (3): 466–76.

Shoup, C. 2017. *Public Finance*. London: Routledge.

Shubert, G. 1957. "The Public Interest in Administrative Decision-Making: Theorem, Theosophy or Theory." *American Political Science Review* 51:346–68.

Shumaker, E. 2015. "Chipotle's Food Poisoning Issue Is Nationwide. Here's A Map." *Huffington Post*, December 10, 2015. http://www.huffingtonpost.com/entry /chipotle-food-poisoning-outbreak_us_56687740e4b009377b235b0d.

Siegel, D. S., and D. F. Vitaliano. 2007. "An Empirical Analysis of the Strategic Use of Corporate Social Responsibility." *Journal of Economics and Management Strategy* 16 (3): 773–92.

Sorauf, F. J. 1957. "The Public Interest Reconsidered." *Journal of Politics* 19 (4): 616–39.

Steenhuisen, B., W. Dicke, and H. De Bruijn. 2009. "'Soft' Public Values in Jeopardy: Reflecting on the Institutionally Fragmented Situation in Utility Sectors." *International Journal of Public Administration* 32 (6): 491–507.

Stevens, M. H., T. Jacobsen, and A. K. Crofts. 2013. "Lead and the Deafness of Ludwig Van Beethoven." *Laryngoscope* 123 (11): 2854–58.

Stiglitz, J. E. 1979. "Equilibrium in Product Markets with Imperfect Information." *American Economic Review* 69 (2): 339–45.

———. 2012. *The Price of Inequality: How Today's Divided Society Endangers Our Future*. New York: W. W. Norton.

Stross, R. E. 2008. *The Wizard of Menlo Park: How Thomas Alva Edison Invented the Modern World*. New York: Broadway Books.

Surowiecki, J. 2005. *The Wisdom of Crowds*. New York: Anchor Books.

Swanson, Judith A. 1992. *The Public and the Private in Aristotle's Political Philosophy*. Ithaca, NY: Cornell University Press.

Tyre, M. J., and E. Von Hippel. 1997. "The Situated Nature of Adaptive Learning in Organizations." *Organization Science* 8 (1): 71–83.

US Department of Energy. 2004. *Competing the Management and Operations Contracts for DOE's National Laboratories. Report of the Blue Ribbon Commission on the Use of Competitive Procedures for the Department of Energy Labs*.

US Food and Drug Administration. 2017. "The 1906 Food and Drug Act and Its Enforcement." https://www.fda.gov/aboutfda/whatwedo/history/origin /ucm054819.htm.

Vakkuri, J., and J. E. Johanson, eds. 2020. *Hybrid Governance, Organisations and Society: Value Creation Perspectives*. London: Routledge.

Valdez, W. J. 2001. "Managing DOE's National Laboratory System: Balancing Accountability and Scientific Creativity through the M&O Contract." Paper prepared for the Annual Meeting of the Academy of Management, Washington, DC.

Van Den Bekerom, P., R. Torenvlied, and A. Akkerman. 2017. "Constrained by Red Tape: How Managerial Networking Moderates the Effects of Red Tape on Public Service Performance." *American Review of Public Administration* 47 (3): 300–322.

Van Den Broeck, A., T. Vander Elst, E. Baillien, M. Sercu, M. Schouteden, H. De Witte, and L. Godderis. 2017. "Job Demands, Job Resources, Burnout, Work Engagement, and Their Relationships: An Analysis across Sectors." *Journal of Occupational and Environmental Medicine* 59 (4): 369–76.

Van Der Heijden, B. I. J. M., and A. H. J. Nijhof. 2004. "The Value of Subjectivity: Problems and Prospects for 360-Degree Appraisal Systems." *International Journal of Human Resource Management* 15 (3): 493–511.

Van Der Wal, Z., G. De Graaf, and K. Lasthuizen. 2008. "What's Valued Most? Similarities and Differences between the Organizational Values of the Public and Private Sector." *Public Administration* 86 (2): 465–82.

Van Der Wal, Z., T. Nabatchi, and G. De Graaf. 2015. "From Galaxies to Universe: A Cross-Disciplinary Review and Analysis of Public Values Publications from 1969 to 2012." *American Review of Public Administration* 45 (1): 13–28.

Varuhas, J. N. 2014. "The Public Interest Conception of Public Law: Its Procedural Origins and Substantive Implications." University of Cambridge Faculty of Law Research Paper, no. 61.

Vecchio, R. P. 1987. "Situational Leadership Theory: An Examination of a Prescriptive Theory." *Journal of Applied Psychology* 72 (3): 444.

Virany, B., M. L. Tushman, and E. Romanelli. 1992. "Executive Succession and Organization Outcomes in Turbulent Environments: An Organization Learning Approach." *Organization Science* 3 (1): 72–91.

Vogel, R., and D. Masal. 2015. "Public Leadership: A Review of the Literature and Framework for Future Research." *Public Management Review* 17 (8): 1165–89.

Volden, C. 2005. "Intergovernmental Political Competition in American Federalism." *American Journal of Political Science* 49 (2): 327–42.

Vroom, V. H., and A. G. Jago. 1988. *The New Leadership: Managing Participation in Organizations.* Upper Saddle River, NJ: Prentice Hall.

Walker, R. M., G. A. Brewer, G. A. Boyne, and C. N. Avellaneda. 2011. "Market Orientation and Public Service Performance: New Public Management Gone Mad?" *Public Administration Review* 71 (5): 707–17.

Weed, F. J. 1987. "Grass-Roots Activism and the Drunk Driving Issue: A Survey of MADD Chapters." *Law and Policy* 9 (3): 259–78.

———. 1993. "The MADD Queen: Charisma and the Founder of Mothers Against Drunk Driving." *Leadership Quarterly* 4 (3–4): 329–46.

Weinberg, G. L. 1995. *A World at Arms: A Global History of World War II.* Cambridge: Cambridge University Press.

Weingast, B. R. 1995. "The Economic Role of Political Institutions: Market-Preserving Federalism and Economic Development." *Journal of Law, Economics, and Organization* 11 (1): 1–31.

West, C. 1989. *The American Evasion of Philosophy: A Genealogy of Pragmatism.* Berlin: Springer.

Williams, C. 1993. *The Last Great Frenchman: A Life of General De Gaulle.* Hoboken, NJ: Wiley.

Williams, I., and H. Shearer. 2011. "Appraising Public Value: Past, Present and Futures." *Public Administration* 89 (4): 1367–84.

Wilson, J. M., S. G. Straus, and B. McEvilly. 2006. "All in Due Time: The Development of Trust in Computer-Mediated and Face-to-Face Teams." *Organizational Behavior and Human Decision Processes* 99 (1): 16–33.

Wong, A. 2015. "The Downfall of For-Profit Colleges." *Atlantic Monthly*, February 23, 2015. https://www.theatlantic.com/education/archive/2015/02/the-downfall-of -for-profit-colleges/385810/.

Wu, Y. 2005. "The Effects of State R&D Tax Credits in Stimulating Private R&D Expenditure: A Cross-State Empirical Analysis." *Journal of Policy Analysis and Management* 24 (4): 785–802.

Zerbe, R. O., Jr., and H. McCurdy. 2000. "The End of Market Failure." *Regulation* 23 (2): 10–14.

Index

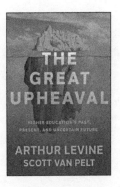